EXCESS

EXCESS

ANTI-CONSUMERISM
IN THE WEST

KIM HUMPHERY

polity

First published in 2010 by Polity Press

Polity Press
65 Bridge Street
Cambridge CB2 1UR, UK

Polity Press
350 Main Street
Malden, MA 02148, USA

ISBN-13: 978-0-7456-4540-7
ISBN-13: 978-0-7456-4541-4(pb)

A catalogue record for this book is available from the British Library.

Typeset in 10.75 on 14 pt Adobe Janson
by Servis Filmsetting Ltd, Stockport, Cheshire
Printed and bound in Great Britain by
MPG Books Group, UK

The publisher has used its best endeavours to ensure that the URLs for external websites referred to in this book are correct and active at the time of going to press. However, the publisher has no responsibility for the websites and can make no guarantee that a site will remain live or that the content is or will remain appropriate.

Every effort has been made to trace all copyright holders, but if any have been inadvertently overlooked the publishers will be pleased to include any necessary credits in any subsequent reprint or edition.

For further information on Polity, visit our website: www.politybooks.com

CONTENTS

For
Sarah MacLean

PREFACE

Western nations are routinely conceptualized by academics, social critics and western populations themselves as deeply embroiled in consumerism – and well they are. At each stage of the boom-to-bust capitalist economic cycle our political leaders insist that high consumption must be maintained or regained. At every economic moment, through good times and bad, unrestrained consumption parades itself as the prize of life. Escalating consumption, despite the peaks and troughs of retail sales, consumer confidence and levels of disposable income, is thus a permanent, systemic imperative: affluent populations must either be rapturously engaged in getting and spending or, as good workers and citizens, must be diligently rebuilding the conditions for economic prosperity and a return to the consumer good life. This book deeply questions this logic. The discussion offered here is not simply about consumption *per se* – as economic activity or individual behaviour – but about contemporary western critiques of consumerism and the ways in which people are

attempting to subvert, escape and remake the economic constraints, cultural values and moral frameworks of the First
World societies they inhabit.

Consumerism, of course, is not merely a phenomenon of
rich nations; during the latter half of the twentieth century
it became increasingly global, coming to pervade certain
developing economies as well. Nevertheless, the world
epicentre of consumption expenditure has been and indisputably remains the affluent West. This is true regardless
of western economic cycles of consumer heaven and recessionary hell or of rapidly expanding, though now tempered,
resource usage and discretionary spending in countries such
as China and India. In global terms, the world's rich nations
can only be described as either consumerist or rampantly so.
At no stage – not even during economic downturn – does
the affluent world merely consume its global fair share of
goods and resources, let alone underconsume them. The
notable feature of the financial market crash of 2008, and
the subsequent end of the long consumer boom, was that
the overconsumption of goods and resources in the West
did not somehow miraculously cease; it has merely been
scaled down for a time – and those who have paid the price
of our economic woes are, as always, those at the bottom
of the social ladder both in the West and beyond. This
permanent, if fluctuating, state of high consumption has
privileged and rewarded many of us in affluent nations at
the same time as it has, at least occasionally, troubled us.
If consumerism has over the past century or more somehow captured a western consciousness, as many contend, it
has also bedevilled a western conscience. As a result, consumerism has perennially engendered public debate and
widespread public unease in the West – and no more so
than over the last tumultuous decade of heady consumer
binge and volatile monetary crisis.

Yet the key terms of this debate are resolutely slippery, and in a book of this nature – one written for a diverse readership – they call out for some preparatory discussion. What, after all, might actually be named and signified by the roll-off-the-tongue phrases that seem always to slip into public discussion about consumption, and particularly the material desires of the affluent world?

The terminology of 'the West' is one such elusive beast. As an entity, the borders of the West seem to contract and expand as we variously define it on the basis of geography, religion, culture, economic development, military alliance, political system and ideology. As a way of segmenting the globe, that which is western is indelibly marked by its juxtaposition to 'the East', and ostensibly includes not only western and northern Europe and parts of southern Europe but also North America and Australasia. Things become somewhat more diffuse, though, if we define our world in terms of affluence. Indeed, countries that enjoy 'western-style' consumption and have a high per capita gross domestic product include most, but not all, nations within the traditionally western orbit, as well as countries such as Japan and Singapore, Brunei and United Arab Emirates. These latter nations are hardly western in a cultural sense but they must be counted as part of the economically developed world. To cloud things further, a number of other countries – particularly China and India, as I have already noted – have been developing a 'consuming class' by way of hitherto extraordinarily high rates of economic growth, industrial expansion and commercial entrepreneurialism.

Historically, however, it is in a readily identifiable set of countries – the USA, Germany, the United Kingdom, France, Norway, Ireland, Canada, Australia and so on – that particular economic frameworks, and particular sensibilities towards the acquisition and enjoyment of the products of the marketplace, have in the modern era developed apace. As such, high consumption has been cemented in the global mind, and particularly in the post-World War II era, as an invention and propensity of these kinds of societies – the societies of 'the West' – above all. This renders the terminology of 'West' and 'western' descriptively useful but inevitably clumsy. The same can be said for the starkly dichotomous language of First and Third World, Developed and Developing World, North and South. In the chapters that follow I thus variously invoke the overlapping terms 'western', 'affluent world', 'rich world', 'First World' and so on, but do so with a degree of caution. At times, also, I adopt the useful recent convention of referring to the Minority World to designate the West, and the Majority World to designate the rest. This linguistically reminds us that, on this planet, the few are rich but the many are poor.

If identifying the West is a fraught exercise, so too is defining consumerism. In everyday parlance, consumerism is not an abstract, academic concept; it is for many people a much utilized and often negative descriptor of a western – and increasingly global – *Zeitgeist*. It speaks of a perceived world that with each new generation becomes more and more embroiled in material gain; and more and more prone to nasty economic shocks because of it. While a perceived right to consume, to unrestrictedly spend one's hard-earned money, has become accepted by many as a marker of personal freedom, power and expression and as the flag bearer of democracy, excessive consumption still presents itself as a social and moral problem. Consumerism is unstintingly spoken of in everyday conversation and in social commentary as an attitude and a behaviour that, while it waxes and wanes with the economic times, remains somehow definitive of historically rising levels of affluence. Attitudinally, consumerism is routinely understood by both the public and the critic as an individual, generational or cultural obsession: an obsession with continually wanting, acquiring and discarding stuff – and with both evaluating others and seeking existential meaning through this process. Behaviourally, this propensity towards abundance is apparently all too clearly demonstrated in boom-to-bust cycles of non-stop shopping and unconstrained spending, and in the mounting levels of refuse left behind as we tire of one product and opt for another. Consumerism, moreover, is often coupled with an ethos of materialism, generally understood as an overvaluing of things and money, and an exaggerated concern with their accumulation and possession. Paradoxically, in the contemporary West, these two phenomena seem to both converge and diverge in that purchasable things have come to be promoted not as objects to be hoarded and cherished, but as items to be transiently experienced and quickly discarded. In this sense, the West has seemingly perfected a form of consumerism that has buckled and twisted almost out of recognition the possessive materialism of which it was born.

In short, then, consumerism is conventionally understood as referring not to the consumption of goods and services *per se*, but to the endlessly desirous and routinely wasteful consumption of affluent economies. This is a form of consumption that is always, to a greater or lesser extent, part of the day-to-day reality of western life; and, at its worst, it is seen to embody the values of profligacy and greed, selfishness and indulgence, irresponsibility and social disconnection. There is, however, a twist: consumerism is almost always invoked by the public and the critic as a foible of others – and only sometimes of ourselves.

This same tendency to both deride and distance oneself from consumerism has been wellnigh perfected by social theorists, who have nevertheless crafted more detailed interpretations of its emergence and meaning. Consumerism

– understood as a culturally manufactured desire for and preoccupation with the getting and having of consumer goods
and experiences – has remained a perennial intellectual
concern across the political spectrum. Scholars have unceas-
ingly portrayed consumerism as paradigmatic of a capitalist
modernity, speaking of it as an ideology, a moral doctrine,
a culture, a syndrome, a mentality and a way of life. This
has yielded a powerful narrative of modern times whereby
consumerism is purveyed by political and economic elites,
embraced by populations and lived by individuals. In an historical era of consumerism, the products of the marketplace
are seen by theorists to have become ideologically and experientially central to self-identity and individuation, personal
status and group belonging, and to social life itself. Thus,
consumerism in the modern world is so often understood
by theorists not only as material overabundance but also as
ubiquitous, as at once everywhere and inescapable. In the
process, consumer society and an accompanying consumer
culture has, it seems, been forged over many decades, if not
centuries. This is a society and culture in which – regardless
of the highs and lows of global capitalism – all of economic
and social life becomes organized increasingly around consumption as function and goal, and in which a consumerist
mentality and sensibility dominates on both a collective and
individual level. Part and parcel of this has been the central
and ongoing phenomenon of commodification: literally the
process of 'marketizing' existence, of rendering ever-more
aspects of our everyday life as commodities – or things and
activities that must be bought and sold through a system of
monetized exchange.

Already, given this lightning tour through the language of
consumption, we can begin to sense what an 'anti-consumerism' might be all about. We can begin to grasp the subject of
its critique and the object of its opposition. This is a political

discourse – and an emergent cultural and moral sensibility – that rests solidly on the public, critical and theoretical understanding of western consumerism sketched above. Yet it is a field of action as well as analysis, one that purposefully and volubly talks of and enacts a partial escape from the enclosing logic of the western consumer present and insists that the task ahead of us is not to return to an era of global hyperconsumption, but to hasten the demise of consumerism itself.

In the text that follows, I explore, question and conceptually extend the perspectives and solutions offered by this essential political critique of the era. I move also towards a reinterpretation of western consumerism – and the pressing task of understanding its reach and dimensions in a world in transition.

ACKNOWLEDGEMENTS

Gratitude, in its deepest sense, is perhaps best expressed with meaningful brevity – and, in acknowledging my many debts, I will keep to this rule. I could not have written this book without the help of three colleagues; Andy Scerri, Ferne Edwards, and Kelly Donati. As researchers, each of them brought an intellectual agility and a political passion to this project that has shaped it for the better. I thank all them warmly. I thank also those who participated in the interviews; both for the generosity of their time and the quality of their insights.

At RMIT University numerous colleagues have, over many years, influenced my thinking and writing. I particularly want to acknowledge the contribution of my friends in the Globalism Research Centre; especially Paul James, Yaso Nadarajah, and Manfred Steger, who was instrumental in bringing this book to publication. On a more formal note, I express appreciation of the financial support offered by RMIT through its small grants scheme, and the considerable support of the Australian Research Council through its Discovery Project program.

The writing of this book has been a wonderful and mostly joyous process, thanks to a handful of people whose involvement made it a much smoother task than it might have been. At Polity, Emma Hutchinson seemed to take to this book from the beginning and, with a gentle and enthusiastic editorial touch, has helped me improve on it immeasurably. My Melbourne-based copy-editor Gill Smith brought a wonderful clarity and lightness to so many of my paragraphs, while Anna Zaranko in the UK saw the manuscript through its final stages. Various colleagues and friends – especially Jo and Neil MacLean, Mandy Brett, Judy Smart, Jeff Lewis, Mary Danckert and Tim Jordan – offered much-needed advice, gave generous assistance or valiantly read the penultimate draft.

Finally, to my family. This book bears the supportive mark of my sisters Jan and Rob. It is a product, most of all, of the forever tangible gaze of my mother, the late Nicky Humphery. It speaks of – and I hope it will eventually speak to – my daughters Rosa and Freya. And it is written for Sarah MacLean. After all, after everything, it could not have been otherwise.

INTRODUCTION: TROUBLE IN
CONSUMER PARADISE

Vancouver in November is a perishingly cold place; Melbourne, Australia, is considerably warmer. Yet both it seems, around this time of the year, are hotbeds of radicalism or at least of civic action and agitation squarely focused on one of the key issues of our time – consumption.

Every year in Vancouver, and in many other cities around the world, Buy Nothing Day (BND) is staged in late November. As the slogan suggests, this annual stint of cultural politics, involving a whole range of activities from street theatre to public lectures, urges people, as the BND website puts it, to 'shop less – live more'.[1] Initiated by the artist Ted Benton, and subsequently adopted by the Canadian-based Adbusters organization in the early 1990s, BND has garnered considerable media attention along with a mixture of support and derision from within the broad global coalition of political movements of which it is a part. This focus on the perils of shopping embodies nevertheless what the North American sociologist Juliet Schor has usefully called the 'new politics of consumption': a politics fundamentally defined by an opposition to the entrenched consumerism of western economies and, more lately, to any return to the global consumer boom of the last few decades.[2]

Actions give rise to ideas, and further action. In December 2006 a group of Melbourne environmentalists launched what they called a 'challenge' rather than a protest event known as the Big Switch Off. The goal here was to enlist people as participants in a collective weekend of minimizing their environmental impact by forgoing the use of electricity, petrol and other energy resources. With their fridges unplugged and by the light of non-petroleum-based candles, this group of concerned citizens hoped in late 2006 that the Big Switch Off, like the BND, would take hold internationally and become an annual event.[3]

There is a purpose in beginning with these two civic actions. Together, they articulate the global and particularly the pan-western nature of a contemporary anti-consumerist politics. Each illustrates also one particular aspect of contemporary consumption: on the one hand, the conspicuous behaviour of shopping for material goods, and on the other, the often inconspicuous activity of consuming resources.

In speaking of the pan-western I'm not suggesting that it is only in the Minority World that the excesses of consumerism are being taken to task. On the contrary, the Majority World has long looked on aghast and with rightful anger at the consumptive greediness of the West, while Majority World commentators and social movements have offered a vigorous rebuttal of global commodity culture. Yet within the world's richest nations it has over the last decade or so become hard for people to escape a now steady murmuring of concern. Here, in the affluent world, our bookshops have been doing a fine trade in critiques of western materialism and our newspapers regularly showcase articles on the perils of consumer culture – sandwiched, of course, between the advertisements and the insistences of politicians that spending equals growth, equals good. By 2008 these warnings had turned to lament and even a 'we told you so' sermonizing, with many a social critic laying the blame for a pulverized global financial market at the feet of the feral shopper 'maxed-out' on easy credit.

In this book, I am especially concerned to focus on these affluent world protests and polemics or, more broadly, on what I will call western anti-consumerism – a field of analysis and action which targets not consumption *per se* but the routine, if currently muted, excesses of consumer economies. While I have, for many years, been engaged in research on consumption in both western and non-western societies, what drives this geographically more modest study is the imperative to explore the singular and recently enlivened intensity with which consumer excess is condemned by western social commentators, challenged by western social movements, and popularly understood by the western public as socially undesirable (at least in its extreme manifestations). Why is this disdain the case? The West, after all, has long been portrayed as an Eden of commodity choice, and in global terms it most certainly is. While, in rich nations, a commodity abundance is accessed in grossly unequal ways, on an aggregate level it is indisputable that western countries are, in commodity terms, wondrous places to be – even in tough times.

But wonder can work on us in many ways. Despite the long-held view that western populations are mindlessly conditioned to shop – a view that will be challenged throughout this book – western individuals have always wondered both privately and publicly about the ultimate desirability of a world chock-full of purchasable things. There is, of course, a long tradition within affluent nations of biting academic analysis and social commentary in relation to the shallowness of a so-called consumer society. There is much evidence also that on an everyday level a majority of individuals within rich world economies experience an ambivalence towards the consumer marketplace – drawn to its luxuries, but repelled by its materialism.

Periodically, in the modern West, concern over consumption comes to a head and bubbles over into a powerful moment of oppositional polemic, public discussion, and social and political action. We in western nations have been experiencing one of the longest of these moments over the last few years, not least because of pressing issues such as climate change. Ironically, just as the wealth of the affluent world achieved an historical high in the late 2000s, also surfacing was trouble in paradise – and not just of an economic kind. This trouble was certainly to emanate from what, in 2008, became the new reality of economic recession, but even before then the dream of endless western abundance was being energetically disturbed by a growing chorus of people offering a direct challenge to the social, moral and environmental values encased in consumer economies.

Over the past decade or more within a number of western countries a new liveliness and urgency has been evident in relation to an albeit long, ongoing debate about the causes, ramifications and future of dominant modes of affluent consumption. Targeting western populations in particular, a resurgent left and liberal opposition to consumerism has focused on what has succinctly, if somewhat vaguely, been called overconsumption.[4] Minority World social commentators, journalists, religious leaders, political activists and academics across the sciences, social sciences and humanities have voiced often impassioned resistance to what is seen as a hitherto increasing, and increasingly global, obsession with the consumption of material goods and commodified experiences. This obsession may well have taken a substantial hit through economic downturn. Yet, as we might now well observe, the western overconsumption of goods and resources remains a stark reality, while western governments remain ideologically wedded even more stubbornly than before to growth economics and accelerated consumption as the sole path to progress.

Overwhelmingly, this resurfaced opposition to consumer abundance has been characterized by an environmentalist ethos – questions of resource usage and waste have been central to this debate. But the latest desire to challenge western (come global) consumerism – and any return to its pre-2008 heights – is also social, cultural and emotional in focus, as such debates have always been. While almost all contemporary critics and activists talk of the need for an environmentally sustainable mode of living, many also focus intently on how the consumerism driving overconsumption undermines our sense of wellbeing and happiness; contributes to a culture of overwork, haste and instantaneous gratification; underscores a bland cultural homogenization of life; and fragments communities and social relationships. In short, contemporary critics argue, overconsumption left unchecked, and potentially shifted back into top gear as recession fades, will ultimately render a world that is socially moribund, one in which nature is subject to its final, irrevocable destruction and in which civic and communal life has entirely dissolved, leaving us to vainly seek fulfilment of our needs and desires in the essentially meaningless plethora of things we can buy.

I have, in beginning to introduce this resurgent political sensibility, articulated its concerns at their most bleak and overgeneralized – and at their most powerful. We can gain an immediate sense of the dominant thrust of this commentary simply through perusing recent booklists. Sometimes, it seems, we *can* read a book by its cover, especially when they are emblazoned with titles such as *The Overspent American*,

Luxury Fever, Affluenza, The High Price of Materialism, The Costs of Living, Your Money or Your Life, Dematerializing and so on.[5] An admirably accessible journalistic style marks much of this recent work, mirroring the broader re-emergence of the 'bestseller' political commentary exemplified by Naomi Klein's *No Logo.*[6] And, lamentably, the contemporary critic of consumerism has a rich field of horrendous statistics and concerning trends on which to draw in underscoring the validity and urgency of their arguments. In terms of global inequality, contemporary commentary can, and repeatedly does, point to the fact that 20 per cent of the world's population – those residing in rich nations – account for around 85 per cent of total global consumer spending.[7] In terms of environmental degradation, critics press home the reality that world consumption, global recession or not, is now far exceeding the Earth's capacity to regenerate the resources feeding production.[8] Moreover, in social and emotional terms, commentators make much of the fact that despite exponentially rising levels of wealth and commodity consumption within many rich nations over the past three decades or more, a sense of subjective wellbeing and life satisfaction among western populations has evidently remained stationary. Conversely, in many rich nations, indices of such things as social isolation, partnership breakdown, stress and depression have risen – in tandem, it would appear, with unprecedented levels of affluence that have only now moderated in face of a major economic downturn.[9]

The new politics of consumption, however, is not only a body of commentary. As an 'oppositional discourse', it informs a set of concrete responses to the conventional treadmill of work and spending. Many of the same commentators who write of a world of consumer emptiness look to a life beyond the glitzy commodity and dreams of a new consumer boom, championing instead an ethos of ethical and responsible consumption and promoting the adoption of lifestyle change embodied in movements for simple and slow living. Importantly, the new politics of consumption thus deals in political practice as well as social analysis.

So also does this book. Indeed, my focus in the chapters that follow is twofold. First, I survey the field of contemporary western critique and activism in relation to western overconsumption. Second, I attempt to further develop this field by seeking to productively rethink both how and why consumerism is maintained over time, and why and how certain forms of consumption are to be opposed.

My interest here is thus both intellectual and political. As a scholar – to use that always rather overblown term – I am concerned to deal with ideas, with how a contemporary critique of consumerism often connects with, sometimes ignores and, at its best, contributes to the long-pursued and ongoing project of theorizing consumption and the material nature of everyday life. But my task is more directly contestational too, since a contemporary western anti-consumerism, for all its possible failings, speaks very deeply to my own sense and understanding of justice, of right action and good judgement.

It must be said, however, that much recent commentary on western consumerism does not connect with a sense of what we might identify as critical humility. More than a few contemporary commentators equate the need to deal with the realities of overconsumption by being overly censorious; diagnosing, chastising or simply lampooning the apparently woeful materialism of the conditioned masses. In fact, a good deal of recent critical commentary on western overconsumption indulges, to varying degrees, in a high moralism, a pop psychologism, and a self-helpism, all directed rather more at the individual as consumer than at the institutions of commercial and political power that drive consumption systems. Moreover, there is a tendency, even in the best of such work, to take the erstwhile excesses and public cultures of consumption in the USA as characterizing western nations *per se*, eliding crucial differences in the way consumption is practised, conceptualized and questioned across western populations. Perhaps most limiting of all, much of the anti-consumerist literature currently available has been so determined to dispraise the 'affluenza' of boom-time economies and the commodity-lust of credit-drunk western citizens, that it has left itself with little to say about overconsumption in a time of rising unemployment, mortgage defaults, and relative shopper restraint. As a result, critics have been relegated to either celebrating the apparent end of global hyperconsumerism (and thus ignoring the brutal hardships of recession) or, more positively though somewhat ineffectually, portraying tough economic times as constituting a 'breathing-space' in which we can reflect on the need for more frugal and less materialistic ways of living.

In alluding to these limitations of a resurgent anti-consumerism, of the new politics of consumption, I am signalling the interrogative thrust of this book, albeit one that is informed – as I shall explain below – by an ethos of generative rather than conventionally critical analysis. The timeliness, importance and resonance of a critique of western overconsumption can hardly be disputed at a moment when our world seems to be under so much pressure environmentally, socio-politically and economically. Indeed, one task of this study is to appreciate the deeply constructive manner in which a renewed politics of consumption has repositioned the economic and social practices of western populations in relation to a whole set of interrelated issues: our attitude towards nature, our sense and use of time, our understanding of life satisfaction, the exploitative labour practices of global commodity production, the imperative to consume in a sustainable manner, and our obligation to ensure a globally equitable level of access to and distribution of the world's resources. This new politics, if it can be so named, is a rich one indeed.

Yet a politics of change must question itself and the ideas it draws on and gives rise to, as much as it must question its object of opposition. The British sociologist Elizabeth Shove has noted the reticence of environmentalist commentators to analyse the assumptions they make about nature, society and the individual. As a consequence, Shove argues, an environmentalist politics often frames debate about resource usage and social change in terms of ignorance and profligacy on the one hand, and individual restraint and action on the other.[10] The same could be said in more general terms about current social commentary relating to the state and impact of western consumerism.

As a field of public intellectual debate, contemporary western anti-consumerism tends to reinvigorate not only critical opposition and purposeful political action in relation to consumer capitalism but also, more perplexingly, an accompanying image of a vacuous mass culture and of individuals as pathologically conditioned to work, shop and, of late, strive blindly towards a rebirth of consumer good times. It tends to reinvigorate, too, a sense that the gearing of western economies to working and spending can be challenged merely through an act of individual will and lifestyle change. This, as we shall come to explore, draws much anti-consumerist commentary into a highly conventional but thoroughly dubious set of assumptions about the nature of consumer culture and the actions needed to transform it. Moreover, contemporary anti-consumerist commentary is, for the most part, drawn into a contradictory, and none-too-attractive, argumentative logic. While espousing concern for the health and happiness of the western individual, many critics in fact simply indulge in moral disdain or, at best, patronising lament for the apparently addictive consumption decisions and actions of the 'great unwashed' – a disdain embedded within a promise of liberation, or at least enhanced wellbeing, for those somehow brave enough to voluntarily turn off the telly and stop shopping.

In these last few paragraphs, I have already begun to prefigure some of the key lines of discussion that are found in this book and to signal how anti-consumerism is both celebrated for its transformative potential and substantially questioned, problematized and prodded. But, as I have already intimated, my task goes well beyond a simple description and review of a renewed critique of consumption. While western anti-consumerism is certainly the key focus of this study, I am concerned by implication to rethink some of the recurring ways in which consumption as a social practice and consumerism as a set of cultural values remain conceptualized within the western humanities and social sciences, and particularly within critical social theory.

Much social theoretical writing on consumption shares with a contemporary anti-consumerism a set of particular – and highly debatable – assumptions about both the ubiquity and dominance of consumerist values and about the central role and manipulability of human consciousness in maintaining consumerist forms of economic and social life. This book thus treats together the 'political' field of contemporary anti-consumerism and the 'intellectual' field of contemporary social theory, at least in respect of what some contemporary theorists have to say about consumption. By the same token, we are concerned here to bridge a gap of recognition and mutual engagement between the more public forms of anti-consumerist commentary and action and the now rich diversity of academic work on consumption and material culture. This gap emanates from a tendency in recent commentary – even when proffered by academic writers – to ignore or draw very selectively from consumption-related research that is seen as too intellectualist, abstract and complex. This is to some extent a favour reciprocated by the academy. Scholars in the humanities and social sciences have, with notable exceptions, been slow to engage with a politics of consumption that raises questions about the morality of consumption practices and, in particular, the environmental impact of consumerism. Thankfully, this mutual disregard is now changing, and this study is part of that change.

What marks this book also is a changed way of understanding the role and usefulness of what academics are apt to call 'critical analysis'. In both championing and challenging a contemporary western anti-consumerism, the chapters that follow move between the descriptive and the analytical, gradually building up a portrait of this field while, at the same time, progressively testing its limits. Indeed, readers will note the refusal here to engage in a conventional, point-by-point deconstruction of anti-consumerism, and a willingness instead to allow a narrative – and a questioning – of the new politics of consumption to slowly unfold. This approach is informed by a set of broader debates on the very nature and purpose of western research and theoretical speculation.

The Maori educationalist Linda Tuhiwai Smith has written eloquently of the links between the colonization of indigenous peoples and western research methodologies.[11] Her work, and that of others, on the politics of research seems a long way from this discussion of anti-consumerism – but it is not. Within a number of western countries both indigenous and non-indigenous researchers working in a diversity of fields have been at the forefront of moves to remake research practice. In part, this has been informed by a long history of resistance to the imperialistic gaze of western research in which indigenous societies have been exoticized and often derided. But it is informed also by a practical need, in the face of the complex issues facing indigenous communities in the West, to readdress the most basic questions of how and why knowledge is produced, communicated and used. As part of what Tuhiwai Smith has referred to as the development of an indigenous research agenda, this questioning involves, among other things, the adoption of alternative conventions of critical analysis and theory construction that always have in view the processes, politics and ultimate point of particular research endeavours.

Such ideas both draw and contribute to western scholarship, particularly as the field of theory experiences – as it is presently – a realignment of purpose. As the British cultural critic Terry Eagleton has argued, the 'golden age' of cultural theory, of a deconstructive postmodernism intent on problematizing the categories of politics, morality and the universal, is long gone. Eagleton, as a cultural theorist himself, does not devalue the postmodern moment, but urges – and indeed senses in the contemporary politics of global social movements – a step well beyond an anti-foundationalist relativism. The time of 'high theory' (though not theory *per se*) is over, Eagleton rightly contends, if only because the global realities we now face require a clear and consensual political and moral response from the intellectual left, not an arcane academicism.[12]

Across the English Channel, similar concerns have been voiced by quite different writers. The French theorist of science and technology Bruno Latour has asked of the humanities – and particularly of social theory – that it abandon its endlessly critical impulse of debunking all within its path, that it transform its excessive questioning of 'good matters of fact' into dealing instead with contemporary 'matters of concern'.[13] This auto-critique from one who has himself forged a deconstruction of modern science is motivated, much like Eagleton's intervention, by a realization that the academy urgently needs to deal with the pressing political issues of our time. In the process, Latour insists, we need to develop a new critical attitude that does not simply deconstruct but *constructs*, that moves beyond iconoclasm and endlessly pulling ideas apart to a position of intellectually contributing to debate around matters of human import. Latour thus writes of the need to 'associate the word *criticism* with a whole set of new positive metaphors, gestures, attitudes, knee-jerk reactions, habits of thoughts'.[14]

Latour is undoubtedly on target, but why, we might ask, continue to privilege the task of criticism at all as the *raison d'être* of socially engaged academic analysis? Why not move instead to simply demote criticism to the status of a method or tool at hand to be carefully utilized, and to envisage the task of social inquiry as fundamentally *generative*, a notion that Latour himself fleetingly invokes? The term 'generative' in relation to the task of writing and theorizing about the social world inevitably signals a dual sense of the productive. A generative form of analysis and theoretical conjecture is certainly one which is constructive of new ideas – ideas that are offered in ways that build not impermeable, obtuse and jargon-filled theoretical edifices but renewed understandings. On another level, however, the task of a generative form of analysis, as understood throughout this book, is not simply 'knowledge production' or the offering of interpretation. It is also the exploration and assertion of possible solidarities of perspective, belief, action and even identities; it is the furtherance of a politics of change in a highly practical sense.

Perhaps all this is a longhand way of saying that analysis and theory should – in a thoroughly conventional sense – matter. And, indeed it should, as many social and cultural analysts would insist. But a turn to a deeply generative form of inquiry, I would suggest, speaks not simply of the obligation of the humanities and social sciences to engage, but of the imperative to adopt – as Tuhiwai Smith proposes – different modes of engagement. To ground this idea in the context of the present study, this does not entail an abandonment of the critical or of the need for firm judgement in dealing with the pronouncements and actions of contemporary commentators and activists in relation to the present exigencies of western consumption. It does, however, entail putting critique in its place, subordinating it to an open and self-reflexive search for new ways of thinking about consumerism, all within the context of maintaining solidarities of mutual understanding, ethical concern and political focus that builds on, rather than ungenerously derides, the ideas and efforts of others. This ethos undergirds the discussion that follows.

1

THE NEW POLITICS OF

CONSUMPTION

In the month I began writing this book I paid a long overdue visit to an old and very dear friend. We lunched round a solid Australian blackwood table that I knew well, though on this occasion I was to be served more than I bargained for. Not far into the first drink and the nibbles I was beckoned to the loungeroom and ushered into a space transformed or, rather, colonized. Obliterating a view of almost everything surrounding it was the latest of gargantuan and impossibly flat TVs. It had just been home delivered, unceremoniously dumped in the centre of the room, and hastily connected-up; we now stood together before the beast – given that sitting down, in what was still a tiny Edwardian parlour, was no longer a viable option. Remaining silent, but sporting a slightly excited and cheeky demeanour, my friend, knowing my work on consumption, seemed to be half insolently bracing for the critical onslaught. For my own part, I slowly, perhaps oddly, sensed what I can only describe as a rising joy, not in response to the flickering, inescapable screen but because what was being played-out in wordless action was a social reality, a human moment, that is rarely captured adequately in commentary, and least of all in theoretical writing. I could, and would, well argue the merits of the purchase, yet what was being impressed upon me was the delightful fact that the 'commodity' in front of us said nothing in particular, or at least not immediately, about the individual who had purchased it. It did not tell me that he was greedy or stupid, immoral or hypermaterialist, acquisitive or status-hungry, uncultured or unthinking. Knowing this individual, I knew also that such knee-jerk assumptions were ludicrous. They were not only wrong as a summing-up of the man, they illegitimately turned his act of consumption into a means of evaluating him. Here, in fact, was a person who, in his gregariousness and community engagement, put me to shame, and who had simply acquired, and was now showing me, a rather large piece of up-to-date and expensive technology – a thing – that would be used and enjoyed, and no doubt come to be a vehicle of good times to be had through watching the cricket with his kids.

Among critics, this way of understanding consumption is not common. There is an irresistible urge for intellectuals and social commentators to make objects say a range of things about the people who possess them. And what they are made to say is, as we have previously noted, often none too flattering towards the 'consumer'. Occasionally, this is challenged. The anthropologist, Daniel Miller, for example, has recently explored with great delicacy the relationships between people and objects and the way in which our acts of acquiring and valuing things, far from defining us as materialistic and superficial, express our constant ability to use the material world in order to forge and foster our relationships with other people.[1] This challenge, however, raises a central analytical and political dilemma. While there is much about material culture and our relationship with things that can be understood as constructive (and we will certainly return to this fact in later chapters) we cannot escape the need also to reflect on and question market systems, consumption decisions, and the ultimate value of particular kinds of objects. It is the preparedness to tackle this latter imperative that has indelibly shaped contemporary anti-consumerist critique. In fact, at no time in the modern period have social observers and political activists sought to be *more* evaluative of consumption and material possessions than they are currently.

For this, there has been a ready audience. There is, indeed, a definite though now perhaps shifting market for polemic on western consumerism. Across the English-speaking world in particular rarely has a month gone by over the last ten or fifteen years without a new book being published on the perils of working, borrowing and spending. Ironically, by late 2008 one could sense this output slowing in tandem with the global economy. Critics of consumerism have scrambled, like everyone else, to rejig their analysis in face of a boom gone pear-shaped. What remains in place, however, is anti-consumerism itself; that is a highly active and well-developed field of resistance to the still globally dominant logic of over-consumption. But just what is this field of opposition? What perspectives and aims partially unify it? In what sense can it be called a new politics of consumption? And what are its limits in terms of its ability to understand western material life and those who consume? In this chapter I begin to explore these questions by way of synthesizing and, at times, challenging a broad but relatively unified body of contemporary western social commentary on the extent, causes and consequences of consumerism.

In this commentary, there have been some prominent voices. This has been particularly so in North America, long the cradle of world commodity consumption. Pre-eminent here are Juliet Schor's skilful expositions of overwork and overspending in the USA, which have been instrumental in reinstating consumption and affluence as a field of public debate in her own country and beyond. Schor's work has constituted a vigorous return to a sense of western levels of affluence as socially problematic – a critical sensibility that Schor rightly identifies as having once been a key part of an oppositional political agenda within western nations during the 1960s and 1970s. What this critical return brings with it, however, is a slightly altered set of concerns embedded in a realization of the urgency with which we must now confront the social and environmental costs of overconsumptive western economies set on fire over the past few decades by a 'new consumerism', and now struggling out of the inevitable recession. In a similar vein, the North American environmentalist Bill McKibben has spoken of 'a new critique emerging', not simply within intellectual circles but by way of the more grounded formation of a movement for 'voluntary simplicity'.[2]

Notwithstanding the quality of Schor's and McKibben's insights, however, the epithet 'new' in relation to a contemporary politics of consumption smacks a little of overstatement. Invoking such an epithet underplays the extent to which contemporary anti-consumerist commentary exists on an analytical continuum, to a large extent reiterating earlier social theoretical, environmentalist and public intellectual arguments in relation to a commodity capitalism. Similarly, beyond the realm of commentary, a contemporary anti-consumerist activism and alternative lifestyle movement plays out a politics with a long pedigree.

It might be more accurate, then, to talk of a reinvigoration of a politics of consumption having taken place in a range of western countries over the last decade or more. And this needs to be placed itself within the context of a broader reinvigoration of the genre of oppositional political criticism more generally. Although it's difficult to ground this claim empirically, there is an undoubted sense among western intellectuals, social commentators and activists that the 'noughties' have signalled a return, in the wake of a post-modern moment of radical doubt, to the stuff of politics. Just as there has been a discernable 'environmental turn' across the field of social analysis in the West, there has emerged also what we might call a 'moral turn' which seeks to rescue questions of value, universal rights and purposive ethical and political action from the clutches of what is seen by many as a debilitating overemphasis during the 1980s and 1990s on cultural and moral relativism.

Already, in introducing this book, we have noted the recent questioning of theory by social theorists themselves, with both Terry Eagleton and Bruno Latour writing of the necessary demise of a mode of late-twentieth-century theorizing intent on endless deconstruction. We noted also in the Introduction the vigorous re-emergence over the past few years of left and liberal public intellectual critique and of a readership receptive to its arguments, particularly concerning questions of global economy and culture. In fact, Naomi Klein was writing by the year 2000 of a political (and generational) shift from an activist concern with questions of discrimination and identity to a new, more globally engaged politics of anti-corporatism. Similarly, the British writer David Boyle, in exploring an emerging desire among western populations for 'authenticity' in opposition to the spin and virtuality of western culture, has written of a new humanism replacing a now defunct postmodernism.[3]

Whatever the status of such claims, recent anti-consumerist commentary is undoubtedly a part of what many see as a renewed political moment, and Schor is right in recognizing this. In fact, the links between rubric critiques of globalization and more focused anti-consumerist polemic are somewhat blurred. Thus, the writings of a varied bunch of thankfully very present contemporary malcontents, from John Ralston Saul, Martha Nussbaum and Richard Sennett to Naomi Klein and George Monbiot – to name but a few – target consumerism and overconsumption as an element of their concerns. Other writers, such as Joel Bakan, David Boyle, Thomas Frank, Carl Honoré and Eric Schlosser – once again a selective list – focus specifically on aspects of current economic life and its alternatives, from fast food and brand marketing to corporate power and slow living.[4] Finally, there is the very particular body of work framing this study: those writers who over the last decade or so have taken on consumerism directly as their principal focus of analysis and opposition.

There are, I want to suggest here, a number of tiers to this latter body of work. Predominantly, commentators critical of western consumerism – from Juliet Schor, Barry Schwartz, John de Graaf and Kelle Lasn to Robert Frank, Paul and Anne Ehrlich, Tim Kasser and many others – have adopted the genre of the concerned public intellectual intervention.[5] This work is resoundingly North American in origin and mostly journalistic in style – even when written by academics.[6] Yet underneath this is another tier of anti-consumerist research and writing that is both more specialist – aimed, for example, at an environmentalist or even business readership – and more avowedly scholarly in that it examines the issue of 'sustainable consumption' with a formality not usually possible in the context of pursuing the pacy syntax of the non-fiction bestseller.[7] Finally, these popular and specialist tiers of anti-consumerist commentary and analysis inevitably draw on and reframe social and cultural theory. Thus, increasingly, contemporary theorists invoke the new politics of consumption in reflecting on the current predicament of late modernity.[8] It is the first and, to a lesser extent, the second of these tiers that I discuss in this chapter, leaving an engagement with recent social theory until a little later.

It must be said from the outset that one of the defining features of the new politics of consumption – particularly as expressed in public intellectual commentary – is its repetition of a limited set of understandings and perspectives and the speed with which a number of its pronouncements on western economic life have become in part irrelevant in the post-2008 era. There should be no mincing of words here. Much contemporary anti-consumerist writing in the West is, in conceptual and analytical terms, a somewhat static conversation in which, with some notable exceptions, one text blends into another, proffering the same arguments, utilizing the same evidence and juggling a similar range of solutions. Emblematic of this is the use over the past few years of the same title – *Affluenza* – for three separate books: one North American, one Australian and one British. Each of these in part constructive books essentially pushes the same pathologizing argument; that consumerism is driven by a conditioned desire to keep up with the Joneses and ultimately results not in satisfaction but personal unhappiness.[9] This minor epidemic of affluenzas does not signal a politics that is, in analytical terms, creative. Rather, it signals a type of commentary that has reached an impasse, uncertain of how to further develop an interpretation of and response to the exigencies of global consumption. Even more damagingly, talk of 'affluenza' has become a dead end in a time beyond the millennial boom; an era that requires a far more nuanced understanding of why and how the West consumes than is evident in a trite, if pithy, labelling of the western individual as manic shopper.

Yet, notwithstanding these difficulties, much recent commentary on western consumption has, on any fair estimation, admirably reframed public political agendas in many affluent nations. Repetition may make for a lack of analytical dynamism but it does at least speak of a certain unity of focus and intent on the part of those who seek to expose and oppose the environmental and social ramifications of western consumerism. It yields also a political perspective that is remarkably synthesized in relation to the identification of the causes and consequences of contemporary western overconsumption. In the remainder of this chapter, then, I trace and explore the contours of this synthesis. In doing so, I focus particularly on how a western consumerism has come to be interpreted and contested in ways that are intensely *socially oriented* rather than simply ecologically framed.

OVERCONSUMPTION

Undoubtedly, the key concept of overconsumption has come to shape contemporary critical engagements with a global consumerism. In the context of decades of rising, if now stumbling, Minority World affluence, commentators have looked to the historical rise in the consumption of goods and services within many western nations as reflective of an inability and lack of will to grasp the pressing realities of environmental 'overreach' and of global economic inequality. But more than this, overconsumption is understood also in terms of a further threshold having been reached in the maintenance of personal wellbeing and, more broadly, of social health. Although the concept of overconsumption is often invoked with a frustrating vagueness, it remains useful in drawing attention, when used in its most politicized sense, to the unnecessary excess of global commodity capitalism. Within contemporary discussions of anti-consumerism, this is an excess variously and interconnectedly understood in terms of ecology, equity, wellbeing, social cohesion and morality. While thus loosely defined, and often mistakenly used as a synonym for the somewhat different processes of consumerism and commodification, overconsumption is made to cover a very broad conceptual ground. Its conceptual importance has also, we might note, been strengthened in face of a world economic downturn; in large part because, while a rampant consumerism is presently a less visible feature of affluent societies, the global overuse of resources and the churning-out of waste has only marginally declined.

The well-known critics of western affluence and global population growth Paul and Anne Ehrlich utilize the term overconsumption in a predominantly ecological sense to designate levels of acquisition that go beyond those necessary to meet 'basic needs' and provide 'reasonable comfort'.[10] This serves as a straightforward starting definition. In considerably more detail, however, Thomas Princen usefully distinguishes between *overconsumption* as an aggregate ecological concept, indicating a level of resource usage that undermines a species' life support system, and *misconsumption*, understood as the taking of poor economic decisions on the part of individuals that results in a loss of personal wellbeing through the stress of debt and overwork. Such a distinction, although contestable, effectively allows us to more clearly envisage a rubric notion of overconsumption dualistically: as a structural and very much ecological problem inhering in particular forms of economic organization, and as a problem concerning the nature of individual consumption decision making.[11]

There is, of course, recognition by many writers that overconsumption is an increasingly global rather than simply western issue, evidenced in the rise of what Myers and Kent have called the 'new consumers' within developing and transitional economies. Similarly, overconsumption, on an aggregate basis, is most definitely related to global and regional population levels as well as consumption rates.[12] Yet, notwithstanding the impact of population growth and the global spread of high-consumption modes of living, it is indisputably the case that western capitalist economies have always been the most highly consumptive on a global per capita basis; and this remains so despite recent First World recessionary trends.

Given this fact, overconsumption has a broad *ethical* meaning in the hands of many contemporary critics that goes beyond a sense of its crucial ecological impacts or the personal psychophysical effects of individual consumption decisions. To return to the work of the Ehrlichs, they offer a clear recognition that a global environmental crisis is embedded in a two-dimensional political reality involving overconsumption on the one hand and underconsumption – or poverty – on the other. As they constructively state:

> Ironically, the world is thus faced with a complex dual problem. If civilization is ever to achieve sustainability it must find ways both to increase necessary consumption in poor nations and to simultaneously reduce wasteful and harmful consumption in both rich and poor countries.[13]

This 'other directed' sense of overconsumption as inequality is undoubtedly a strong theme that runs throughout the contemporary body of western critical commentary on consumerism. This work has been marked also, however, by a certain analytical irony. While informed by ecological and global equity perspectives, so much of the recent western literature on the perils of consumerism has attended almost exclusively to its impact on the western life-world. This focus has not only privileged questions of personal wellbeing and the life satisfaction of western individuals, but also emphasized the related impact of hyperconsumerism on the social cohesion and moral state of western populations above all.

In relation to the question of wellbeing and life satisfaction especially, this approach is evident in the considerable attention given by recent commentators to a range of other important areas of excess: namely, overspending, overwork and overscheduling. As accompanying notions to the phenomenon of overconsumption, overspending invokes a sense of people living beyond their means (a propensity that has now hit home for western economies), while overwork and overscheduling speaks of the contemporary nature of paid labour in the West and of the so-called 'velocitization', or speeding-up, of working and everyday life.

These notions concerning work and speed importantly shift the focus of attention from consumption to time, while signalling the deep interconnection of these facets of everyday existence in the Minority World. Thus, the North American critic and simple-living theorist John de Graaf has identified 'time poverty' or 'time famine' as the key issue facing US citizens. As de Graaf, Schor, Stephan Rechtschaffen and others have powerfully argued, increased postwar productivity in the USA resulted by the mid-2000s in a highly stressful work-and-spend cycle in which economic growth translated into higher incomes but, at the same time, brought with it increased working hours and higher consumer spending rather than greater leisure. Commentators in other western countries that have also maintained high average working hours, such as Australia and Britain, have similarly advocated a need to tackle the issue of overwork – a phenomenon that remains a lived reality for many despite high levels of unemployment.[14]

A related but somewhat different confrontation with an overvaluation of speed and efficiency – with the velocity of the western life-world – is embedded in the Slow Food movement and in the advocacy of 'slow living' generally. As Carlo Petrini, one of the key founders of Slow Food, passionately argued in 2001, a globalized consumerism – symptomatic of which is the incipient globalization of fast food – extinguishes local agricultural–culinary production and traditions as well as a personal ability to sense and celebrate the pleasures, conviviality and taste of local cuisines. Such concerns remain current, and they easily translate into and connect with notions of slow living – or taking greater control of social and personal temporality – as a way of resisting what the British journalist Carl Honoré has called the cult of speed. This cult is bound up, Honoré argues, with a consumeristic and ultimately unsatisfying cramming of life with commodified goods and experiences. [15]

Of course, to return to the point raised earlier, it is a little problematic to utilize terms such as 'poverty' and 'famine' in relation to the lives of working westerners, and to emphasize their need for increased leisure and pleasure in the context of an anti-consumerist politics informed in part by a concern for global economic inequalities. At work here is a heavy paradox – involving a focus on the western self as a way of expressing a concern for the global other – that often goes unrecognized or is poorly handled within recent commentary. It is not, however, a paradox that entirely eclipses the importance of identifying the varied, including personal, dimensions of western overconsumption as being of both local and global significance. And in this vein, it is of equal import to emphasize the manner in which tackling issues of individual wellbeing necessarily translates into a broader confrontation with the socio-moral meaning of overconsumption for western populations.

Just as ecological concerns underlie and run throughout the contemporary field of western anti-consumerist critique, so too does a concern for the social and moral state of western countries. As such, the always ongoing consumptive excess of affluence is interpreted by many contemporary public commentators as breaching a socio-cultural, not simply an ecological, threshold. Here, attention to the individual and the social meanings of high consumption combine. Overconsumption, driven by the imperative to maintain or regain a national state of hyperconsumerism, is almost universally recognized within contemporary anti-consumerist commentary as essentially depleting the 'social health' of affluent nations from one generation to the next. Indicative of this is an impairment of a sense of civic connection, a fragmentation of personal relationships and social networks, and a diminution of support for collective consumption, or public provision, in relation to welfare spending and the maintenance of state services.[16] This is intensified, as the psychologist Barry Schwartz has argued, by a debilitating excess of choice within wealthy nations which, instead of bringing freedom, brings a socially destructive individualism. The 'time poverty' wrought by overconsumption is implicated in this process also. As the North American writer Jonathan Rowe has nicely put it, in demonstrating a concern for what he calls the 'temporal commons', 'The market has been claiming more and more of the nation's time [for the work of citizenship], just as it has been claiming more of nature'. Finally, and in perhaps the most strongly normative terms, overconsumption is understood as having, to use Herman Daly's words, a corrosive effect on moral standards and as impairing, to cite Paul Wachtel, our sense of 'love, friendship, being part of a community, being committed to or part of something larger than oneself'.[17]

Clearly, a contemporary questioning of dominant western approaches to nature, wealth and time draws on a long tradition of critiquing affluence, advocating the limits to growth and lamenting the rise of consumer society. I am largely confining discussion in this chapter to the most recent public intellectual commentary. Yet, as most writers would readily admit, there are loud echoes within contemporary commentary of J. K. Galbraith and Vance Packard, of Donella Meadows and E. F. Schumacher, of André Gorz, Fred Hirsch and William Leiss, and of many other twentieth-century critics of affluence as social and environmental destruction.[18]

Indeed, a number of the writers already mentioned in this chapter, have themselves proved honourable contributors to this broad body of research spanning many decades.[19] What, then, has driven an apparent rejuvenation and intensification of critical concern as we have entered the new millennium? Undoubtedly, as many commentators insist, a moment of truth has been reached whereby both western and non-western societies can no longer ignore the environmental consequences of their actions. But it is also the case that as the western life-world, and indeed that of the globe, has seemingly become more and more geared to consumption as a path to progress, the utter dependence of the Minority World on a permanency of consumer excess somehow becomes more noticeable – and perhaps even more so as the West both reaps the consequences of financial crisis and yet struggles still to revive the consumer boom of old. Recent commentary on consumerism thus offers a range of evidence to substantiate the charge of endemic western overconsumption. This evidence is often couched in ecological terms. Yet, a contemporary anti-consumerist critique provides abundant discussion as well of the social meaning of excess.

OVERCONSUMPTION AS CONSUMERISM

In his 1992 book *How Much is Enough?*, the environmentalist Alan Durning provided one of the immediate precursors of the latest swag of books on consumerism and 'enoughness'.[20] In fact Durning's contribution remains one of the best of these texts, combining a predominantly environmental focus with a concern for the global and socio-cultural consequences of affluence. Identifying what he called a 'global consumer class' (living in both western and, to a much lesser extent, non-western nations), Durning contrasted this stratum with the 'sustainable middle', or the then three billion plus of the world's population that achieved reasonable wellbeing on moderate income and resource usage. Much of his book was taken up with offering a convincing range of statistical – and now well out-of-date – evidence on consumption expenditure and its environmental impact. And in the years since its publication, that evidence and the use of the 'shock statistic' to drive home the realities of world ecological decline and global resource inequality has developed apace.

Many shock statistics are now offered in contemporary commentary, and some are mind-boggling indeed. We have noted already the fact that roughly 20 per cent of the world's population – mostly those residing in rich nations – is responsible for roughly 85 per cent of world consumer spending. Of course, such figures, while useful in pointing to distributive imbalance, say little about aggregate overconsumption on a global level. It is on the terrain of environmental evidence that claims of overconsumption become most well grounded. Thus a sense of gross excess and imbalance is often evidenced within contemporary critique by recourse to the notion of the Earth's 'carrying capacity'. As William Rees has demonstrated, this concept is crucial to the notion of ecological sustainability. Writing in 2000, Rees insisted that

> the fundamental ecological question for sustainability is whether remaining natural capital stocks (including other species, populations and ecosystems) are adequate to provide the resources consumed, and assimilate the wastes produced by the anticipated human population into the next century, while simultaneously maintaining the general life-support functions of the ecosphere. In short, is there adequate human carrying capacity?[21]

In environmental terms, at least, there appears to be clear supporting evidence for invoking notions of global ecological overreach and of a rich-world propensity towards routine overconsumption, regardless of economic conditions. Indeed, it is regularly observed by commentators and activists alike that by the late 1970s global consumption levels already exceeded the Earth's capacity to provide the resources necessary for sustaining current commodity production and dealing with the resultant pollutants and waste. Even more powerful has been the emergence of the overlapping and more refined concept of 'ecological footprints', a measure developed by Rees and his colleague Mathis Wackernagel in the mid-1990s. Citing Rees once again, the concept of ecological footprints simply indicates 'how large an area of productive land and water is needed to sustain a defined population indefinitely, *wherever on earth that land is located*' (author's emphasis).[22] This concept, too, has been further developed by researchers connected with the US independent public policy organization Redefining Progress (with which Wackernagel is associated) in order to 'measure and analyse human natural resource consumption and waste output within the context of nature's renewable and regenerative capacity (or biocapacity)'.[23]

This measure is especially useful for providing insight into the differential as well as aggregate global use of resources and the production of waste. Thus, in comparing the footprint of nations, the Redefining Progress group found that by the year 2000 Western Europe and North America had maintained by far their status as having the highest per capita footprints of any regions on earth.[24] At the same time, the world's collective footprint had increased its state of so-called 'overshoot': that is, the global use and degradation of ecological assets continued to surpass the sustainability mark.[25] Of late, this reality has become even more complex. The industrial and urban expansion of China has certainly begun to gradually change this picture (at least in terms of resource exploitation). More to the point, the world economic deceleration of 2008 and 2009 has marginally slowed the clock of ecological decline. The question is: for how long?

Unsurprisingly, ecological impact measures remain imperfect and controversial just as the overused language of sustainability (as well as simplistic conceptualizations of limits to growth) remains problematic. Nevertheless, these measures are drawn on extensively by contemporary critics, and their use and usefulness needs to be understood in the context of a struggle within the sustainability field over a number of decades to insist that consumption, not simply population levels and industrial processes, is one of the primary factors underlying environmental unsustainability.[26] This debate has gone to the heart of how to define a notion of global sustainability itself, distinguishing those who have rejected notions of exponential economic growth, and advocated for a 'strong' model of sustainable consumption and its implementation, from those who continue to emphasize 'sustainable development' in which the problem is envisaged not as overconsumption or growth, but as bound up with the need to environmentally improve production and distribution methods and manage population levels. The latter perspective is often associated not only with development economics but also with the so-called 'natural capitalism' approach, one driven in part by notions of the 'technological fix' in which capitalism can be maintained and aggregate global growth pursued through new production processes that radically increase resource productivity.[27]

To broach issues of the global in relation to overconsumption, however, is to entertain concerns beyond those of ecological limits, population growth, resource-use inequality and sustainability. Much of the recent anti-globalization literature has in fact emphasized the exploitative transnational labour practices underlying the production of western commodities, the unregulated power of expanding multinational and transnational corporations, and the construction of a homogenized global commodity culture. The work of Klein, Monbiot, Bakan and others might be noted here, along with writers such as Benjamin Barber and Jeremy Seabrook, both of whom have talked of the construction of 'McWorld', to use Barber's term, in which a thin global democracy is conceptualized as rooted in market-based individual choice, and in which local and national cultures are reshaped according to the demands and values of the global economy; an economy driven by western needs.[28]

These sentiments steer us directly to the social, rather than environmental 'diagnostics' of much of the recent anti-consumerist literature. While the foregoing discussion of global environmental impact measures has briefly immersed us in the field of environmental research, contemporary anti-consumerist debate in the West sits both inside and outside this field. In fact, much of the literature dealt with here, while informed by environmental concerns, is far more socially oriented and borrows mostly from the disciplines of sociology, economics and psychology. To reiterate, overconsumption, for many critics, is thus not simply to be understood in technical, ecological terms, but is a socio-moral concept – and 'measurable' in socio-cultural ways. Overconsumption is in fact understood as a corollary of a western, and increasingly global, consumerism, as the quantitative marker of a cultural attitude that places commodities at the centre of life. In the work of Schor, Schwartz, de Graaf, Lasn, Kasser, Oliver James, Robert Frank and others, the environment and global equity is a sometimes important but far from central concern. This is what, in part, strongly connects contemporary critique to a critical social theoretical tradition – and renders it of continuing relevance to a world that is being economically realigned.

As a socio-moral notion overconsumption is speculative rather than easily proven. It is also intensely human, invoking a sense that affluent populations and individuals do not simply consume beyond a level of necessity or reasonable comfort but at a level that does demonstrable harm to self and society, besides that of ecological damage. Even excess and waste is not simply to be merely environmentally interpreted, it is indicative rather of an entrenched western consumeristic sensibility involving an overvaluing of material pleasure and monetary status and a lack of care for the personal and social consequences of our action. In grounding this broader and much more amorphous sense of overconsumption as the product of a historically formed and ever-present consumerism, the 'shock statistic' once again comes into play, though perhaps somewhat more problematically than its use in environmental research.

There are many gobsmacking figures to juggle with and North American critics, especially, have been adept at throwing them in the air. As one text informs us, there are more shopping malls in the USA than there are high schools, while another insists, somewhat improbably, that US citizens, as of the late 1990s, spent on average six hours a week shopping and only forty minutes playing with their children.[29] It does not end there. Many critics in fact draw an important if slightly tenuous link between the human body and the social body, particularly in relation to the 'supersizing' of food products. The USA, commentators routinely point out, has the highest rate of obesity in the world, with other western nations not far behind.[30] The mind, too, is understood by critics as highly vulnerable: one author reports that US citizens encounter up to 3000 advertisements per day, a mind-forming exposure experienced by other rich-world populations.[31]

Reading across the last decade of western anti-consumerist commentary, such statistics crop up again and again. At times, critics are keenly aware of the apparently North American nature of a postwar consumerism. Far from generalizing, many North American writers portray overconsumption as very much a part of the 'American Dream' gone feral in the decades of boom-to-bust prosperity from the 1950s on. Yet, these statistics are also sometimes understood transnationally, somehow speaking of a general western life-world, or they are mirrored by the search for similar evidence within other countries.[32]

Fortunately, a somewhat more substantial grounding of a socially oriented notion of overconsumption in the West – and by implication consumerism – is offered through measures relating to income, expenditure and debt. It is well documented that per capita incomes in rich nations have, at least until 2008, risen significantly, and in some countries dramatically, over the last few decades – although these increases have been experienced inequitably across socio-economic groups.[33] When coupled, as in a range of wealthy nations, with declining household savings rates and rising household debt levels, this resulted in unprecedented increases in consumer spending over the final decades of the twentieth century and into the new millennium.[34] To be sure, as Yiannis Gabriel and Tim Lang have noted, the steady rise in western affluence and discretionary spending over the last thirty years has been uneven. The western economic boom of the 1980s was followed by the recessionary period of the 1990s and, by the early 2000s a major resurgence in consumption expenditure was being experienced in many Minority World countries and beyond.[35] This volatility has clearly been momentously capped-off as the first decade of the twenty-first century comes to an end and the long, upward spiral of western consumer spending, global resource exploitation and world financial speculation falters.

These cyclical economic trends will no doubt continue as

western economies shimmy between 'slow-down' and 'recovery'. However, as critics rightly maintain, the long-term logic of increasing consumption will clearly remain in place without fundamental socio-economic change beyond that of massive financial bailouts, economic stimulus measures and more 'responsible' corporate regulation.

But just what is this logic? What is it that drives western consumerism over the long term, maintaining it as a goal – and often as a highly visible activity – irrespective of the economic climate? In many ways the latter question has dominated the field of socially oriented anti-consumerist commentary, with almost all critics feeling the need to identify a limited set of 'causes' driving consumption behaviour and shaping the mentality underlying it. Overwhelmingly, recent commentators have returned to theories of emulation, of 'keeping up with the Joneses', and to notions of mentalist manipulation, particularly through advertising, as preferred explanations for the development of western consumerism over the last half century. At its most direct, recent commentary has opted for the uncomplicated causal portrait, particularly when the aim is simply to advocate for individual and social change in consumption patterns. Thus, in their influential and highly accessible book *Affluenza*, John de Graaf, David Wann and Thomas Naylor dissect what they variously refer to as the virus, disease, infection and syndrome underlying overconsumption. While couched as a tongue-in-cheek account, which provocatively uses the lingo of the medical condition to explore consumerism, there is nevertheless a definite implication here that the pathology is real, that the consumerism – both rampant and more subdued – underlying overconsumption is driven by a false consumer consciousness resulting in damaged individuals and a damaged society.

Many other critics across the western world agree, although there are nuances of interpretation. In adopting the affluenza model (and book title) both the Australian writer Clive Hamilton and the British commentator Oliver James emphasize the emulative nature of modern western consumption and interpret the origins of 'affluenza' as lying in a culturally driven and essentially pathological confusion between wants and needs. The French critic of market economy Christian Comeliau similarly writes of the historical dominance in the West of 'imitative consumerism'. While Kalle Lasn, the Canadian doyen of culture jamming, is even more direct in writing of western nations as long peopled by 'consumer drones' formed through, and ever more susceptible to, marketing messages. Returning to the USA, Paul Wachtel invokes the pervasive force in American culture of an irrational overvaluation of money and of a consumerism driven in part by advertising and constant product innovation but equally by the psychology of comparative expectation.[36]

Working with similar ideas, Schor and Frank have been particularly concerned to reinvigorate Thorsten Veblen's late-nineteenth-century notion of consumption as embedded in comparison and emulation. While notions of consumption as status are invoked here, Frank and Schor offer slightly deeper readings of recent North American consumerism. Frank's notion of 'luxury fever' names the nature of North American conspicuous consumption over the past few decades, particularly the spending habits of the affluent sections of his society. For Frank, consumerism in the US is bound up with a sense of relative expectations that, in the context – at least until recently – of ever-increasing wealth, fosters an ever-upward shift in the benchmark of both desire and socially acceptable consumption levels. However, for Frank, an erstwhile luxury fever has not been a product of marketing, the result of a simple striving for class status or the outcome of a declining sense of public responsibility. It has, rather, been the very product of the economic, and insufficiently regulated, logic of higher income levels.[37]

Others, such as Schor, offer more socially conceptualized explanations. Schor, in referring to the USA, talks of a 'national culture of upscale spending' having emerged since the 1980s in which people increasingly attempt to emulate not simply those one rung above them on the socio-economic scale but, in the context of a changed and globally oriented sense of belonging, those who are wealthy. As evidence of this, Schor draws on a range of surveys which indicate that North Americans have increasingly defined 'the good life' in terms of material luxuries, that over the last three decades, through a process of adaptation, a whole range of once exclusive commodities have taken on the aura of necessity, and that people on even high incomes report feeling that they do not have sufficient money to buy all that they really need. For Schor this ratcheting up of consumption is in part a product of advertising and, to a lesser extent, continual technological innovation, but it is driven as well by the changed nature of social norms in relation to perceived needs and appropriate spending, and the requirements of modern labour markets. This has intensified the felt necessity to work long hours and to engage in competitive or comparison consumption. Schor thus works, drawing on the work of the French sociologist Pierre Bourdieu, with a theory of emulation as social practice and an understanding of consumerism as framed by given social norms.[38]

There are other perspectives, however, beyond – though not in opposition to – theories of emulation and manipulation. Rosenblatt talks of a human yearning driving consumption, of a relentless acquisitive impulse that can only be reined in by examining the self. Alternatively, Schwartz – while also emphasizing processes of adaptation in relation to overconsumption – writes of a heightened culture of increasing individualism, autonomy, liberty and marketplace choice as driving consumerism, the origins of which, Schwartz has insisted, lay in the very chaos and openness of modernity itself.[39]

A very similar range of explanatory arguments inflect environmentalist writing and frame some of the more scholarly literature on sustainable consumption. The environmental analysts Norman Myers and Jennifer Kent write of high consumption being driven in the West – and on a global level – by a 'Coke and McDonalds culture', and they invoke the affluenzic impact of emulation and the key role of advertising. Similarly, within one of the more reflective collections of essays available on anti-consumerism and sustainable consumption, these arguments are reinforced: the communications expert Marilyn Bordwell confirms Lasn's contention that advertisements are 'conditioning us to a false reality', while the environmental politics specialist Michael Maniates reiterates the role of relative expectation and manufactured wants in maintaining overconsumption.[40]

There is no reason to assume that these various writers would now, in face of an uncertain economic future, disavow an understanding of consumerism as driven by emulation, as the product of manipulation or as the uncontrollable progeny of a human acquisitive impulse. Taking a longer-term view, most critics would no doubt insist that although consumerism in its most rampant guise may be in retreat for a time, it remains an essential propensity of affluent societies – and, as such, must continue to be challenged. They would be right. And yet, much western anti-consumerist polemic over the last decade or more has been for the most part disappointing when it comes to telling the story of *why* we consume. The recourse by critics to conventional notions of emulation, manipulation and acquisitiveness simply hasn't delivered, as the opening narrative of this chapter makes clear, a dynamic understanding of contemporary western

material life – though I shall leave it until chapter 4 to argue
this further. Moreover, any assumption – now emerging in
some critical camps – that recession might give rise to a collective retreat from materialism is appealing but tenuous.[41]
After all, the experience of economic uncertainty (and, for
an increasing number of people, plain hardship), can result
in a longing for an erstwhile prosperity as much as a preparedness to willingly opt for living with less. The continuing
strength of recent anti-consumerist polemic, however, surely
lies in its all-important impetus to wrestle overconsumption
away from purely environmental definitions, conjoining them
with a deeply socio-cultural understanding of its dimensions.
The same impetus is evident when critics have shifted from
naming the supposed causes of consumerism to identifying
the possible effects of consumer desire.

CONSUMERISM AS ILL-BEING

Already, throughout this book, I have alluded to the ramifications of western consumerism beyond that of the environmental
damage and global inequality to which it gives rise. In relation
to the western life-world we have noted the extent to which
contemporary commentators, mirroring a long tradition of
social critique and theorizing, deeply implicate consumerism
in the psychological disturbance of individuals, the breakdown
of family and community life, the unanchoring of cultural
traditions and social bonds, and the undermining of civic
and moral values. These warnings about the consequences
of material excess point towards the principal philosophical dualism underlying the contemporary western critique of
overconsumption – that of disequilibrium versus balance; of
ample versus too much. An Aristotelian sense of striving for
balance in the material, physical, emotional, ethical and spiritual aspects of life, of a striving to live well and in morally good

ways, irrevocably frames the way that contemporary critics interpret the broad individual and social impact of consumerism. And, in this, they are in good company.

As many commentators point out, countless surveys of various Minority World populations indicate very clearly that people perceive western societies as having become over the past few generations too materialistic, too disregarding of nature and too consumeristic.[42] Influential here has been the work of Ronald Ingelhart and the longitudinal research of the World Values Survey. These investigations into the beliefs and values of a wide range of national populations have found that as countries become more affluent there is a movement also towards 'post-materialist' (or quality of life) values – values that place great emphasis, not on the things money can buy but on democratic freedoms, strong communities, meaningful relationships and so on.[43] Such evidence, although rightly contested, tends to suggest that affluent populations are not, in principle at least, quite as accepting of consumerism as it may seem.[44] Indeed, too great an emphasis on consumerism is generally perceived in the West as ultimately having highly negative personal and social ramifications – and here the public majority and the study-bound critic tend to concur.

In dealing with these personal and social ramifications, and in the context of largely adopting emulation and manipulation as causal models, western consumption has been widely – and far too simplistically – interpreted by recent critics as a realm of addiction. In mixing metaphors, commentators have turned from the language of the virus to the language of obsession, fetish and dependency in relation to the western playing out of overconsumption. Here, commentators have tended to focus their attention on shopping and on the acquisition of concrete material commodities rather than on less conspicuous consumption activities such as energy use. Indeed, shopping – the hunt for and purchase of material goods – looms large within contemporary critique and is often seemingly understood as the main vehicle of consumption, not least because theories of emulation require an attention to that which can be seen. The communitarian thinker Amitai Etzioni encapsulates this understanding well when he states that 'Consumerism sustains itself, in part, because it is visible'.[45] An attention to consumption as a form of socially sanctioned – and governmentally encouraged – addiction has led some commentators to rather wildly extend the clinical concept of 'compulsive shopping', or oniomania, identified by psychiatrists as a specific obsessive-compulsive disorder, to western populations *per se*.[46] For others the treatment of consumption as addiction remains largely metaphorical rather than overgeneralized as a 'real' condition defining western economic behaviour *in toto*. Whatever the slant, individual entanglement with consumerism as a culture of acquisition, display and disposal is placed at the core of a radical disintegration of self and society in the West. Like so many forms of dependency, and as embodied in the very term itself, consumption is understood as destruction.

As Comeliau has put it, perhaps articulating the concerns of many critics, 'wherever market rationality acquires dominance it transforms *social relations in their entirety*' (author's emphasis).[47] This transformation, for Comeliau, actively promotes individualist and materialist values destructive of social cohesion. More particularly, Schor by 2005 was, with characteristic clarity, delineating the impact of consumer society – understood as a society in which 'the vast majority of people have a consumerist attitude or are living consumerist lifestyles' – as fourfold in nature. Besides that of its ecological impact, Schor spoke of late modern consumerism as diminishing people's ability, through overwork, to engage in non-market social activity, as having almost entirely replaced public consumption with private expenditure, and lastly, although more speculatively, as having undermined a collective ability 'to construct durable community'.[48]

Once again, there is no reason to assume that critics would shy away, in light of recent economic change, from visions of consumerism as addictive. In fact, anti-consumerist critique might well claim a prescience in alerting us to the negative trajectory of rich-world economies dependent on reflex borrowing and spending. What is more, in relation to the lived experience of individuals, the insistence that we must confront our 'dependency' on consumption and seek fulfilment beyond the realm of material acquisition has substantial and continuing relevance across and within a range of Minority World nations. Perhaps the most grounded evidence of this, emanating from a field of research that is made much of in the new politics of consumption, relates to a sense of life satisfaction, often understood interchangeably with the notions of subjective wellbeing or happiness. In narrow economic terms, particularly within measures such as Gross Domestic Product (GDP), life satisfaction has been simply identified with income, wealth and prosperity. As the contemporary critique of consumerism has ably pointed out, GDP is still taken by governments as an overriding indicator, at least at a national level, of wellbeing. Moreover, within conventional, and still dominant, utilitarian economic theory the ability of people to satisfy their needs and wants through the marketplace remains almost the sole measure of life satisfaction. The critique of this position is now decades old and well founded. Economists such as Richard Easterlin and Amartya Sen long ago problematized the assumed connection between money and wellbeing (not to mention the fact that a similar perspective animated much of classical western thought).[49] Similarly, philosophers and historians of happiness have long explored its dubious linkage with wealth – and this critical perspective has been reconfirmed as one of the principal organizing arguments of a contemporary anti-consumerism.[50]

As Bill McKibben writes of US society, despite the growing affluence of the past three or four decades (and per capita disposable income in the USA more than doubling in real terms between 1960 and the late 2000s), 'The number of people who described themselves as very satisfied peaked somewhere in the mid-1950s'.[51] Variants of this sentence, often drawing on similar data about other western populations, appear repeatedly in almost all recent anti-consumerist commentaries. Understandably, such survey evidence is interpreted as a 'trump card', demonstrating that despite the rhetoric of affluence as the path to happiness, this is not borne out by the research. While some writers have come a little too close to blandly restating a 'poor but happy' interpretative line, most are far more careful. As Etzioni has observed, while the data on subjective measures of wellbeing is conflicting, the bulk of studies clearly suggest that 'income does not significantly affect people's contentment, with the important exception of the poor'.[52] This has been found to be the case across a range of wealthy nations, including Japan, Western European countries and Australasia.[53] It must be said that commentators are not always so quick to point out that, as the Australian psychologist Bob Cummins has established, a general sense of life satisfaction – as opposed to a more affirmative claim of being 'very happy' – is the norm across western populations and is remarkably stable over time. On average, western citizens rate themselves as being about 75 per cent satisfied with their lives, and this result appears to fluctuate little from year to year.[54] Nevertheless, operative here is most certainly a phenomenon of diminishing returns. As the North American psychologist David Myers observed in his offering to the now long list of books on wealth and happiness, while there is a tendency for wealthy countries to have a larger proportion of people who are more satisfied with life in comparison to economically impoverished nations, beyond a certain level of national wealth subjective feelings of life satisfaction do not seem to increase with greater national prosperity. Even within individual nations, beyond a certain level of affluence, increases in personal income and wealth do not contribute significantly to subjective wellbeing.[55] This suggests that, within western nations, the rich are no more likely to be happier than those possessing more moderate wealth and this in turn underscores the now much-articulated argument that of greater relevance to people's subjective measurement of their wellbeing, at least in economic terms, is their *relative position* in comparison to others.

This body of survey data concerning the plateauing of the (already high) average levels of wellbeing within affluent nations is often conjoined with a contention that happiness levels may well have actually declined within western countries over the last few decades. Although there is little conclusive evidence of this, commentators point in a more speculative vein to a rise in rates of anxiety, depression, suicide and divorce across the Minority World.[56] A related, though even more speculative, concern is with the supposed prevalence of a so-called materialistic 'personality type', open to such anxiety. Social psychologists in the USA, Britain, Germany, Australia and elsewhere have psychometrically tested individuals for materialistic values and have calibrated these values against states of psychological wellbeing.[57] Using 'materialism scales' and surveying various population groups, this field of research suggests that people with highly materialistic aspirations – those who greatly value the pursuit of money and the acquisition of possessions – show a lack of civic sensibility and social connectedness and report, to cite Tim Kasser, 'lower psychological wellbeing than those who are less concerned with such aims'.[58]

Taking recent 'happiness research' as a whole, the overall implications of stagnating, even diminishing, rates of subjective life satisfaction seem clear. If increasing affluence fails to translate into personal happiness and collective wellbeing then why pursue exponential economic growth? This is a crucial socio-political question, and in posing it – or rather in loudly raising this question again, as so many have done in the past – a contemporary anti-consumerism demonstrates the intelligence and integrity of its approach. It also, of course, demonstrates its tendency to focus above all else on the self-fulfilment of the western individual, and to rely on often dubious survey and psychometric data in doing so. Posing individualized questions of life satisfaction, though, undoubtedly makes for good short-term political strategy. As the North American environmentalist Betsy Taylor states, the goal of a new politics of consumption 'is to make an emotional connection with people and then persuade them to take action'.[59] The terrain of the self is the perfect terrain of this persuasion.

Yet the self and the social are obviously inextricably intertwined; and a contemporary anti-consumerism thus moves between personal and collective life-worlds. To be sure, in moving from a focus on personal and aggregate scales of wellbeing to a concern for the social and moral health of western nations, contemporary anti-consumerist commentary becomes highly attenuated in strictly empirical terms. It also becomes highly schematic, offering only glimpses of the broader social and moral impact of our apparent obsession with commodities. Schor, for one, recognizes this in noting and questioning the extent to which critics argue that consumerism has destroyed community. For Schor, as for Schwartz, Comeliau and other writers, a more generalized and complex force such as capitalism, modernity or postmodernity may well be the culprit.[60] Yet notwithstanding this more general outlook, recent anti-consumerist discourse as a whole has worked, whether intentionally or not, to place the act of consumption at the dead centre of western socio-moral decline. The two key issues that frame this centrality are, on the one hand, a loss of a sense of community and social connectedness and, on the other, a loss of a moral sense of care beyond the self.

In relation to the former issue, commentators have turned to the notion of social capital, and particularly the work of the North American sociologist Robert Putnam in discussing the impact of consumerism on community. Consumerism has been deeply implicated by many critics in the progressive loss of social capital – understood as resources of trust, shared norms and mutual networks. As explorations of this concept have contended, there has been within western countries a steady dissolution of the integrity of local communities over the past few decades, resulting in increased levels of social isolation and civic disengagement, an undermining among people of a sense of mutual trust, an increased sense of life as marked by risk, and the fragmentation of sense of place and coherent belonging. For contemporary anti-consumerism, these developments are tightly bound up with dominant modes of consumption. At the level of observation a disintegration of local place is evident in the corporate commercialization of streetscapes and shopping precincts and the retail domination of the mega-mall. Similarly, an increased sense of risk and distrust is demonstrated by the investment in so-called 'gated communities' or the growth of residential and consumption enclaves. Finally, a consumerist-driven turning away from a civic sensibility is underscored by the privatization and marketization of government services within many western nations, as well as reductions in the provision of state welfare.[61] Beyond the observational, there is some quantitative evidence for these concerns. Many commentators, particularly in the USA, point to alternative measures to that of GDP that attempt to assess not simply the economic state of western nations, but their generally declining social and environmental development in relation to such factors as income inequality and unemployment, crime rates, and resource depletion and pollution levels.[62]

These social changes are seen to be bound up, as we have previously noted, with a concomitant transformation of individual moral values. Here, however, anti-consumerist polemic enters a most uncertain terrain, one which returns to a sense of consumer culture as productive of a certain type of person, a certain widely ascribed-to morality. Once again, in justifying these claims, somewhat scant survey evidence is drawn on by a number of commentators to indicate a shift in the aspirational values of rich-world citizens over the last decade or so from an earlier primary aim of pursuing a meaningful and fulfilled life to a more recent one of achieving material wealth and success.[63] Perhaps, with the credit bubble now having burst, these unedifying aspirations have been tempered. Yet consumerism is still resoundingly understood in much of the new politics of consumption as reflecting not simply a culture of excess and endless desire, but as speaking of populations that have let or are letting go of virtue. As the Australian wellbeing researcher Richard Eckersley has uncompromisingly stated: 'Once we have met our basic needs, most consumption today is located within the vices, little within the virtues – feeding off envy, to say nothing of greed, lust and other moral hazards'.[64] While we can, and should, take issue with this heavy moral tone, we must also recognize a central point. Contemporary anti-consumerist commentary, a body of work driven by a deep ethos of concern, has been instrumental in insisting that we finally face up to a reality – the world of western consumerism in ecological, global equity, socio-cultural and ethical terms is an ugly one indeed. As contemporary critics rightly insist, it is a world which we desperately need to escape, rather than re-energize – and the following chapter explores the politics of doing so.

2

ANTI-CONSUMERISM IN ACTION

In the previous chapter, I identified the rise of a reinvigorated critique of consumption in the West and explored what contemporary commentators have to say about the extent, causes and consequences of consumerism. One of the most notable aspects of anti-consumerist analysis, however, is not simply its determination to expose the true costs of working and spending but also its preparedness to offer concrete solutions to the problem of western overconsumption.

Contemporary critics have not shied away from the programmatic; many discuss extensively the steps that might be taken in order to combat the environmental, social and personal consequences of western consumerism. Indeed, recent public commentary has been energetically marked by a 'last chapter' interventionism whereby the writer shifts from interpretation – or telling us why consumerism occurs and what it does to nature, society and the individual – to outlining a response.[1] Overwhelmingly, this interventionism has focused on individual change, but it has not by any means ignored other forms of action such as the implementation of regulatory measures to curb consumption and address environmental degradation. In fact, it is possible to identify within anti-consumerist commentary – and more specialized scholarship – at least five intertwined strands of political response.

One such strand, referred to as "culture jamming", invokes a *cultural politics* of consumption, focused on challenging the ideology of consumerism purveyed through advertising. In a somewhat different vein, a *civic politics* of ethical consumption is embraced within much recent critique, whereby individuals are encouraged as responsible citizens to consume in ways that are mindful of the effects of their consumption on others and on the environment. Contemporary commentators have even more vigorously advocated a *life politics*, insisting that individuals enact fundamental lifestyle change. This involves people achieving greater existential satisfaction through working and spending less, a process that has been variously named as downshifting, slow living and voluntary simplicity. This attention to modes of living is at times extended by way of adopting a *community-oriented politics*. Here, individual change is coupled with a more encompassing affirmation of local collective initiatives to create or maintain alternative economic practices and to construct or maintain particular communities. Finally, a *systemic politics* of varying dimensions pervades anti-consumerist literature. This extends from the advocacy of legislative measures to control advertising, impose environmental taxes on consumer goods and regulate production to more radical calls for the reorganization of work practices, the subordination of market imperatives to social goals and the tackling of economic inequality and social fragmentation.

Clearly, these overlapping responses – and we will explore each of them in this chapter – move between what theorists are now apt to call macropolitical and micropolitical aims and actions. That is, they focus both on the achievement of the grand, abstract goals of ecological balance and global justice and on the more immediate aims of individual self-fulfilment and the cultivation of an attitude of care towards both others and nature. Moreover, anti-consumerist texts inform and are informed by a continually developing anti-consumerist activism embedded in a whole range of responses from ethical consumption decision-making and simple living practices to the construction of alternative economic spaces and communities supportive of 'the good, the low and the slow' (that is, responsible purchasing, low consumption and slow living). The British geographers Andrew Leyshon and Roger Lee have written of such individual and collective activities as representing 'practical, day-to-day experiments in performing the economy otherwise'.[2] But I would add that what is performed here also are different possible life-worlds, different ways of thinking about self, other, nature and society, and of acting out a life. In no uncertain terms, then, a contemporary anti-consumerism exists both on the page and on the ground. As a set of solutions and responses, rather than simply a genre of social critique, the new politics of consumption might also be said to be relatively 'timeless'. That is, whether affluent economies are experiencing boom or bust, the insistence that we purposefully opt for forms of consumption that embody the good, the low and the slow remains of pressing relevance.

CULTURE

The strategy-cum-art of culture jamming, as we noted in the introduction to this book, has garnered considerable media attention and constitutes an important element of the current critical response to overconsumption. Mostly now associated with the work of Kalle Lasn and the activities of the Canadian (but globally networked) Adbusters Media Foundation (which publishes *Adbusters* magazine and auspices BND), 'jamming' in relation to consumption has roots in the long history of cultural politics and of what has been called 'semiotic terrorism': a 'cultural warfare' aimed at challenging the dominant symbolic codes that actively enforce given behaviours, mores, attitudes and mentalities. As the British-based theorist of social movements Tim Jordan has put it, 'culture jamming is an attempt to reverse and transgress the meaning of cultural codes whose primary aim is to persuade us to buy something or be someone'.[3] In relation to consumerism, the dominant jamming strategy has been to graffiti and parody commercials. In the case of the Adbusters Media Foundation this has involved the rather slick and professional production in print of 'subvertisements' and on television of 'uncommercials'.[4]

In essence, such strategies, by using the form and language of commercialism to convey anti-consumerist messages, attempt to bring to consciousness the commodification of everyday life and the dominance by advertising of public and mental space. At times this can involve also a play with conventional 'soft' protest action as in BND, an event that has been matched with other annual Adbuster protests such as TV Turn-Off Week, World Car-Free Day and Buy-Nothing Christmas. It is at the level of street theatre, however, that anti-consumerism as cultural politics has perhaps proved most confronting – and humorous. Notable here is the work of the US Church of Stop Shopping, headed by the Reverend Billy (Bill Talen). Parodying both the saccharine religiosity of US Christian fundamentalism and the consumer fundamentalism of North American society, the reverend, along with congregation and choir, regularly blitzes major retail stores offering pavement sermons that promise shoppers salvation from their consumer addiction. Of late, this has turned to eulogies for the death of luxury fever and an insistence that the 'shopocalypse' of 2008 (i.e. the global credit crunch), was a time of revelation; the West, the Rev. Billy intones, literally shopped till it dropped.[5]

Anti-consumerism can be playful stuff. Yet, as creative as this may be, there are very real limits to culture jamming as a political strategy, and the Media Foundation especially has been the subject of criticism for what some see as a lack of radicalism and its apparent incorporation into the very commercialism it opposes. As Jordan has noted, culture jamming as a political weapon is almost always ambiguous given the extent to which it can become compromised through using the promotional language and attention-getting techniques of the very 'enemy' it seeks to subvert.[6] Conversely, the oppositional messages of culture jamming can be all too easily appropriated and tamed by marketers and corporations, ever skilful at using signs of rebellion, particularly of the generational kind, to market products as cool, non-conformist and culturally on the edge.[7]

What is equally notable is that culture jamming by no means defines the nature of anti-consumerist politics. On the contrary, most anti-consumerist commentators, advocates and activists in the West, while sharing with culture jamming an attention to challenging a perceived consumer consciousness, emphasize civic and lifestyle responses far more so than cultural protest action as a means to achieve a more moderate and equitable level of consumption.

Within much contemporary commentary, then, people are principally urged to confront the dominant ideology and practices of consumerism not by way of symbolic subversion but through ethical or sustainable consumer behaviour and through lifestyle change. And here we reach the core of a present-day anti-consumerist response. The emphasis within anti-consumerist critique is resoundingly placed on individual practice as politics. This is accompanied by a move beyond, and sometimes a rejection of, conventional notions of group resistance, orthodox protest action or even of social movement identification. A Minority World anti-consumerism is, at least as articulated in recent commentary, an activism focused on the self, albeit a self thought of in relation to others and the natural environment. Although highly individualist, such a perspective nevertheless courts a form of collectivism – one in which the collective is constituted predominantly through the adoption of common consumption decisions and through shared sentiment and life-course direction rather than through the explicit membership of or identification with groups, organizations or even political networks. This is not to suggest that older forms of political organization and action have been somehow abandoned by those seeking to alter the nature of western consumption economies. It is merely to recognize that a contemporary anti-consumerism mirrors the shift across the whole field of oppositional politics towards what the Italian theorist Alberto Melucci has recognized as the *experiential*.[8] Western anti-consumerism illustrates very clearly the manner in which a politics of change in the West is now deeply enveloped with individual experience, with the micropolitics of everyday life in which questions of personal conduct – but more especially of emotion, feeling, embodiment and selfhood – are central. It is for this reason that a dual – and politically productive – focus on *ethics* and *life* dominates in the new politics of consumption.

ETHICS

Very few critics of consumerism fail to acknowledge the role of ethical or 'good' consumption as a strategy for change. Indeed, advocacy of responsible consumer choice is found in the work of Schor; de Graaf, Wann and Naylor; Farrell;

Eckersley; Kasser; Myers and Kent; and Durning to name but a few.[9] It is the more specialized academic literature, however, that has provided the most detailed exploration and advocacy of ethical consumption as a growing western phenomenon and as a potentially effective political strategy in transforming the nature of markets.

While acknowledging that notions of 'socially responsible' and 'green' consumption have a long pedigree, the founders of the British *Ethical Consumer* magazine, Mary Rayner, Rob Harrison and Sarah Irving, write of a new wave of 'ethical consumerism' arising in a number of western countries since the 1980s. This is in part connected, the authors argue, with the ascendancy of the global free market and the demise of government regulation of corporate activities. In this context, citizens themselves have more vigorously than ever before been drawn into the role of watchdog and regulator in relation to issues of animal welfare, environmental sustainability, and workers' and human rights.[10] Elsewhere, Harrison and his colleagues Terry Newholm and Deirdre Shaw have further suggested that as consumption has become a more prominent part of life in the West, and as post-materialist values have apparently strengthened, the consumer marketplace necessarily becomes a field for the expression of political opinion and ethical self-actualization as much as a place of hedonistic desire.[11]

Clearly, an ethos of ethical consumption can be expressed in a number of ways, from purchasing sustainable, organic or cruelty-free commodities to buying fair-trade goods that guarantee reasonable terms of exchange for small-scale and Majority World producers, to investing in ethical shares and to participating in consumer boycotts of particular products. Ample evidence suggests that 'thinking ethically' about consumption resonates in western populations. At the level of survey data there appears to be a high degree of public support across the Minority World for the availability of green, cruelty-free and no-sweat products, and for the enforcement of corporate social and environmental responsibility. While most analysts acknowledge that particular ethical goods and services usually achieve within western nations only a very small market share, there is clear evidence nevertheless of rapid growth in the production and purchase of organic foods, of the increased utilization of farmers' markets and of the rising popularity of fair-trade products and buying local.[12]

One of the key contradictions, however, is a disconnection between the expressed interest of western populations in factoring into consumption decisions environmental, social, global and health concerns and actual purchasing behaviour. For most of us there is always a trade-off between broader socio-political concerns and convenience, accessibility, quality, taste, familiarity and, most of all, price. In relation to food especially, the ethical commodity, given its comparative expense and inaccessibility, has thus earned its reputation as 'yuppie chow', as a vehicle of altruism for the well-off. Ethical consumption advocates insist with some justification that a *desire* to 'consume consciously' is widespread among a western populace and that, even in practice, ethical consumption is not exclusively middle class.[13] Yet the ethical commodity retains its image as a salve for the wealthy western conscience.[14]

In part because of this issue, ethical consumption, like culture jamming, has been thoroughly questioned as a political strategy. There is now a concerted critique of the ethical commodity not only as marked by socio-economic privilege but also as effectively commodifying dissent. The best of these critiques are supportive but analytical, recognizing the potential value of practices such as fair trade in challenging consumer ideologies, but drawing attention also to the manner in which conscientious consumption buys into an often unquestioned support for a 'vote-with-your-dollar' consumer sovereignty, commodifies the nature of ethical behaviour and conflates civil protest with tokenistic market choices.[15] Just as problematically, advocacy of ethical consumption can be puritanically divisive in that it often fails to recognize that ethics is not simply the domain of the politically conscious, but that all consumption decisions in some way invoke a day-to-day ethics of care, concern and altruism – in relation, for example, to what we see as good for our family and friends, for our local area, or for our own wellbeing. [16]

Much of this questioning of ethical consumption, of course, rests on an assumed division between consumption and citizenship in which genuine civic engagement and political activity is seen to take place only outside the market and beyond what we buy. This is a division between purchasing and politics, and also between consumption and collectivity. Yet this very opposition has been challenged by those who defend the links between, to use the words of the Swedish political scientist Michele Micheletti, 'political virtue and shopping'. A number of writers, Micheletti among them, have explored notions of 'political consumerism' and 'consumer citizenship' in ways that challenge orthodox left and liberal conceptualizations of political action and relate closely to ethical consumption as a political model.

Micheletti in particular argues that western citizens increasingly act as *political consumers*, taking into account social and ethical issues in their shopping decisions. Far from being a minor phenomenon, Micheletti and other writers insist that this is remaking notions of political action by dissolving the assumed barriers between public and private interests, and between economics and politics. So-called political consumerism gives rise to a form of action that is citizen-based and market-oriented and that enables what Micheletti calls *individualized collective action*. Here, politics takes place as a form of democratic 'responsibility taking' by individuals acting outside the confines of the 'collectivist collective action' embodied in older forms of social movement opposition and beyond the realm of state-based regulatory intervention. Politically driven individual consumption decisions thus express self-interests but also link us to others making similar consumption choices and articulate the collective goals of justice, human rights and environmental sustainability. Consumption in other words becomes what Micheletti calls a form of *phronesis*, or virtues in action in everyday settings.[17] The dimensions of this have been further explored by the Italian sociologist Roberta Sassatelli, in a recent analysis of the rise of 'critical consumption'. Sassatelli has suggested that the emergence of the morally responsible consumer represents a form of 'sub-politicization': a process 'whereby politics is emerging in places other than the formal political arena (sub-politics) because citizens no longer think that traditional forms of political participation are adequate'.[18]

Directly allied to this formulation of consumer activism is the notion of consumer citizenship, a concept energetically invoked by a range of writers, particularly the British philosopher Kate Soper. Soper has explored in detail the manner in which consumption can be a terrain of civic virtue and responsible action where citizen-consumers can pursue their conceptualizations of the good life in a manner that is nevertheless deeply linked to their citizen concerns for fair trade and environmental sustainability. This form of consumption, Soper interestingly contends, is more broadly linked to the rise of 'alternative hedonism' within western nations which serves as a rationale for a gradual shift to ethical and green consumption. Alternative hedonism, for Soper, 'points to the way in which enjoyment of affluent consumption has become compromised by its unpleasant by-products (noise, pollution, danger, stress, health risks, excessive waste, and aesthetic impact on the environment) and has thus prompted revisions in thinking about the good life'. Faced with diminishing returns from a fast-paced and materialistic lifestyle, the pleasures of existence have, for a small but increasing number of people, become empty, leading to an emerging ethos of counter-consumerism whereby pleasure is pursued through the adoption of different levels of, and attitudes towards, consuming.[19]

As with ethical consumption more generally, a note of caution has been sounded in relation to overpoliticizing such alternative consumer practices. As Sassatelli rightly observes, responsible consumption is an activity that gestures towards change rather than being a form of political practice which, in any comprehensive way, challenges 'the functioning principles of the entire economic and political system'.[20] Other writers, such as Andy Scerri, rightly point to the dangers of celebrating a 'stake-holder citizenship' in which meeting the ecological challenge is reduced to the 'ethics-lite' of buying green.[21] In an important sense, Soper's work implicitly recognizes these potential limits. It recognizes as well that any insistence that politics can be expressed through the purchase of 'morally good' commodities must inevitably confront the reality of consumption as excess. In other words, ethical or political market behaviour cannot simply be about making better product choices in the context of continuing to consume at high levels; it also entails a deep questioning of consumption itself as part of any civic responsibility. This constructively responds to those who, quite rightly, accuse the more shallow forms of ethical consumption of ignoring the need for western populations to consume less, not just differently.[22] This is a point now acknowledged by the more reflexive advocates of the ethical commodity. Newholm and Shaw, for example, identify anti-consumerism as a key ethical consumption strategy, drawing a direct parallel between this 'radical' form of ethical consumption and so-called voluntary simplicity.[23] Here, the emphasis shifts from market behaviour to life itself.

LIFE

Contemporary western polemic on consumerism can in many respects be defined as a celebration of alternative ways of achieving life satisfaction, meaning and purpose beyond the realm of consumption. At its least challenging, this involves simply advocating that people adopt environmentally sustainable behaviours or take personal steps to control their spending and better organize their working life. This is often combined, however, with advocacy of downshifting or, in a somewhat more encompassing vein, of simple living and forms of frugality. Although less well formulated than ideas of simplicity, slow living is emerging also as a life paradigm.

The concept of *phronesis* captures the ethos informing these responses. Given the focus on life satisfaction and happiness in much of the recent anti-consumerist literature, self-fulfilment is one of the overriding goals of resisting consumerism and refusing the 'velocitization of life'. But public virtues are, it is assumed, enlivened by the very process of discovering the authentic and contented self with other altruistic goals – sustainability, community cohesion and global justice – made more attainable as a result. As we noted previously, this emphasis on self-development and life satisfaction is, in some way, strategic. Soper usefully encapsulates this intent in recognizing that calls for an altruistic dedication to sustainability are unlikely to be as successful in reducing consumption as emphasizing 'the personal interest of affluent consumers in improving the quality of their own lives through consuming differently'.[24]

But the turn to the self and to life within western anti-consumerism is not just a nifty piece of political footwork. It does not simply disguise a continued and unreconstructed allegiance to older forms of social democratic or socialist politics intent on state reform of the market or collectivist struggle against capitalism (although these influences remain present). Rather, there is an overriding sense in a contemporary politics of consumption that existential questions of self-fulfilment and happiness are crucial. This is hardly surprising given that, as the British sociologist Anthony Giddens has influentially formulated, a 'life politics' – in which individuals view the construction of their personhood and life course as a reflexive project of personal decision making and self-actualization – is characteristic of a globalized, post-traditional and risk-filled late modernity.[25] This does not imply that the self-orientation of anti-consumerist politics is, at least in its more radical clothing, unchallenging or simply complementary to the ideologies of neo-liberal globalization. On the contrary, no sympathetic reading of the new politics of consumption could fail to acknowledge its productive connection to the whole trajectory of post-1960s radical theory, from the feminist emphasis on the personal as political to what Melucci has identified as the political possibilities embedded in a conception of deep individual experience as motivating of a social energy for change.[26]

Yet this in no uncertain terms means that a good deal of recent anti-consumerist advocacy rather awkwardly straddles the divide between notions of personal growth and visions of social transformation. There is much of the self-help manual about many a recent text, underscored by the popularity of offering a series of steps to personal enlightenment. That this is potentially constructive is not in question, but there is a wide variation in the degree to which critics explicitly connect individual change with a broader social, political and ecological project. A number of texts, for example, simply refuse to move beyond a self-help focus on happiness and life satisfaction in the context of assuming that more challenging responses are too conflictual.[27]

Many other commentators, however, more explicitly connect practices such as downshifting or simple living with broader political aims and significant socio-cultural transformation. Amitai Etzioni has suggested that a voluntary shift towards 'simplicity' among western populations is at present both limited in impact and takes place on various levels, but is nevertheless a rich potential source of reduced consumption and social change. Etzioni portrays downshifting as a moderate, indeed rather shallow, form of voluntary simplicity engaging mostly the well-off, who tone down their consumption – almost as a fashion statement – to a limited degree. This is contrasted with 'strong simplification' through which people give up both income and socio-economic status in order to pursue a more encompassing form of economic moderation and non-material pursuits. Finally, 'holistic simplifiers' for Etzioni adopt comprehensive life change informed by a coherent philosophy of voluntary simplicity and identified with simple living as a social movement.[28]

Useful as this typology may be, the lines between these different forms of simplification are perhaps not as clear-cut as Etzioni suggests. Indeed, downshifting in the hands of Schor, one of its principal advocates, looks much like a hybrid of Etzioni's soft and strong simplification. Schor recognizes that downshifters are not necessarily self-consciously anti-consumerist. They are people seeking a work–life balance, a slower pace of existence, more meaningful social relationships and 'daily lives that line up squarely with their deepest values'. While many are 'yuppies', jumping off the work–spend treadmill, downshifters, Schor insists, are found at all income levels. The common denominator is that they all *voluntarily* earn less money than they could, and thus presumably place less emphasis on consumption. Schor and other advocates of downshifting are keen to normalize this lifestyle. Downshifting is not portrayed as dropping out, communitarian, anti-urban or even based on a shared identity. Nevertheless, it is a phenomenon in some way connected, Schor argues, with a diminishing belief in materialism and consumerism, and with an act of 'soul-searching' and a 'coming to consciousness'. This involves a process of taking control of our desires and behaviours through voluntarily restraining our consumption patterns.[29]

Such advice clearly blends with other forms of simplification, and Schor readily acknowledges the importance of the voluntary simplicity movement. Where downshifting is identified as a process involving a conscious decision to trade off money for time and quality of life, simple livers, Schor notes, transcend this, coming to celebrate sufficiency and frugality not as a trade-off, but as a positive life statement.[30] This is really to suggest, as with Etzioni, that voluntary simplicity is the more politicized and encompassing form of downshifting, though Schor, not inaccurately, portrays it also as even more white and middle class in nature. Simple livers, in other words, tend to be already rich in economic and cultural capital.

Unlike downshifting, voluntary simplicity is by no means a recently minted concept. Simple living advocates in the USA – and it is very much a North American movement in origin – are quick to demonstrate the historical and philosophical roots of frugality in the life and writings of the nineteenth-century transcendentalists Ralph Waldo Emerson and Henry David Thoreau, both of whom emphasized the pursuit of a rich inner life rather than the attainment of possessions.[31] What is more, in the North American context, voluntary simplicity sources various elements of a puritan and non-conformist

Christianity, as well as traditions of thought in Gandhianism, Buddhism and other non-western philosophies.[32]

The work of the North American social scientist Duane Elgin, stands as the definitive and influential late twentieth-century statement of the need for simplicity. For Elgin, to live simply is to seek a balance in one's life between the material and the spiritual in order to find greater purpose, harmony, fulfilment and satisfaction. This is to construct a life-world in which emphasis is placed on experiential rather than material riches. Far from valorizing poverty (that is, an imposed frugality or involuntary simplicity) simplification seeks the golden mean of 'a creative and aesthetic balance between poverty and excess'. This clearly has an environmental implication, and Elgin routinely refers to voluntary simplicity as 'ecological living', contrasting the industrial era, and its emphasis on material progress, with an emerging ecological era, emphasizing a harmony between the material and the spiritual. This is necessarily embedded in a transformation of societies, such that we collectively live a life of sustainability, efficiency, peacefulness and equity. Elgin thus writes of voluntary simplicity as involving a 'revolution in fairness'.[33]

In the USA, more recently, writers and 'simplifiers' such as Cecile Andrews, and Vicki Robin and Joe Dominguez have published much-cited bestsellers on the simple way. In *Your Money or Your Life*, Robin and the late Dominguez outline a nine-step program to frugality, all in the interests of enabling people to gain financial independence, escape from a culture of consumerism and achieve greater fulfilment through drastically reducing working hours and consumption expenditure.[34] It is a similar story in the work of Andrews, a Seattle-based simplicity advocate, who has become widely known for her promotion of 'simplicity circles'; or locally organized and controlled study and support forums. As with other voluntary simplifiers, Andrews conjoins a critique of

ANTI-CONSUMERISM IN ACTION 65

consumerism in terms of its environmental impact with a focus on time – or the manufactured lack of it seemingly experienced by many in the Minority World.[35] Indeed, theorizations of frugality, as with downshifting, work with a deep sense of consumerism as bound up with the velocitization of contemporary life in the West; and it is this very temporal–material bind that is escaped through opting for 'the examined life' of simplicity.

Clearly, in relation to both downshifting and a more encompassing frugality, the key word is 'voluntary' – indicating the need to experience the simple life not as a consequence of economic recession or underprivilege but as a purposeful choice. Indeed, Etzioni has described voluntary simplicity in its purest guise as representing a 'new culture' embodying a willingly adopted appreciation of the benefits, both personal and social, of modest levels of work and consumption. Unlike other supporters of simplification, however, Etzioni remains cautious about both the degree to which downshifting has actually taken hold in western nations and the possibility of a more thorough voluntary simplicity becoming widely adopted.[36]

This caution speaks directly to the tendency within much of the new politics of consumption to constitute particular subcultural trends and lifestyle preferences as indicative of the rise of new social groupings on a broad scale. Much has been made by Schor and others of the limited but useful social survey evidence which suggests that in the 1990s up to 20 per cent of the US public downshifted or 'made a voluntary lifestyle change, excluding a regularly scheduled retirement, that entailed earning less money'.[37] Similarly, it has been claimed, once again on the basis of limited survey results, that 25 per cent of British adults aged thirty to fifty-nine downshifted in the decade to 2003 and 23 per cent of Australians in the same age range did so in the decade to 2002.[38] What is most probably being identified here, however, is, as Schor observes, mainstream lifestyle alteration rather than 'ideologically motivated' opposition.[39] It is thus difficult to interpret this evidence in any substantial way as indicative of socio-cultural change, let alone anti-consumerism. Even more importantly, there is a lack of comparative data on previous time periods making it difficult to assess whether the percentages cited above indicate a decrease or increase over time in the prevalence of so-called downshifting.[40]

Despite these difficulties, many commentators, drawing on lifestyle change data, imply or simply assert that downshifting is a major contemporary trend that speaks of a strengthening post-consumerism in the West; a post-consumerism driven not simply by the realities of economic downturn but by a growing rejection of the mainstream. This contention is undergirded by the continued popularity among many commentators of a social typology and social segment approach. The classification of individuals and demographic groups into types and segments – one of the oldest and most basic of sociological techniques – has never diminished as a favoured interpretative strategy within 'pop soc' critique.[41] Nor has it diminished as the central tool of investigation in marketing research – it was, indeed, the field of marketing that created the notion of downshifters. Blurring the boundaries between marketing and social science, much social commentary has been intent on working with categories such as 'cultural creatives', 'inner-directeds' and 'new realists', terms that designate more or less the same thing. Thus the 'cultural creatives' are identified as that one-quarter of the North American population who hold post-materialist values. These are individuals who are intent on self-realization through striving for a healthy, happy, spiritually rich life and whose vision of the future promises a remaking of cultural mores.[42] In Britain, up to half the population apparently exhibit signs of being inner-directed – a term coined in the 1950s by the sociologist David Riesman.[43] Inner-directeds are, once again, those who seek self-fulfilment beyond materialism and who value autonomy, self-expression, individuality, self-improvement and, as David Boyle has put it, authenticity.[44] Indeed Boyle, in his very readable book on what he calls 'new realism', sees the desire for authenticity, for a world free of domination by the fakery and emptiness of commercialism and mass culture, as the key to understanding the social emergence of inner-directedness and a possible renaissance of humanist values.[45]

This talk of the emergence of 'new' cultural attitudes and social practices in western countries is not without empirical foundation, and the preparedness of writers like Boyle in particular to find in people's everyday concerns and actions signs of struggle and change is welcome. Yet such talk unfortunately slides all too often into a 'minority populism'; that is, into making wildly overgeneralized claims about the novel and oppositional nature of apparently emergent social trends and the supposedly enlightened activities of privileged social strata.

This brings us squarely to the problematic nature of the whole turn to a life politics in contemporary anti-consumerism. I have alluded already to a number of the limitations of any insistence on changing individual lifestyles and life-ways in opposition to overconsumption. Those who celebrate downshifting in particular can be seen as over-imbuing the current life-course decisions of individuals with political and sociological significance. Even more worryingly, advocacy of downshifting invariably underplays the extent to which such lifestyle change is essentially an option far more readily open to those who are economically secure and well educated. Most pointedly of all, as a form of politics downshifting is profoundly self-oriented and, as such, may constitute little actual challenge to the ideologies of individualism upon which notions of consumer choice are themselves based. The voluntary simplicity movement has been similarly questioned. In supportive, but nevertheless highly critical terms, Michael Maniates has suggested that voluntary simplicity offers a constructive alternative to consumerism yet in its current guise is rampantly individualistic, middle-class in nature and nostalgic for a pastoral life.[46]

We must question as well the way in which a politics of simplicity is so often conceived and conveyed. Advocacy of both downshifting and frugality has, after all, shown itself to be thoroughly voluntaristic in outlook and vanguardist in delivery. The adoption of particular lifestyles and life-ways is portrayed by many commentators as a matter of personal will, while the failure of individuals to jump off the consumer treadmill is interpreted as a product of brainwashing, irrational fear or simply moral laxity. In the process, a 'groupism' is privileged as a way of championing social change; the contemporary social field is divided into two kinds of individuals: those with an 'affluenzic' consciousness and those possessed of an enlightened 'mindfulness' – with the latter constituting the vanguard of cultural transformation. There is a stark failure, also, in much anti-consumerist polemic, to explore, rather than simply assume, the potential connection between attending to the health, happiness and wellbeing of oneself as an individual and reanimating the wellbeing of communities and of a collective sense of responsibility towards the welfare of others. The mooted link between the existential contentment of western individuals and the achievement of sustainability, social cohesion and global justice is thus an article of faith, rather than a process explained. It is crucial to note, however, that none of these concerns provides grounds for simply rejecting a focus on the politics of everyday life in the context of addressing overconsumption. The personal is indeed political, and the promotion of different behaviours, attitudes, lifestyles and 'simplified' life-ways must clearly be central to any anti-consumerist politics.

The same can be said for the rise of interest in 'slow living'. Conceptually, this is most directly associated with the advent of the Italian, but now international, slow food movement. Formed in 1986, Slow Food arose as a leftist attempt to preserve local agricultural production and regional cuisines in the face of globalization, and to foster a sense of the pleasures and sociality of local foods and communal dining. By 1989, and in response to its campaign of opposition to the opening of McDonald's outlets in Italy, Slow Food emerged as a global network-cum-movement, emphasizing opposition not simply to fast food, but to 'fast life'.[47] Slow Food, however, rather than emphasizing frugality, quite purposefully promotes 'quiet material pleasure', viewing pleasure itself, in the words of Slow Food founder Carlo Petrini, as 'a universal right'.[48] This celebration of a moderate hedonism places a slow-food philosophy in a tangential relationship to a movement such as simple living, with its more puritan emphasis on the non-material, the spiritual and 'traditional' American values.[49] Nevertheless, like simplification, Slow Food, as a worldwide network, champions the personal benefits of lifestyle change and mindful practice, and the environmental and social importance of resisting globalized consumerism.

As the New Zealand-based writer Wendy Parkins has argued, the 'slow' in Slow Food conveys an opposition to homogeneity, globalization and corporate dominance but it also signals a promotion of 'pleasure, taste, authenticity, connectedness, tranquillity and community'.[50] For Parkins, Slow Food is but one element of an emergent set of responses evident across the Minority World that attempt to revalue time and to offer an alternative sense of its perception and use in opposition to the temporal pace of late modernity. She thus points to the emergence of groups such as the Society for the

Deceleration of Time in Australia and, in the USA, the Take Back Your Time campaign, the latter being closely allied with the work of de Graaf (of affluenza fame) and the simple living movement.[51] The British journalist Carl Honoré has, as I mentioned previously, surveyed this field in his enjoyable bestseller *In Praise of Slow*, suggesting that the emergence of such groups, as well as the myriad attempts of people to 'decelerate' their lives, reclaim their time and challenge 'the cult of speed', indicates a 'global yearning for Slowness' and promises an escape from 'time-sickness', from our addiction to 'doing more and more in less and less time'. Animating this is a philosophy of balance, of seeking to live *tempo giusto*, or at the right speed, allowing individuals to 'make meaningful connections – with people, with culture, with work, with nature, with our bodies and minds'.[52]

Elsewhere, Parkins and her co-author Geoffrey Craig, writing in more academic terms, have described slow living not as a nostalgia for an Arcadian past but as 'a process whereby everyday life – in all its pace and complexity, *frisson* and routine – is approached with care and attention, as subjects attempt to negotiate the different temporalities that they daily experience'.[53] Yet Parkins and Craig acknowledge that the forms of slow living are diverse and that there are, as yet, no firmly prescribed 'slow' practices.[54] As a consequence perhaps, a focus on time, and on slow food in particular, becomes entrapped in some of the same limitations plaguing responses such as ethical consumption or downshifting. Sympathetic critiques of Slow Food, for example, have rightfully noted that while the slow food movement has become an important global voice on food issues, its focus on promoting culinary knowledge and its celebration of gastronomic pleasure renders the movement politically amorphous and thoroughly bourgeois in address and appeal.[55] Similarly, as Kelly Donati – herself an Australian Slow Food activist – has carefully argued, the celebration of the local and the slow is at times expressive of a nostalgic romanticization of tradition and of a 'fetishistic consumption of cultural diversity'.[56]

What is notable about Slow Food in particular, however, is that it constructively attends to consumption *and* production in forging its politics, and as an organization it pursues this on an international level through initiating collaborative campaigns supporting biological and cultural diversity in opposition to the global corporatization of agriculture.[57] For Parkins and Craig this and other actions distinguish Slow Food from voluntary simplicity which, they rightly argue, mistakenly tends to reject consumption as a site of pleasure and overemphasizes changed consumption behaviour as the means to social transformation.[58] This latter observation importantly highlights the extent to which a contemporary western anti-consumerism, particularly in its strong focus on the escape from consumer consciousness, does indeed reduce social change to a politics of the purchase. Moreover, this politics is mostly envisaged within recent critique as pursued through the mindful, self-actualizing individual acting as either responsible consumer or frugal non-consumer. Here, the personal is not simply understood as political, rather politics itself is rendered almost entirely a product of personhood – and one which is publicly expressed through making particular income and expenditure choices. It is perhaps not surprising then that the subject on which much western anti-consumerist commentary becomes frustratingly timid is that of systemic economic and political change, beyond that of attending to the self.

ECONOMY AND COMMUNITY

To be sure, there is no shortage of calls within recent work for broad legislative and social change designed to both curtail overconsumption and restore everything from quality of life to social and global justice. Time and again, commentators insist upon the need also for the restoration of community. Thus Schor – who has long sought to link questions of work and consumption – writes of the need for 'coordinated inter- vention' involving consumption and income taxation measures targeting luxury and environmentally damaging commodities and addressing income inequality and working hours.[59] Like many others, Schor calls as well for a 'civic reengagement' and a return to community, while emphasizing the role of the sustainability and simplicity movements in modeling social change.[60] These visions of legislative and community-level intervention to curtail the excesses of consumption econo- mies are perhaps even more apposite now, given the current struggle to extract western nations from recession and the opportunity this creates for a change of direction.

Yet, notwithstanding the breadth and integrity of these suggestions, such intimations of systemic or structural change remain, in the hands of many critics, curtly outlined wish lists in the context of an overwhelming focus on, to use Barry Schwartz's words, 'exploring what individuals can do, despite societal pressure, to overcome the overload of [consumer] choice'.[61] This draws much anti-consumerist lit- erature across the Minority World into a stark contradiction in which the fragmentation of the social and the dissolu- tion of community in face of global commodity culture is lamented but the individual – and the search for happi- ness – remains at the dead centre of the solutions offered.[62] Schwartz's work on the downside of endless consumer choice is a case in point. Schwartz writes of his culture as rampantly individualistic and of a lack of a sense of belong- ing plaguing the North American psyche, but each of the eleven steps he offers towards accepting the need for limits on market choice are entirely individually focused strategies of rethinking the value of money and consumption.[63] Even when broader steps are proposed, advocacy of collective change seems muted in a many a recent text. In the final three pages of the Australian version of *Affluenza*, for example, Clive Hamilton and Richard Denniss, in acknowledging that they have 'talked only about individual responses', belatedly shift to what they call a 'political response' that consists of promoting a philosophy of wellbeing embodying a turn to fulfilling work, vibrant communities, environmental protection and market regulation.[64]

This relegation of structural change to the status of an addendum is not just the product of an effort to appear moderate and thus appeal to a broad sector of the public in order to 'sell dissent'. In many respects the new politics of consumption, particularly in the USA, is hostage to its own liberal individualism. But beyond this, the whole discourse of anti-consumerism across the Minority World invokes an underformulated conception of late-modern personhood that, at one and the same time, both embraces and rejects a privileging of self over other – ever hopeful that what is truly beneficial for the western individual (i.e. material moderation) will be good for all. Moreover, the apparent obsession with individual strategies of escape by contemporary critics of western consumerism is a direct product of a culturalist focus on consciousness. If consumerism is essentially a product of mentality, if it is a cultural logic that works on individual minds, then this eclipses in importance an attention to consumerism as an *economic logic* and a field of enforced social practice undergirding the control of capital, the organization of production, the design of urban and suburban environments, the nature of transport, the uses of communication technologies, the structure of households and the processes of retail distribution.

Undoubtedly, much of the new politics of consumption in the West is marked, as Maniates insists, by an 'individualization of responsibility'.[65] But, to return to the earlier point, we can perhaps even more accurately portray an attention to downshifting and simple living in particular as a refusal to dichotomize the structural and the individual – as a belief that self-actualization also actualizes the social. This politics is clearly driven by a sense that the only really effective ground left for the enactment of social change under conditions of globalized modernity lies in the realm of life. This has been put in its most sophisticated terms by Etzioni, who insists that ideological arguments championing the need to confront injustice, along with organizational attempts to address social issues through political parties, unions and progressive government action, have largely failed. In this context, although Etzioni most certainly does not reject a role for public policy, a life politics involving a shift to simplification provides the best hope of change, not least because simplification produces non-materialistic individuals who are not coerced into supporting equity but freely share wealth.[66]

Not all, however, have been so happy to place such trust in personal transformation. Taxation responses to overconsumption in affluent nations have been strongly emphasized by a number of writers. Robert Frank, in fact, rejects life politics as an effective strategy for change, advocating instead a graduated or progressive tax on consumption as a means of controlling competitive spending, increasing savings and reducing work hours.[67] This, unlike a value-added tax, involves changing the incentives to overconsume by differentially taxing the expenditure patterns of individuals. Others, in suggesting that this might reduce Minority World consumption levels but do little to curtail the purchase of environmentally damaging products, suggest alternative forms of taxation that factor in the environmental and social costs of particular commodities. Thus, Paul and Anne Ehrlich support individual lifestyle change, but urge the implementation by western governments of so-called 'Pigovian taxes' that take account of the environmental and social costs of production (or the 'externalities' of which economists speak) so as to direct purchasing towards goods that are less destructive.[68]

These forms of tax-led intervention readily overlap with advocacy of new forms of commerce, particularly by those promoting 'natural capitalism' and sustainable business practice; a perspective now increasingly beloved by western governments. This pro-growth approach portrays change as emanating not chiefly from regulation but from commerce itself, and urges the adoption of a new philosophy of business attuned to sustainability. This involves the pursuit, among other industrial and commercial strategies, of 'closed loop' systems in which wastes themselves become commodities to be recycled, the implementation of so-called 'full-cost accounting' that adds the full environmental and social costs of production to product pricing, and the adoption of a 'service and flow model' whereby goods are temporarily hired rather than owned and are thus maintained from 'cradle-to-grave' by producers themselves.[69]

A somewhat broader and more contestational literature, focused on the very nature of national and global market economies rather than anti-consumerism *per se*, has given rise to vigorous advocacy of concepts such as the stationary state and the critique of growth. In the USA, the work of Herman E. Daly has been instrumental in promoting the notion of achieving 'stability in material throughput rather than growth' designed to maintain a sustainable economy that delivers reasonable prosperity and a high quality of life, but one which is not focused on the continual overexploitation of resources and undifferentiated or aggregate economic expansion for its own sake. In policy terms this entails ceasing to treat natural capital – the Earth's resources – as free goods and moving to calculate their exploitation as a cost rather than income within measures such as GDP; taxing resource consumption rather than simply income; maximizing the productivity of the Earth's resources and investing in increasing their supply; and abandoning the ideology of global integration through free trade, capital mobility and export-led growth.[70] Similarly, the French development economist Christian Comeliau has rejected the process of 'global marketization', arguing for a more ecological and ethical form of economics that addresses collective needs – freedom, dignity, democracy, health, education – and responds to the imperative of global equity. Comeliau pushes for differentially encouraging economic growth in some contexts but controlling it in others, *contra* a neo-liberal ideology, and developing a 'new style' planning that reinstates social rather than market-oriented goals as the central aim of public policy and global governance.[71]

These ideas seem eminently poignant and even prescient in the post-2008 era; they also touch the ethos of contemporary global activism – and, to a lesser extent, an ascendant social democratic interventionism – with its emphasis on a renewal of democracy and the creation of an alternative or, at the very least, better regulated global trade and finance system.[72] Indeed, it is at this point that anti-consumerism overlaps with the critique of corporate power. The Canadian commentator Joel Bakan, for example, has strongly backed the national and global regulation of corporate activities, suggesting that laws must be 'at the heart of any effective strategy to curtail corporate harms and exploitation'. In fact, Bakan tackles head on the notion that institutionalized political solutions to social and environmental problems are ineffective, suggesting that lifestyle and protest-oriented responses alone, while crucial, can play into the hands of corporate elites by abandoning national government and global regulatory bodies as a still potent source of enforcing democratic rule.[73] This warning now rings undeniably true and underscores the continuing efforts of networks such as the Association for a Tobin Tax for the Aid of Citizens (ATTAC). Formed in France in the late 1990s, ATTAC advocates for measures such as the control of market speculation, the regulation of international banking and finance, the taxation of income on capital and the restoration of democratic control of the world financial sphere.[74]

Far from tangential to anti-consumerism, such concerns merely demonstrate the permeable analytical and political boundaries of any critique of overconsumption. So too does the emphasis given by at least some writers and activists to alternative economic space, localism and intentional communities – a subject on which I end this chapter. I have noted already the somewhat muted promotion of a collectivist response to overconsumption in contemporary anti-consumerist literature, or at least that tier of it that constitutes public commentary. Contemporary writers promoting strategies such as ethical consumption, downshifting, work–life balance and even simple living mourn the demise of social solidarity but, fearful of being seen to return to dead ideologies, offer little sense that power might be appropriated and new forms of life constructed through direct, highly collectivist, possibly confrontational, and ongoing action rather than as a consequence of consumer choice, lifestyle change and personal growth.

Once again, others have sounded a very different note. Increasingly, there have been efforts to explore the workings and possibilities of alternative economic networks, venues, organizations and events particularly those forged collectively. Within cultural and economic geography, for example, there has been a surge of interest in documenting and promoting 'the efforts of individual and collective actors to imagine and, more importantly, to perform economic activities in ways that mark them out differently from the dictates and conventions of the mainstream economy'. Motivated by a desire to provide 'practical visions of a non-capitalist world', a number of researchers have sought to demonstrate that alternative economic practices embodied not only in lifestyle change and ethical consumption but also much more broadly in cooperatives, credit unions, worker-owned enterprises, local trading schemes and small-scale industrial and agricultural production continue to challenge the conventional.[75] As the geographers Kathie Gibson and Julie Graham have argued, contemporary economic reality involves a diversity of capitalist and non-capitalist activities (a fact that is forgotten in overemphasizing the commodification of the life-world) – and this informs their concern to identify and advocate for alternative economic arrangements already within our midst that demonstrate different ways of working, spending and living.[76]

In a not dissimilar vein, the North American environmentalist Thomas Princen has interrogated the concept of sufficiency. Princen writes in part through frustration with what he sees as the tendency in environmentalist discourse to combine doom-and-gloom scenarios of the future with platitudinous thinking in terms of offering thin solutions that rest on insisting that people be less greedy, buy green, recycle, think globally, grasp spiritual awakening and so on. Princen emphasizes instead the need to explore how 'industries or markets or communities should be organized' and how they can embody 'principles of social organization consonant with long-term, sustainable resource use' – sufficiency being one such principle.[77] He thus seeks to ground a sense of 'enoughness' in relation to work and consumption by exploring the economic and social structures, not simply the individual actions, necessary for its enactment. Much like in the economic geography discussed above, Princen examines in detail existing attempts at worker-managed and ecologically informed industry and primary production, which model what he calls an 'ecological rationality' embedded in a sense of locality and place.

This brings us finally to the issue of community in combating overconsumption. For some critics, the two are intimately bound together. The Australian environmentalist Ted Trainer, for example – who in 1985 published one of the early critiques of late-modern affluence – celebrates simple living in the context of promoting the global ecovillage movement.[78] For Trainer, simple living necessarily involves the formation of 'intentional communities' at the local level in which people collectively pursue – and model for the wider society – an alternative way of living that is just and sustainable.[79] Trainer acknowledges that such communities can be insular and self-indulgent, and can constitute little challenge to the mainstream economy. Yet he sees their presence as being of crucial symbolic importance. A similar, though perhaps more constructive response has been the turn to a less exclusivist localism that echoes in many ways Princen's recognition of the need to directly focus on community maintenance and change as a step towards sustainability. The British activist Helena Norberg-Hodge has been one of the significant recent voices here. Norberg-Hodge articulates an opposition to economic globalization in the context of advocating for localizing economic activity or, as she nicely puts it, promoting small scale on a large scale. This signals a return of sorts to ruralized communities dependent on small-scale, diversified, locally adapted agricultural production, industry and sustainable energy infrastructure. It involves also a rejuvenation of and reinvestment in public space and community services and the adoption of alternative finance and trade practices. All of this for Norberg-Hodge speaks to the personal as well as the systemic; it involves 'rediscovering the deep psychological benefits – the joy – of being in embedded community'.[80] Here, community is not regained principally via individual lifestyle change. Rather, community is directly identified, taken hold of and reorganized, while the personal is transformed in the process – not vice versa.

This more expansive sense of how tackling overconsumption entails broad socio-economic change speaks, in the context of this study, of the need to fundamentally challenge some of the dominant suppositions of the new politics of consumption. There is, in fact, so much more to be said, and that should be heard, about why consumerism occurs and how to confront it, beyond the dominant and increasingly repetitive narrative that western populations are prone to affluenza, are now paying the price of consumer obsession, and that all of us should simply be content to downshift. Notwithstanding the energy and commitment with which contemporary critics have placed overconsumption on the political agenda, there is a need to search out new paths for the interpretation of consumption, particularly in new economic times, and to formulate clearer understandings of what an anti-consumerism is opposing on the one hand, and seeking to achieve politically on the other. We can begin this task by first shifting from the page to everyday action, from the person as commentator to the person as activist and advocate.

3

ENCOUNTERING

ANTI-CONSUMERISM

Long before bequeathing the world his Star Wars mytho-
logy, the American movie director George Lucas made the
film *THX 1138*. The title did not, as we might suppose, refer
to some kind of intergalactic starship coming, complete with
merchandise, to a cinema near you, but to an individual,
played by Robert Duvall. Numbered rather than named,
Duvall portrays a dissident who rebels against a totalitar-
ian society dominated by western-style consumerism. This
is a world of ultimate elite control where the worker-masses
are placated through mood-enhancing drugs and rendered
content through the provision of ultra-violent TV and tacky
products. Produced in 1970 by a then experimental film-
maker, this was Lucas's dystopic – and anti-consumerist
– polemic. And, as if to echo the recent reinvigoration of a
politics of consumption, the film underwent restoration and
was re-released as the 'director's cut' in 2004.[1] The world
Lucas put on film almost four decades ago has thus lost none
of its resonance. It is, it would seem, all the more salient in

face of an intensely globalized, if recently wounded, commodity capitalism. Rebellion also has lost none of its import, and in this chapter we focus our attention on the arena of political opposition across the western world.

Contemporary anti-consumerism is, at least in some respects, indicative of what the Australian sociologist Kevin McDonald has identified as a new form of worldwide protest and political action arising in the context of globalization. For McDonald, contemporary social movements are now often better conceptualized as *global movements*; ones that are formed transnationally and are animated by a collective desire for different ways of experiencing the self and living in the world.[2] This certainly sheds light on aspects of the so-called new politics of consumption, yet it does not mean that a contemporary anti-consumerism somehow itself represents a newly born or unified political project, nor that it rejects forms of organized and programmatic political intervention. As I have so far intimated throughout this book, western anti-consumerism is usefully understood as an ongoing dialogue and field of alternative practices. As such, it is a political understanding that converges with a range of movements and projects aimed at personal and social change.

In light of this, the present chapter draws selectively on a wide range of conversational interviews conducted with consumption activists in Europe, North America and Australia in order to both situate anti-consumerism as an international agenda yet illustrate also the mistakenness of treating it as a 'first-order' politics that is able, in and of itself, to provide a conceptual focus for social change.[3] A global political agenda is thus explored here, but, in keeping with the purview of this book, I restrict my discussion to the pan-western aspects of contemporary consumption activism. Moreover, this chapter contributes only tangentially to social movement theory. Somewhat more modestly, I am concerned here to treat interview material as an alternative field of commentary, rather than as the basis of conducting a sociological analysis of contemporary consumption activism *per se* – valuable as such a task may be. The responses and statements documented in the following pages are thus used journalistically rather than ethnographically. The term 'activist' – like the word 'movement' – is also used advisedly, not least because a number of those interviewed remained wary of this descriptor as either portraying them as too oppositional or as inaccurately defining the impetus for and meaning of their actions. In fact, 'activist' does now have a rather hackneyed ring to it. While it is an identity that some politically involved individuals and groups may continue to claim, it is a term that also categorizes and names in a manner that can both over-politicize certain actions and fail to give due attention to the highly varied nature of contemporary political engagement. In relation to consumption this is an engagement that can be designated radical, oppositional or interventionist. But it might equally be understood as simply critical, alternative or even playful.

Questions of terminology aside, however, anti-consumerism and the activism to which it gives rise must be seen as both a politics in the making and, perhaps rather oddly, not really much of a stand-alone politics at all. Analytically, rubric terms such as the 'new politics of consumption' or 'anti-consumerism' make sense – and remain useful – as convenient descriptors of a critical sensibility and a focus of political argument. But can these terms really be understood as referring to a politics in the round; a politics in its own right somehow able to provide a philosophical underpinning for social change and a source of identification and solidarity for those who strive after it? Undoubtedly, anti-consumerist commentary is marked by a dance around this question. Overconsumption, as we have seen, so often makes an appearance in anti-consumerist polemic as the kit and caboodle of social and environmental problems while frugality and slowness announce themselves as the be-all and end-all of personal and social transformation. Yet it is clear that the new politics of consumption constantly looks to a set of political values and hopes – ecological balance, social justice, global equity, democratic rights – that move us way beyond overconsumption and consumerism as the problems to be confronted. The very fact that the new politics of consumption works, as I have argued, on a number of both individualist and structural levels of political response is testament to this conflicting sense of consumption as both the key problem to be addressed and not the real problem at all.

No such difficulty seems to mark anti-consumerism when it is brought to life through conversation. It is, in fact, through encountering anti-consumerism on the ground, so to speak, through moving from critical text to activist talk, that we can gain a firmer sense of this oppositional dialogue not as a politics *per se* but as a political stance, and one for which consumption is often not the overriding issue to be confronted. This essentially is to recognize anti-consumerism as a second-order politics that, at its best, is informed by and bound-up with much more comprehensive and challenging forms of political theory – environmentalism, human rights, anti-capitalism and so on. It is to acknowledge also the status of anti-consumerism not as a coherent movement but as a political current informing, to various degrees, the actions of an array of alternative organizations and networks.

It is for this reason that the internet now abounds with the websites of political groups and alliances critical of western consumerism and overconsumption. In terms of the western world, these range from well-established environmental organizations and consumer associations to specific campaign groups, centres of research and information, alternative living networks and less conventionally organized nodes of cultural and economic activism. These groupings and networks are nationally based but often internationally engaged and interconnected. To talk, for example, of Friends of the Earth, Greenpeace, Slow Food, Adbusters, Consumers International, the Fair Trade Federation or the Association for a Tobin Tax for the Aid of Citizens (ATTAC) is to invoke both a local and a global field of political organizing and activity.[4] Many such organizations and networks simply target consumption – and related issues such as waste – as part of a wider programme of campaigns; others concentrate squarely on interrogating and seeking to transform western material life.

The World Wide Web, as social movement scholars have adeptly explored, provides the virtual terrain for a highly fluid and amorphous form of political expression, identification and solidarity, especially in relation to the central issue of corporate globalization.[5] This is equally the case in relation to contesting consumption. This virtual terrain is one that is often connected with or conducive of grounded action but which rests on letting such action 'unfold' by way of disseminating information, reporting on local and global political events, providing forums for debate, offering models of lifestyle change and, in particular, facilitating shifting moments of solidarity around both localized and international political actions. In the broadest sense, 'book-based' sites such as those attached to Klein's *No Logo* or Bakan's *The Corporation* are a prominent means of articulating a critique of western consumerism within the much wider context of opposing corporate globalization.[6] Somewhat differently, research and education-oriented organizations offer a wealth of specific information on the negative impacts of high consumption and on how to address issues of environmental and social sustainability. The list of these organizations is long (and expanding) but includes Redefining Progress, the International Society for Ecology and Culture, the New Economics Foundation, the Ethical Consumer Research Association, the Center for the New American Dream, the Worldwatch Institute, the Consumer Citizenship Network, and the Association of Conscious Consumers.[7]

Just as vigorously, it is the numerous nodal internet sites – acting as the voice of small groups, regional and national organizations, and alternative living networks – that articulate much of what contemporary anti-consumerism is all about. These sites both report and incite action at the level of consumer citizenship, cultural intervention and life politics. In taking a broad view, though remaining focused on the West, we can identify a wide array of such groups and networks centred on aspects of consumption. These include those targeting particular corporations and retail chains such as Delocator, Sprawl-Busters and Whirl-Mart Ritual Resistance.[8] More general forms of consumption activism and cultural opposition to commercialism is evident in the widely varying activities of groups such as the Church of Stop Shopping, Résistance à l'Agression Publicitaire, Action Consommation, Food Not Bombs, ConsumeHastaMorir and the Associazione per i Consumi Etici ed Alternativi.[9] Finally, a life politics of frugality, simplicity and slowness is purveyed by numerous nationally based groups and information portals such as Freegan Info, the Simple Living Network, the Compact, and Bilanci di Giustizia.[10]

Members of a number of these and other consumption-related groups and networks were generous in agreeing to participate in the research on which this book is based. Over a three-year period, hundreds of western political groupings were identified and about forty of those that predominantly targeted overconsumption and consumerism were approached for information. Subsequently, nearly thirty detailed conversational interviews with individuals connected to these groups took place.[11] In an effort to explore the personal dimensions of consumption-related political action, these interviews briefly covered people's upbringing, career and chosen lifestyle. More particularly, however, the interview sessions involved detailed discussion of the perceived sources of and reasons for consumerism and overconsumption. Equally, discussion focused on people's understanding of the nature and purpose of contemporary 'anti-consumerist' politics – and on the prospects of achieving economic and social change.[12]

It was no surprise that most of those participating in this research were from middle-class socio-economic backgrounds and possessed university level degrees. This merely reflects the still highly classed nature of active political participation in movements such as environmentalism. There was, however, much greater diversity in terms of family background and political formation, and this demonstrated the dubious validity of constructing simple typologies of the contemporary consumption activist. A number of people mentioned deeply religious family backgrounds; others spoke of a 'mainstream' family life or, in stark contrast, of a 'radical' upbringing. What is more, in terms of political outlook, participants varied from those who described themselves as liberal to those who espoused neo-Marxist and anarchist views. A certain spirituality was invoked also by a number of those with whom we spoke.

Yet, interesting as these findings are, my purpose in this chapter is to focus on a specific set of perspectives and opinions rather than on personal history. I am concerned, here, to move the narrative of this book forward by examining how activist talk demonstrates a less self-assured and insular form of consumption politics than is often evident in anti-consumerist literature. Inevitably, I draw below on a mere fraction of the interviews undertaken, but in doing so I join with a number of those we spoke with in challenging some of the ideas of causality, change and future that pervade the new politics of consumption.

US AND THEM

I have explored already the interpretative framework of much anti-consumerist polemic. In doing so I have acknowledged the timeliness and importance of a renewed critique of consumerism, but also identified its interpretative limits particularly in relation to its penchant for bland causal explanation. Indeed, stripped down to its basics, recent commentary has consistently offered a powerful but frustratingly partial vision of 'consumer culture', routinely identifying the manipulative power of advertising and the imperative to keep up with Joneses as the central forces underlying over-consumption. For many critics the person has thus given way to the gormless consumer, who is now no longer prepared or able to exercise a moral strength to forego immediate gratification and material reward. A more empathetic, though still somewhat patronizing, side to this vision emphasizes consumption as cultural entrapment, seeing the western individual as bound up in a competitive cycle of chasing status and security through the dollar, and as hopelessly lost in a futile search for personal efficacy and existential meaning through the commodity.

Not unsurprisingly, many of those we spoke with in researching this book reiterated elements of this interpretative perspective, particularly when dealing with notions of mass culture and popular consciousness. The manipulative and culture-framing power of advertising – and people's acceptance of a culture of acquisition – was emphasized by many we spoke with. Indeed, whether situated in North

America, Europe or Australia, participants, at various moments in conversation, readily vented frustration at what they saw as people's 'unbridled need to buy'. Western populations, especially the young, were variously spoken of as 'constantly duped by advertisers and by the media', as leading lives 'without moral underpinning', as 'unthinking', as 'passive', as 'self-indulgent', as 'driven by cash and greed', and as having 'an almost exclusive identity as consumers'. This rather bleak picture of the late modern western individual was most forcefully put by Kalle Lasn of Adbusters in Canada, who has made no bones about adopting an orthodox 'mass culture' position:

> I quite openly say that the bulk of us are caught in a media–consumer trance; that we basically sit down in front of our TV sets every night and absorb consumption messages . . . And then on Saturday mornings we hop into our cars and dash off to the malls and do exactly what all those ads have been telling us to do. I think most of us are living lives of mindless consumption. I think we are dupes.[13]

Importantly, Kalle ultimately tempered this line of argument by adopting also a psycho-social perspective common to almost all those who participated in this research: a sense that people, beyond brainwashing and greed, are driven to consume as a way of relieving the apparent stress and meaninglessness of contemporary western existence. Clearly, this latter perspective complements the more empathetic approach noted above; that is the effort of a number of critics to see people not simply as dupes but as, quite literally, shopping for something beyond what the consumer marketplace offers. Critics have now moved also to a recognition that western populations are currently shopping somewhat less than previously.

Numerous interviewee comments that speak of these interpretative parallels between anti-consumerist polemic and activist dialogue could, of course, be reproduced here. Yet, this would be to go over ground already covered. Far more interesting to note is the point at which participants began, often in an openly contradictory way, to double-back on these kinds of perspectives, to depart from the orthodox narrative of the new politics of consumption and, indeed, to gently pull this politics apart.

This was nowhere more apparent than in discussing an activist relationship with a public. At various stages in conversation, many of those we interviewed sought to partially unravel the 'us and them' dichotomy that runs throughout anti-consumerist commentary and politics; that is, the assumed divide between an enlightened vanguard, on the one hand, and an entirely befooled majority, on the other. In a highly productive way the very act of informal dialogue, as opposed to the formal constraints of writing polemic, allowed interviewees to reject one-dimensional constructs such as 'affluenza'. Indeed, perhaps the most interesting facet of the interviews was the effort made by many participants to come to grips with consumption as a double-sided phenomenon: as driven by both reasonable and unreasonable desires, and as involving concrete pleasures, not just undelivered dreams. In the process of discussing this double-sidedness, the very notion of anti-consumerism itself was sometimes brought into question. As Joel Bakan, author of *The Corporation*, thoughtfully observed:

> I have to say I'm not anti-consumerist. I've always seen that being interested in comfort, a good bottle of wine, some nice clothes, etc., is part of human nature, and they are things that I don't think we should hate in ourselves or in others or feel that that is the source of the problem. I think that the source of the problem is when those values occlude

all other values, when we start to believe that that's all that we're about and that that's all we should be concerned about . . . That's where I think the left ends up getting itself into knots, sometimes. I think we're mistaken for condemning consumerism and [insisting] that we should completely eradicate the desire to consume anything. So the label of 'anti-consumerism' itself is very tricky . . . because what we really want to say is that we're anti-fundamentalist consumerism. We're against our society *only* valuing consumerism, or we're against [the] eradication and occlusion of values of compassion and sympathy and trying to be a good citizen. That's what we're against.[14]

Across the Atlantic, a similar point was made by Rob Harrison of the Ethical Consumer Research Association in the UK. In response to a question about the usefulness of terms such as 'consumer society', Rob insisted that

I honestly don't use that term [consumer society], really. I kind of call them capitalist economies . . . old-school Marxist, really, in terms of terminology. I guess I feel we're battling against consumer society . . . to some degree . . . [but] I don't have a big problem with consumers and shopping . . . I don't see consumer society as necessarily a bad thing, so long as it pays for its impact, if you see what I mean. As long as it takes responsibility for its impacts and minimizes them, or eliminates them ideally, and constructs itself in such a way that they're not negative.[15]

In some respects, this questioning of the ethos of 'anti-consumerism' is no doubt a matter of semantics. Joel appeared to use the term 'consumerism' to refer to the practices of modern consumption *per se*. In this sense, his comments fit with the distinction invoked throughout this book between consumption as a perfectly reasonable and indeed essential human activity, and consumerism as a practice and ideology of ceaseless acquisition and disposal. What is of greatest relevance here about Joel's and Rob's comments is that they speak of a major tension within a contemporary politics of consumption between those who portray the western consumer as essentially irrational, amoral and misguidedly seeking meaning in the wrong place and those who more readily accept consumption as a vehicle of pleasure, expression and self-identity, but who wish to transform it as an economic and social activity. This returns us to the distinction, noted elsewhere, between the ostensible puritanism of practices such as frugal living and the celebration of pleasure embodied in movements such as Slow Food.

Just as the interviews problematized the image of the consumer as entirely duped, and contemporary consumption as unrelentingly negative, so too – and even more importantly – did they bring into question a focus on individual culpability. Once again, this challenged notions of 'us and them' born of a belief that most western consumers lack the moral fortitude to change their ways. A number of interviewees were at pains, often in direct critique of the current anti-consumerist literature, to reinstate a sense of the highly institutionalized and systemic nature of overconsumption. This entailed moving beyond censoriously identifying the manipulated, status-hungry and uncaring individual as the source of consumerism. Instead, consumerism was seen as the result of a complex interplay between the subjective and the structural, the cultural and the systemic. Helena Norberg-Hodge, founder of the UK-based Institute for Ecology and Culture, put this well:

> This for me is one of the most important and most insidious characteristics of consumer culture. I see that it provides for

a very natural inclination to want to belong and be loved, to want to be seen and respected. It provokes that in-born desire into a path that actually leads to separation, alienation, competition, envy and social breakdown. Concomitantly, with the changes that are introducing consumerism, you also have economic pressures beyond the psychological pressures as part and parcel of consumerism. They are systemically linked, and they are increasing the need to move for jobs. They are increasing mobility, and that also breaks down families and community relationships. So you have both psychological and structural pressures.[16]

Across the globe, Suzie Brown of the Australian Conservation Foundation made a similar observation in the context of critically reflecting on her own highly individually focused work as a coordinator of workshops on sustainable living:

I can talk [to people] a lot about the social and psychological drivers [of consumerism] . . . but the block I always get to is the economy and the way it's set up . . . I think that's really the root of the problem . . . I'm not saying that the only answers lie in the economy – you need to tackle all areas – but the one that's not being addressed at all and really is the root of the problem in my mind, is the economic structure, I guess – the structural situation.[17]

Still in Australia, Danni Zuvela of Food Not Bombs, while talking of consumerism as driven by an acquisitive culture and individual desire, was at pains to take issue with those who would emphasize these factors to the exclusion of a more systemic approach. To speak of consumer culture, as she put it,

is not to say that people are brain washed or stupid. I accept that a lot of people can be exercising a great deal of personal power [through consuming] and might be making very critical and informed distinctions between what they're buying. I don't think [this] changes the fact that it's a real crisis and that we are consuming way too much . . . But this [fact] is partly due to the complicity of industry, government, multinational corporations . . . I would [thus] put the blame at a higher level. I don't think it [overconsumption] is generated by individuals, or people.[18]

Finally, speaking from a very different socio-historical context, Lewis Akenji, a founding member of the Hungarian Association of Conscious Consumers, noted, like Helena above, the intense interplay between the political, the economic and the subjective:

It [consumerism] has to do a lot with politics and business, and, on the other hand, with psychology and people's appetite . . . On the one hand, it's in the nature of the state to promote business and thus consumption . . . These are really strong systemic forces which you just can't step out of: business and politics. These are grand frameworks that people are shrouded in. It's hard to avoid [these pressures]. Then there are people at the individual level. I think consumerism [at this level] comes from a lack of ways to define [oneself]. It's like people have limited ways of defining who they are . . . showing who they are.[19]

These discussions about the systemic origins of consumerism provided some of the most refreshing moments in undertaking this research. These and other comments were certainly marked by contradiction in that participants often seemed to want to keep hold of a sense of consumerism as driven by consumer acquiescence but to also puncture this assumption by offering a quite different perspective.

This took a politics of consumption beyond much of the published commentary on the perils of affluenza and the virtues of downshifting – while not necessarily dismissing entirely this now dominant public intellectual approach. Such comments simply gave voice to what, as Suzie Brown well recognized, must be seen as the realities of structural enforcement and the imperative of fundamental systemic change. Here again was illustrated a major tension within a contemporary politics of consumption, this time between analyses that privilege a view of consumerism as the product of socialization, consciousness and existential malaise, and those that give equal or more accent to an understanding of consumerism as driven by the organizational logic of contemporary capitalist economies.

What was demonstrated also was a geographic tension, or rather, a difference of political cultures. Notably, interviewees in the United States, as opposed to those in Europe and Australia, rarely moved beyond notions of cultural conditioning and the psychology of materialism as an explanation for consumerism. This partial elision of structural explanation is, as we have seen, equally characteristic of much recent anti-consumerist polemic – and this reminds us of the extent to which the unmistakeable dominance of American voices in constructing the new politics of consumption, at least at the level of published critique, has so far shaped this politics as strongly liberal in orientation, notwithstanding the importance of these North American interventions.

A BROADER POLITICS

In the introduction to this book I signalled the perhaps inevitable contradiction into which many critics of consumerism are drawn. Within much contemporary public intellectual critique the western individual is envisaged as both a mindless purveyor of consumerism and, at the very same time, as a potential agent of individual, social and cultural change. Here, a vision of consumerism as an iron cage of domination and manipulation rests alongside an insistence that people can attempt to – and achieve – escape from the forces and frameworks of the consumer marketplace. Within the very midst of consumerist complacency, critics thus identify an emergent field of hope either in the form of those few who have opted for strong simplicity or as represented by the significant and growing minority who express a will to life and politics through practices such as downshifting, ethical consumption, consumer citizenship or, more broadly, 'cultural creativity'. The new politics of consumption, at least within the more polemical and advocatory literature, thus courts the perennial problem of all false consciousness and vanguardist arguments. Change is seen as the product of enlightenment, but enlightenment is seemingly precluded by the overarching hegemony of the dominant culture and thus is only truly to be achieved by a minority who drive social change.[20]

To be sure, no politics of reform can entirely escape this logic, nor is it possible to think of social transformation without recognizing it as inevitably shaped by communities of people, both small and large in number, who think and live differently. Yet much of the contemporary popular literature on the new politics of consumption has failed to grapple with the contradictions inherent in portraying western populations as pathologically conditioned to shop while somehow also desirous of a life beyond consumerism. This failure is compounded, as we have previously noted, by the tendency of a wide array of critics to promote the goals of environmental sustainability, social justice, global equity and personal happiness as somehow complementary, and to envisage these deeply variant goals as in large part achievable through individual attitudinal and behavioural change.

As with the question of how to interpret consumerism, those we interviewed for this study juggled sometimes contradictory visions of political action and social reform. In mirroring key elements of contemporary anti-consumerist polemic, western populations were spoken of by interviewees as problem and hope, while change was envisaged as a product of both dedicated vanguards and of an emerging post-materialist social stratum. Yet once again, and perhaps because of the dynamic nature of conversation, participants, in speaking of change, went beyond this – and it is these sentiments, rather than simply those acknowledged in previous chapters, that I want to highlight here. A number of interviewees well recognized the intense ambivalence, rather than simply acceptance, with which many western individuals participate in the consumer marketplace. Some of those interviewed spoke also of the sheer difficulty of enacting personal transformation under conditions of consumer capitalism, given the constraints placed on people to conform. Indeed, this led to critical reflection on the ultimate value of a politics of consumption that focuses predominantly on behavioural and attitudinal change; a position already echoed in comments cited above. Equally, more than a few participants implied, and sometimes directly insisted, that a discourse of anti-consumerism must move beyond a limited focus on the achievement of lower levels of consumption and the pursuit of personal wellbeing. For others, a politics of consumption itself could only really be made sense of by constant reference to much broader political traditions and values.

What was particularly notable within a small number of discussions undertaken for this study was the identification by interviewees of an already-present *majority discontent* with consumerism. Here, a consciousness of consumerism as damaging and undesirable was in fact seen as already generalized across western populations rather than as being the property of the politicized few. Indeed, this generalized consciousness was understood as eclipsed, repressed and frustrated, rather than as absent. This was expressed succinctly in conversation with Helena Norberg-Hodge, who observed that

> actually, I'm convinced that a good majority of people within the industrialized world are showing signs that they would prefer something else [to consumerism] . . . We [in the International Society for Ecology and Culture] believe that the crisis we face is not born of innate human greed or that the major driver is overpopulation. We have a very positive outlook in that we believe that human beings inherently prefer collaboration and peace and that they have a desire for deep community and contact with nature.

Reaffirming this sentiment, Joel Bakan spoke just as eloquently of the need to see western individuals as being more than one-dimensional consumers and as inherently open to constructing a better society:

> We are, as human beings, as individuals, very complex and contradictory. There's a large element of self-interest in terms of what drives us to act. There's a large element of consumer desire. There's also a large element of compassion, altruism, the capacity to love and not to see other people and the environment as simply things to be consumed and exploited for our own purposes. So we exist as individuals in this complicated mix of motivations and desires.

Others wholeheartedly agreed, suggesting that amongst western populations there is a more generalized preparedness for change than is sometimes supposed. This was put well by Erika Lesser of Slow Food in the USA. She spoke not only of select individuals opting for lifestyle change, but also of a widespread desire for alternatives (an argument perhaps now reinforced, in the context of her own country, by the election of President Barack Obama):

> I think that a *lot* of people are hungering for an alternative. I think we see all the time little pockets of people finding outlets for doing something that feels much more real and grounded and that isn't just about being a consumer . . . I definitely think change is possible. It's not just that it's part of my job to be optimistic about that [as a leader of Slow Food USA], but I really do believe that there are so many people that are hungry for a more authentic experience and way of life.[21]

Of course, the question is: how to achieve it? On this point a number of participants vigorously tackled both notions of structural constraint and the imperative to emphasize much more than lifestyle choice in tackling overconsumption. As Helena observed of the structural constraints working against people effecting change in their lives:

> I think that for many people [change] is very frightening psychologically as well as economically. But I believe that the main reason that more people don't do it [attempt to opt out of consumer frameworks] is economic. It's a [reasonable] fear of not being able to provide for themselves and their children economically. I think . . . people *can* [change] if they turn much more consciously towards local community building . . . that is the number one step, that connection with other people . . . We have this very complex globalized system which, structurally, is simply too big . . . I believe this calls for an overview that spells out how crazy that is, and this argument for localization is extremely commonsensical and appeals to a lot of people.[22]

This clearly returns us to the issue of localization raised in the previous chapter and it explicitly recognizes that change, for many people, is not a matter of simply 'choosing' frugality, responsibility or slowness, nor a matter of either having or lacking the moral strength to opt for a different way of consuming, working and living. It recognizes that such change involves palpable risks and potential losses and is, above all, a collective rather than individual effort. In a similar vein, Véronique Gallais, of the French group Action Consommation, was at pains to insist that western societies are characterized, as she wonderfully put it, by 'a lack of coherence between what people think and *the possibilities they have to act* [my emphasis]'.[23] In other words, while many western individuals clearly express support for notions of responsible consumption and wish perhaps to alter their working lives, social and economic infrastructures, not simply hypocrisy, actively work against such change. Suzie Brown, echoing her previous comment, moved towards this same emphasis on the need to recognize and tackle the concrete constraints on realizing alternatives to consumerism:

> I know that people can only achieve a certain amount of change in their own lives and then they'll hit structural barriers . . . What we really need is large-scale change at an economic and whole-of-society level because individuals can only go so far if they want to operate in this society we live in. I mean, yes, there are downshifters . . . or maybe people living in eco-villages. There are lots of examples of people who have opted out. But they're a tiny proportion of our society and not everyone wants to do that and nor should they have to. So we need to change our cities, our whole society. That's what brings me to the big picture view.

Suzie's invocation of the big picture is, of course, an all-important theme. For all of those we interviewed, tackling consumerism and overconsumption was seen to be connected with and conducive of the achievement of a much broader set of political aims. For some interviewees, however, this did not simply hover as a kind of wish list, it informed their political reasoning to the point where it became obvious that altered consumption behaviours and the pursuit of personal wellbeing was, for them, simply not the main game. As conversations with a number of participants in this study progressed, consumption became displaced as the subject of debate, and attention turned to the issues of empowerment, emancipation, democracy, and social and global justice. A politics of consumption gave way, in other words, to a much more encompassing vision of change – and anti-consumerism morphed into the kind of systemic politics discussed in the closing pages of the previous chapter. Indeed, escaping consumerism and refusing overconsumption was implicitly repositioned as an *outcome*, rather than a vehicle, of a more fundamental political and socio-cultural transformation.

In clearly demonstrating this – and in echoing themes of localization – Véronique Gallais made the case for a highly politicized form of responsible consumption.[24] While Véronique spoke of the adoption of alternative ways of consuming as inevitably transforming one's life, her comments targeted the need for civic engagement and political contestation much more so than lifestyle change. In fact, consumption behaviour as a site of politics was brought into question:

Well, what we [Action Consommation] advocate . . . is that we make the link with political issues. Because responsible consumption is like sustainable development, it is now on everyone's lips, including big companies who offer a few products to give consumers something to play with while they continue with their practices without changing really very much. What we try to push is a political consciousness. We definitely cannot change the world with only consumption. We cannot pretend to change the world only with our purchases and our behaviours, so we have to have political consciousness . . . and [pursue] active citizenship . . . We basically have to question globalization and the policies which are carried with the free circulation of goods and the world finance system . . . And, in the microeconomic field, it [responsible consumption] is about reorganising procurement systems, developing local companies and re-localizing economies.

Just as strenuously, others emphasized altruism and duty as key elements of a politics of consumption, while also insisting that it was a striving for greater global equity and human flourishing, not individual happiness, that must drive this politics. Thus, Victoria Thoresen, of the Norwegian Consumer Citizenship Network commented that

Our network has chosen to use the words 'responsible consumption' and 'just and fair consumption' in reference to global things . . . We have a definition of a consumer citizen which is all encompassing, but it talks about the consumer citizen being an individual who makes choices in daily life on the basis of ethical and critical assessment that also takes into consideration the local, national and global consequences of their choices . . . Sustainable or responsible consumption [can be understood] in terms of removing extremes of poverty and luxury in the world, [allowing] a better distribution of wealth and opportunities throughout the world. Our definition of sustainable, responsible consumption is based on human development. And this is important . . . [it is not just about consumer choice] it says that people should be empowered to participate in defining and making decisions that affect their lives.[25]

Finally, a similarly encompassing vision was articulated by Aiden Enns, the editor of *Geez* magazine in Canada (and former editor of *Adbusters* magazine), who spoke not simply of contesting consumption but of addressing both social justice and participatory citizenship:

> I'd like to see greater wealth distribution, and part of that should come from a stronger national government which can regulate the concentration of wealth and the redistribution of wealth for social welfare. But a very significant part . . . of that change towards challenging the concentration of wealth should come at the consumer level or, I'd prefer to say, the citizen level, or at the level of the people or civil society. I think there should be a new consensus where civil society should not tolerate the current economic structure, which is not in their best interests. [26]

Comments such as these from Suzie, Véronique, Victoria and Aiden are clearly a long way from much of the current discourse of consumption politics as lifestyle change and self-fulfilment – though I do not wish to suggest that these people are hostile to such ideas. I would suggest instead that what these comments work to overcome is the political evasiveness that has tended to characterize the new politics of consumption. This evasiveness might be said to be an overall effect of recent anti-consumerist polemic rather than an invariable product of the often constructive individual contributions that comprise it. It is an evasiveness born of a desire to appeal to a western post-materialist and individualistic outlook, but which often simply fails to actually level with a western public; to make it plain that, in abandoning overconsumption, it is hard won social and economic change that is on the agenda not personal contentment through shopping less. Working, wrongly I believe, with the assumption that western populations will prove unreceptive to altruistic and confronting visions of change based on the invocation of abstract values rather than on the promise of immediate personal benefit, anti-consumerist polemic has often simply reduced politics *to* consumption rather than produced a more daring and edgy politics *of* it. The result has been a certain timidity amongst critics in venturing 'too far' beyond the realm of individual market behaviour. This, in turn, has led to an unpreparedness both to decentre consumption as a source of social and environmental destruction and to move beyond the 'responsible purchase' as a vehicle of personal and social change. It was this kind of timidity and reticence that was, above all, implicitly abandoned by a range of participants.

A KIND OF MOVEMENT

Abandoned also perhaps was the imperative to define anti-consumerism as an identifiable social movement, or at least one with a political autonomy and a coherent identity. As Lewis Akenji constructively observed:

One of the toughest things we've had [to deal with] in the [sustainable consumption] movement, or one of the biggest criticisms we've had, is not having a concrete vision of what a sustainable society should be. On the one hand, I think that's a very valid criticism. On the other hand, I think it's the kind of critique that comes with not necessarily needing to be productive, but wanting to criticise . . . But if I have to talk internally, there *is* some sort of a vision that is needed [of what] a post-consumerist society should be. And yes, I guess I have to admit, we don't have a concrete one, but we do have elements of a vision.

For some, such as Danni Zuvela, this 'vision' was essentially fleshed-out by giving anti-consumerism a type of 'sub-movement' status through its key relationship to the broader, governing political discourse of environmentalism:

> There is [with anti-consumerism] a kind of overarching ecological perspective that I would belong to that says that we need to work on reversing ecocide and making our lives sustainable, and use that as a template to go into all the other struggles; like gender, class, race and so on.

For others, anti-consumerism was far more eclectic; a political matrix, rather than an expression of one movement in particular. Xtine Hanson, one of the creators of the original Delocator project in the USA, put it thus:

> you could quite easily talk about the politics of consumption and look at any one of those categories [of nature, class, gender, race]. I think the politics of consumption includes production. It includes people. It includes locations. It certainly includes . . . the destruction of most landscapes, and these are most likely non-Western world landscapes. Then there's fairness in wages and conditions. So a politics of consumption is *very much* overlapped with other areas. [27]

All of these participants, in speaking of the underformulated and often eclectic nature of anti-consumerist politics, openly recognized it as a sometimes frustratingly ill-defined field of alternative values. Their comments touched as well on some of the quite practical ways in which this ill-definition played itself out, particularly in terms of the highly diverse organizational forms taken by contemporary consumption activism. Danni and Lewis, especially, represented two ostensibly opposite poles of a contemporary consumption politics; one emphasizing the experientialism and spontaneousness of dumpster diving and similar 'street-level' actions, and the other, the programmatic tenor of the educational and advocacy work undertaken by formal, membership-based organizations. This polarity showcased the slippery nature of attempts, particularly theoretical ones, to characterize and name contemporary fields of political contestation; including that of anti-consumerism. Indeed, it reminds us that a contemporary western politics of consumption courts, both ideologically and organizationally, a unity in diversity – so much so that, in bringing this chapter to a close, we might well ask what kind of 'movement entity' do the critics, advocates and activists discussed throughout this study actually belong to?

Over the past three decades, intellectual work on social movements has followed divergent paths. So-called political process theory, particularly dominant in North America and emanating from the work of Douglas McAdam, Charles Tilly, Sydney Tarrow and others, has focused on movement politics as expressed through the organization and strategic actions of political associations.[28] These bodies are seen to purposively represent and articulate collective interests, particularly of the marginalized and disenfranchised. Through various forms of political strategy, movement associations are understood as seeking to mobilize material and non-material resources – from money to public support – in order to effect policy reform and social change. This attention to organized social movements as a crucial, rational and institutionalized part of democratic political processes is routinely contrasted with the work of European theorists, especially Alberto Melucci and Alain Touraine. The concept of life politics –

of negotiating, contesting and reshaping one's experience of the social world – is central here. With an eye on postmodernity rather than political process, European theorists have looked to the emergence, from the 1960s on, of new social movements working beyond the frontier of labourism and more traditional forms of political association and mobilization. These have been, and are, movements intent on challenging particular forms of knowledge, language and communication in relation to issues such as gender, sexuality, race, disability, nature and so on. They have contested and contest cultural values and social mores as much, if not more, than social institutions and governmental policies. Above all, these movements have problematized the personal, insisting that politics is and must be inextricably bound up with people's personal experience of the world and their striving to construct a subjectivity – or sense of selfhood, identity and personal agency – that emancipates them from the dominant power relations and constraining cultural mores that govern everyday life. This disturbs an orthodox sense of oppositional politics as one that promotes policy reform and structural change. Instead, it recognizes politics as having become personalized into a struggle over how we live, relate to others and experience our very existence.[29]

Notwithstanding these different intellectual approaches, however, North American scholars of social movements have hardly ignored the personal dimensions of political action. Moreover, the work of theorists such as Melucci and Touraine has been further developed. Two of the best recent examples of this are provided by the American sociologist Francesca Polletta and also by Kevin McDonald. Polletta has ably sought to overcome the entrenched distinction between the strategic and personal elements of movement activism through documenting the deep allegiance to participatory democratic forms of decision making – and highly personalized forms of politics – within North American labour, civil rights, new left, feminist and anti-globalization organizations over the last century. In doing so, Polletta has demonstrated the manner in which these groups have sought to both prefigure egalitarian, non-hierarchical forms of social organization and challenge an understanding of politics as public and impersonal.[30] Following a very different path, McDonald writes of contemporary movements that are neither nation-based nor conventionally organized. As noted in the introduction to this chapter, he theorizes a move from social to global movements; the latter being understood as 'experiential movements' that, far from emphasizing organizational formality, collective identity, political unity and the public representation of interests and identities, principally express a collectively felt experience of the world. That is, what animates these movements – of which the amorphous anti-globalization movement is the best example – are shared and highly embodied affective responses to the world that lead to a personalization of commitment and to forms of politics that focus on liberatory actions, projects and orientations rather than on formal intellectualized goals. [31]

Social movement theory – and I have but touched on it here – certainly provides us with tools to understand the new politics of consumption; a politics so energetically articulated by those interviewed for this study. Yet, in drawing on such theory, it is crucial to emphasize that a contemporary anti-consumerism in the West is characterized by *layers* of social and cultural interpretation, political intention, strategic and social action, and affective response – and this layering warns against an easy typification. Indeed, the political ideas and responses explored throughout this book move between conventional notions of political activity as organized and programmatic and more fluid notions of movement politics as grappling with questions about what it means to be and act in the world and as deeply connected with the embodied experience of the self. A contemporary politics of consumption, then, is not – at a grounded level of activism and advocacy – a homogenous interpretative and political schema, nor is it, when all is said and done, a particularly concrete political force or identifiable political form. It is rather, to return to the opening remarks of this chapter, a field of alternative social and economic practices, a political stance and current, that traverse movements of various kinds – from the strategically oriented to the experientially based – and invokes an array of political perspectives and strategies – from the liberal to the libertarian, and from the planned to the impetuous.

In this sense, anti-consumerism is not quite 'graspable' as a movement entity at all. And yet, we do not have to look hard among those who oppose a western consumerism for the expression of shared ideas, hopes, identities, emotions and solidarities. Indeed, the new politics of consumption in the West is clearly much more than a set of divided and disparate voices. Even more so, it is a political understanding and approach that is, as I have sought to demonstrate in this chapter, clearly reflexive rather than simply dogmatic, unfolding rather than simply formulaic. It is this dynamism that drives its continued relevance in a world of economic change and that, in moving on to the remaining chapters of this book, points the way to generating more exacting interpretations of and responses to western material life.

4

INTERPRETING MATERIAL LIFE

When I first began studying material culture in the early 1990s, I embarked on what has turned out to be an ongoing exploration of people's responses to consumerism – not least because it struck me then, as it does now, that most of us who live in affluent nations readily strive to achieve material wealth yet object to being labelled a rampant consumer. I am not alone in recognizing this conundrum. There is, as we have noted earlier, mounting evidence to suggest that western individuals are clearly drawn towards the riches offered by a consumer economy but are also perplexed by the moral and emotional poverty of a social world overly geared to consumption. As a novice ethnographer in the 1990s, I was in fact struck by the force with which people of widely varying backgrounds often expressed to me disdain for the consumer economy in which they themselves fully participated. This was nowhere more evident than in a comment from Zoe, then a young, working-class retail assistant of migrant Australian parents who, during one memorable interview in 1994, matter-of-factly observed that 'consumer-ism is a substitute for living'.[1]

This book is, in many respects, a detailed unravelling of this comment. As the previous chapters have made plain, Zoe's observation, over the past decade or so, has had new life breathed into it. A renewed politics of anti-consumerism has emerged in a range of affluent nations through a mixture of concerns relating to the environment, human rights, social justice, global equity, democracy and quality of life. In many western countries which have, at least until the economic tur-moil of 2008, been experiencing economic boom, critics have contested dominant patterns of work and expenditure against a backdrop of unprecedented, though now off-the-boil, consumer spending. Without doubt, economic downturns hurt those the most who should be hurt the least. However, recessionary forces, on the whole, do little to reduce overall levels of global, and particularly western, consumption in the medium to long term. Even less does recession disturb capi-talism's premise that high consumption is to be maintained and, when lost, regained. For this reason, anti-consumerism remains an essential political current of a now economically troubled era and Zoe's pithy adage stands as apposite still. But her comment, offered in the context of acknowledging her own intense attraction to consumption, reminds us also of the need to seek out dynamic ways of interpreting mate-rial life in the Minority World and beyond; dynamic ways of telling the story of why we consume. Indeed, if we are to both comprehend and contest the place of consumption in people's lives – in our own lives – we must resist falling back on tired explanatory paradigms that simply rehash the notion that consumption turns us all into drones and com-prehensively vandalizes our cultures.

In taking up this interpretative concern, and offering a different take on our involvement with a world of things, I move below through three interconnected discussions. First, this chapter briefly situates anti-consumerist commentary in the context of the recent history of western scholarship, and particularly social and cultural theory, relating to consumption and commodification. Second, I challenge and partly displace the dominant focus of the new politics of consumption on consumer consciousness and consumerist culture. In doing so, I take full hold of the fact that so many people in affluent nations seem to live a set of conflicting values – and I let this contradiction guide the way to better grasping the varied, rather than one-dimensional, origins of consumerism. This entails constructing a broader sense of contemporary western consumption as bound up with particular material arrangements, practices and conventions rather than as simply expressive of a 'pathological' individual and collective consciousness. Last, I move to the question of impacts, suggesting that a contemporary politics of consumption becomes more adept and useful as it both modifies vaguely evidenced claims about the individual and social effects of consumerism and abandons a vision of consumer culture as a ubiquitous force, colonizing and cancerous of all that is worthy and human.

DESTRUCTION AND PRODUCTION

I have noted already the extent to which a reinvigorated critique of consumerism in the West draws deeply on the work of earlier social observers. In fact, the new politics of consumption sits squarely within a broad critical tradition – taking in both Marxist and liberal theorists as well as ecological thinkers – that views the commodity affluence of western modernity in overwhelmingly negative terms. Yet over the past four decades or so western critical approaches to consumption have been marked by a notable interpretative dichotomy, one that needs to be briefly unpicked as a means of theoretically situating contemporary anti-consumerist debate and moving to further identifying its explanatory limits.

When, in Stockholm in 1972, the UN Conference on the Human Environment identified affluence – rather than simply Third World population growth – as the primary source of environmental degradation, overconsumption was placed firmly on the international political agenda. Influential at the time was the publication by Donella Meadows and her colleagues of *The Limits to Growth*, widely recognized as one of the key texts underpinning the modern environmental movement.[2] Twenty years later, at the 1992 Earth Summit, overconsumption, particularly by affluent populations, remained a central issue, though it was – following the publication in 1987 of the Bruntland report – reframed in terms of the need to pursue sustainable consumption and economic growth driven by technological innovations designed to minimize the ecological impact of production.[3] This is not the place to enter into the complex politics of enviromentalism and North–South relations that were fleshed out during these decades. We need simply to recognize that these events and publications paved the way for the contemporary politics of consumption now espoused by environmentalist, alternative lifestyle and global justice movements. Notwithstanding the different emphases placed on the need to either abandon or 'sustainably' pursue economic growth, what has been consolidated over almost four decades is a resoundingly coherent portrayal of consumption, particularly in the West, as environmentally damaging and as underpinning global economic inequality. Here, consumption is interpreted in the most direct of terms as depletion and waste, carelessness and destruction.

This, however, was not to be the only story on offer. Almost at the same moment as Meadows and others were urging recognition of environmental limits, the social sciences and humanities were rediscovering the consumer. This was not the consumer of old – the one already well known to conservative, liberal and radical critics alike as greedy, manipulated and falsely conscious – but the flesh-and-blood person with desires, identity and social relationships, eager to use the products of the marketplace as carriers of meaning and vehicles of communication. Here, consumption was given qualities way beyond those of destruction – and in the process the rather laboriously named field of 'consumption studies' burgeoned.

And burgeon it did. In anthropology, Mary Douglas and Baron Isherwood enlivened the study of material culture by turning their attention in 1978 to the *communicative use* rather than simply functional nature or status-oriented importance of western commodities. Writing in the shadow of what they saw as an endless stream of commentary on 'overconsumption and its vulgar display', Douglas and Isherwood did not reject this critique outright but insisted that 'moral indignation' was not enough, that we must better appreciate the socially complex ways in which material commodities are crucial to the construction of human culture and are used by individuals to convey meaning.[4] A year later, in the realm of sociology, Pierre Bourdieu published his exhaustive study of French bourgeois taste, demonstrating the extent to which consumption habits were integral to the communication and maintenance of social distinction – and, more broadly, to the very constitution of the social.[5]

In cultural studies by the 1980s these kinds of ideas – now deeply inflected with postmodern theory – had taken full flight, and the environmental realities of overconsumption simply cut no figure. This analytical ethos was best summed up in the influential work of Michel de Certeau, who rightly observed that consumption was not simply a passive

or mindless act but '*another* production'. While acknowledging the potentially mind-numbing effects of capitalist
economic systems and culture, de Certeau emphasized the
political importance of attending to what people '*make* or
do with the products of these systems', insisting that people
use commodities in ways that create meanings and pleasures beyond and in resistance to a framework, 'imposed by a
dominant economic order', of status, conformity and political acquiescence.[6] During the heyday of the cultural studies
of consumption from the late 1970s to mid-1990s, these
and similar theorizations underscored a swag of texts on the
active, pleasure-seeking and resistant postmodern consumer.
Influential here also was the work of Jean Baudrillard, for
whom late-twentieth-century consumer capitalism had irre-
versibly transformed life into a Disneyland flow of hyperreal
media and shopping mall experiences, leaving western populations with no other option but to ecstatically embrace their
own veritable destruction through hyperconsuming.[7] For all
the fanfare surrounding Baudrillard's work, however, few
took the study of consumption in this nihilistic direction.
Rather, consumption was rethought by most cultural analysts
as an intensely contradictory process and as involving agency
much more so than manipulation. In consuming, people certainly performed a capitalist function, but consumption itself
offered open-ended, rather than rigidly determined, avenues
of self-identity, social connection, gender identification,
bodily pleasure and cultural contestation (the latter through
the adoption of confronting modes of dress, bodily adorn-
ment, music and other forms of generational or subcultural
expression).[8] Clearly, this revisioning of the consumer as
productive positively sidelined an environmentalist language
of limits, waste and destruction.

So too did work in the field of material culture studies
in which a similar emphasis on consumption as complexity

framed interpretation. By the mid-1980s research on material culture had turned its attention to, in Arjun Appadurai's
wonderful phrase, the social life of things. Here, it was not
only people's use of material objects that was the focus of
analysis but also the manner in which objects themselves
develop – as they move from being commodities to useful
and valued things, to family heirlooms, to museum items or
to just plain junk – their own 'life history' and, in the process, shape our everyday existence.[9] Somewhat differently, the
communicative status of the commodity was, by the 1990s,
being further explored particularly in relation to the mundane ways in which material objects and shopping behaviours
are made by individuals to express fundamental aspects of
human interrelationhip. Thus, in exploring supermarket
shopping, Daniel Miller – one of the most prolific writers
in this field – contended that wandering the aisles was not
simply fulfilling one's role as a capitalist consumer, or even
constructing cultural meaning, but was, through provisioning one's household and family, objectifying relationships of
care, devotion and love.[10]

For historians and geographers also, the rediscovery of
the consumer reshaped interpretative approaches. The 1980s
gave rise to a spate of work seeking to document, not simply
deride, the birth of 'consumer society' – and by the 1990s
there had emerged a vigorous historiography of past consumption traditions and shopping environments. This work
sought to position life in and around the shop, the mall, the
department store and the supermarket not as meaningless and
blandly determined, but as an important and dynamic ingre-
dient of social history.[11] In geography, too, scholars proved
equally adept at rethinking material life. By the 1990s human
geography was fusing an attention to the contradictory cultures of consumption with an ethnography of consumption
practices in the shopping centre, the high street and the

household. Moreover, geographers were not only exploring what consumers did in the places where they shopped, but also were developing a somewhat different focus on so-called commodity chains, circuits and networks. In doing so, geography forged an immensely important reconceptualization of consumption as but one step in a continuum of fluid events from production to distribution, marketing, purchase, use and disuse.[12]

Without exaggeration, this move – right across the humanities and social sciences – to reappraise the social meaning and cultural importance of consumption fundamentally remade the terms in which material life in the West was able to be discussed. Yet with hindsight – always an unfair vantage point from which to write – it is extraordinary to now sense the utterly disjunctive western intellectual narratives circling around consumption in the closing decades of the twentieth century. Scholars in the humanities and social sciences were excited by, even enthralled with, everyday consumption as a field of human action and material culture; their counterparts in environmental sciences, development studies and alternative economics were simply angered by consumer excess. To be sure, these schools of thought did not entirely ignore each other, but any engagement remained marginal.[13]

The turn to consumption as productive must, however, be understood in the context of the long history of western social theory and critical commentary relating to the consolidation of consumer modernity. There is no purpose in rehashing this intellectual history here. We need merely to note, in accord with the British sociologist Don Slater, that the new 'consumption studies was almost paradigmatic of the cultural turn in social thought'.[14] In relation to consumption, this was a turn towards a view of culture – of language and the symbolic, of belief and the attitudinal – as the dynamic product of everyday life, not the reflex expression of a capitalist mode of production or the concoction of advertising. It was thus also a turn away from mass culture theory, from the portrayal of western populations as having become an undifferentiated herd, materialistic in aspirations, undiscriminating in taste and passive in relation to civic and moral engagement. Yet, paradoxically, this very determination to tackle the interpretative inadequacies and politics of past theory eclipsed an engagement with politics elsewhere. For a time, at least, the new consumption studies, in its understandable determination to put a positive spin on people's willingness to consume, failed to address the key global environmental and equity issues of the era. It failed, in other words, to grasp that the question to be confronted was not simply *how and why* people consume, but *how much*.

This indeed is why, by the mid-to-late 1990s, the cultural turn in relation to consumption was increasingly challenged from within the field of consumption studies itself as having turned too sharply. In geography, history, sociology and cultural studies, by the end of the century, the terms of debate had shifted anew and were now marked by an explicit return to questions of political value. Writers thus re-emphasized the obligation of politically engaged theorists to '*judge* consumer culture' not just analyse it, to tackle 'the benefits and disbenefits associated with specific kinds of commodification', and to acknowledge the limits of material abundance by seeking to recapture 'the complexities explored by . . . critics in the countercultural and ecological traditions'.[15] There was a return also to portraying consumption in a structural context, particularly by those seeking to more forcefully connect questions of material acquisition and affluence to issues of production, work, inequality and social division.[16] This latest of shifts has, though, heralded no rejuvenation of mass culture theory. What has marked this work, and continues to frame much contemporary scholarship on consumption, is an effort to retain the earlier insights gained into the contradictions and intricacies of our engagement with the consumer marketplace, while forging a re-enlivened and politically astute sense of the material nature – or materiality – of the world. This has involved, among other things, the exploration of themes already flagged in previous chapters: consumer citizenship and alternative economic spaces in particular. Equally, writers have sought to tackle the ethics of consumption, still rejecting moralistic critiques, but insisting on the need for normative evaluations of the consumer marketplace. Even more enervating has been the continued exploration of the embodied relationship between people and material things, especially in relation to conventions of acquisition and practices of disposal; in relation that is, to how we think about and relate to the things we keep and the things we waste.[17]

What has, however, certainly lingered in the work of much contemporary analytical and ethnographic work on consumption since the onset of the cultural turn is the tendency to invoke what various writers have referred to as 'weak theory' or a 'weak ontology'. The North American political scientist Jane Bennett, has, in her quite beautiful book *The Enchantment of Modern Life*, described this sensibility well. To deal in weak theory is to accept that one must work with certain general ideas about human existence and the world in order to offer ethical and political perspectives. But it is to write and converse also in a way that accepts the contingency and speculative nature of these ideas and thus does not attempt, *à la* strong or grand theory, to offer rigid, generalizable truths and certainties, or, we might add, to seamlesly describe *a priori* how and why people act.[18] Whether contemporary scholars of consumption utilize this language or not, most remain intent on resisting the 'cultural meltdown school of thought' – to borrow

Louise Crewe's pithy phrase. Most, that is, reject a view of consumption as an utterly ubiquitous and entirely homogenizing force necessarily destructive of social bonds and local cultures, precisely because this is a form of theorizing that is too strong and overarching in its pronouncements.[19] As a consequence, contemporary consumption studies, now more squarely than ever before, occupy an intellectual position of analytical 'in-betweenness' in which western consumption remains understood as a culturally complex and open process but as demanding also of political and ethical evaluation. Consumption, in other words, remains dynamically envisaged as *both* productive and destructive.

And yet, it is surely strong theory – the very notion of cultural meltdown – that has proved most long-lasting and perennially popular as an explanation of 'consumer society'. The critique of overconsumption, the anti-consumerism, explored throughout this book testifies to the longevity and explanatory appeal of meltdown theories; they have said, and continue to say, something that is more tangibly oppositional than an analytical 'in-betweenness'. Moreover, in their propensity to speak in certainties, grand theories of consumption as destruction touch people in ways that an interpretative hesitancy or 'weakness' cannot. The 'strongness' of strong theory, then, is not simply an epistemological issue. It does not only reside in the making of grand knowledge claims; it is also embedded in the drama and affective impact of forthright pronouncement through which the gravity of the world is conveyed. This is why, in relation to consumption, grand theory – or let us simply refer to it in less perjorative terms as encompassing theoretical generalization and statement – has in fact never disappeared, nor has it been particularly weakened by the relativistic moment of postmodernism. Indeed, a number of writers, less enamoured of theories of consumption as complexity, contradiction and agency, have over the past decade in particular maintained the critical tradition in relation to consumer society, opting for a highly generalizing interpretative approach that, more readily than much consumption studies, complements a reinvigorated anti-consumerism.

The American sociologist George Ritzer has been one of the most prominent theorists in this regard. Writing in 1993 of the 'McDonaldization' of society, Ritzer contended that the McDonald's fast-food chain symbolized the perfection of a long process of instrumental rationalization under conditions of consumer capitalism. The Big Mac spoke not simply of a business but also of a deep, homogenizing and dehumanizing commercial process seeping into all social spheres and reorganizing life along the vectors of efficiency, calculability, predictability and control. In Ritzer's more recent formulations, this process of rationalization has progressively rendered contemporary affluent societies a desert of 'non-places': of planned and controlled environments, from fast-food outlets to shopping malls, that are both devoid of social content and progressively eradicate local community-embedded places of meaningful interaction. This connects directly with a contemporary anti-consumerism, and Ritzer – always a politically engaged scholar – sees in movements such as Slow Food the possibility of defending the local.[20] Similarly attentive to the encroachments of consumerism, the British social theorist Zygmunt Bauman has also forged a powerful vision of consumption as social decline. Writing in 1998, Bauman posited a transition in the West from an early-modern 'society of producers' to a late-modern 'society of consumers'. The implications were social as well as cultural. Socially, poverty becomes defined, not primarily through being unemployed but through being a 'flawed consumer', unable to participate in the aesthetics of consumption through which contemporary identity is forged. Culturally,

the rise of a 'consumer mentality' yields, among the western populace, a socially destructive compulsion to consume.
Bauman would later come to more extensively theorize this
in the context of discussing his evocative notions of liquid
modernity and liquid life. This is the modernity, the life-
world, of the western present in which the only constant is
technological and social change so rapid that we must always
be looking ahead, redirecting our lives, *consuming anew*.
These imperatives are undergirded, for Bauman, by the
'consumerist syndrome', a condition that valorizes the novel
product and devalues the old, reducing life to the pursuit
of individual happiness through instantaneous gratification
within a consumption system that is based on fostering permanent non-satisfaction.[21]

If this sounds much like the anti-consumerism discussed
throughout this book, it is indeed similar. One of the virtues
of Bauman's work (as with Ritzer's) has been his propensity
to engage very directly with the public intellectual critique
of consumption. In fact, it is with the most recent work of
Bauman, and with that of the American political theorist
Benjamin Barber, that I bring this section to a close, since
both authors demonstrate the convergence of certain social
theoretical and anti-consumerist paths of interpretation.

In titling their recent books *Consuming Life* and *Consumed*,
both Bauman and Barber convey immediately the sense in
which consumption must be understood as predatory.[22] For
Bauman, the society of consumers in liquid modern times has
become 'a set of existential conditions' through which people
unthinkingly embrace consumerist culture. This is a culture
that defines us as consuming subjects, meets little resistance
in doing so, and plunges us into an 'economics of deception'
that falsely promises happiness through consumptive excess
while undermining social bonds and community cohesion
in the process. For Barber, liberal rather than left in out-

look, the scene of consumption is equally as bleak. Western consumerism has set a wayward capitalism against democracy, infantilized First World adults by reducing us to beings who seek continual entertainment through all that is novel, simple, easy and fast, and violated our children by training and exploiting them as shoppers. Neither Bauman nor Barber, however, offer entirely bleak diagnoses – and both write on the cusp of global recession. Bauman insists that he is envisaging consumer culture as an 'ideal type', portraying it – in order to invoke further thinking – as far more dominating than it may actually be. Barber, on the other hand, rejects false consciousness arguments, suggesting that people are not entirely duped into consumerism but suffer a 'divided consciousness'; they are drawn to ideas of community and social responsibility, but allow their consumption addiction to hold sway. Both writers look also to a future – and one perhaps now more tangible in a post-2008 era: Bauman to the continued relevance of the 'social state' as a means of controlling the damage reaped by consumerism; Barber to the restoration, in part through consumer citizenship, of a pluralist, democratic capitalism and to the global governance of its activities.

When all is said and done, however, these theoretical treatments of western consumption are a long way indeed from theories of the productive consumer. They bring us full circle, returning us in fact to notions of consumption as destruction. In doing so, they deliver a powerful and important political message, but they tend also to entrap us once again in the interpretative dichotomies – between consumption as either determined or agential, consciousness as either manipulated or self-governed, and theory as either strong or weak – that have come to dominate intellectual debates of the last four decades. Yet surely, we might ask, there is now space for interpretative change. In further generating a

dynamic understanding and politics of consumption the challenge, in fact, is to let our grip on these dichotomies loosen
and to energetically widen terms of interpretation; a task I
will pursue in the remainder of this chapter by returning to
the field of contemporary anti-consumerism itself.

ENCIRCLEMENT, ENABLEMENT AND ROUTINIZATION

If the new politics of consumption has much in common with
a broader social theoretical approach to consumerism it must
be seen also as now reshaping this thinking – and as providing, into the bargain, a vital political ground on which to
revisit some of the perennial issues plaguing all theorizations
of consumption and modernity. In no uncertain terms, then,
we must take a current politics of consumption seriously as
theory, as a dialogue to be reckoned with, offering both substantive interpretations of overconsumption and grounded, if
uncertain, visions of a non-consumerist future.

Yet in treating recent anti-consumerist analysis and
advocacy with theoretical and political regard, we are drawn
inevitably into recognizing its limitations: ones that reflect
the analytical tendencies and prejudices of a deeper tradition
of critical theory. The new politics of consumption, it must
be observed, tends to settle far too readily for a strong theoretical approach that lacks interpretative creativity, draws very
selectively on the now rich array of consumption scholarship
sketched above, and works with an intensely culturally oriented story of consumerism as a product of consciousness and
ideology. This, in part, stems – as we have earlier recognized
– from its inability to move beyond well-worn, if undoubtedly
still useful, theoretical paradigms. So many critics, it seems,
are content to proffer a vision of the consuming person as a
child of socialization, manipulation and emulation. Reigning

supreme, here, is a view of market behaviour as expressing a relentless, obsessional desire for and preoccupation with possessions and social status: an obsession that is nursed by a skewed consciousness of oneself as an individual and of the social and material contexts in which one lives. This damaged consciousness is governed by a mentality that reflects a deeply ingrained consumerist culture: one that has literally captured attitudes, beliefs and values. Whether described by recourse to the now done-to-death and presently somewhat irrelevant term 'affluenza' or by invoking some other epithet, consumerism is seen as a way of thinking, feeling and spending that speaks, at one and the same time, of conditioning, addiction and conformism.

Clearly, this is a type of commentary that radically distances the critic and activist from a populace; it stands back and judges from an assumed position of enlightenment based on a rather rigid set of assumptions. Cast in this light, the new politics of consumption is none too appealing at all – and yet we can and should accept at least some of the tenets of this ever-recurring interpretation of consumerism as a product of manipulated consciousness and hegemonic culture. Not to do so merely condemns us to reasserting the utterly tired dichotomy of consumption as determination or as agency. There is simply no denying the long process through which the subjectivity of western individuals has been, as Barber would have it, consumed. In no uncertain terms, we in the West are indeed subjects of consumption. Our values, our desires and our imagined futures are inextricably bound up with the very particular ways in which western societies have historically conceptualized, produced and related to the material world. Consumerism is thus undoubtedly an ideology, a hegemonic force that has, over time, partially framed the mentality of western individuals and partially constructed the cultures they live through. Moreover, the treatment of human consciousness as damaged or diminished in relation to consumerism can, in its statement of a commonsense position shared by many, take on great rhetorical effect within contemporary polemic. We are compelled to use metaphor in understanding our world and, as the North American writer Susan Sontag so ably demonstrated, metaphors, particularly those of illness, are powerful.[23] So too are metaphors of domination, manipulation, addiction and so on. To utilize these notions within a critique of consumerism is undoubtedly effective in engendering recognition of overconsumption as leading us down a dangerous path.

But consumer consciousness and consumerist culture are not the only – perhaps not even the main – stories with which we must deal. We can and should refuse to settle for these interpretative constructs alone if we are to further generate an intelligence of contemporary affluent world overconsumption and a politics of opposing it. Quite simply, consciousness and culture are made by contemporary critics to do so much interpretative work, to carry so much of the weight of explanation in relation to consumerism, that the very process of social commentary becomes, to use Sontag's apt phrase, *anti-explanatory*.[24] It is at this point that the impetus to grasp consumerism as all mentality and ideology simply fetishises these constructs and closes off the possibility of parallel explanations as to why particular forms of consumption and overconsumption occur. The continued recourse to consumerism as a product of skewed consciousness and culture does not, then, speak of the endless explanatory usefulness of such a perspective but, rather, of *interpretative habits*, of the way in which naming and defining western consumption has become enmeshed in conventions of thought that allow it to be always already known and easily explainable. This leads ultimately to a misrecognition of – and lack of deeper reflection on – the very object of analysis: contemporary western, indeed global, material life. It stymies a willingness to tackle consumerism without explaining its occurrence predominantly by recourse to a base intelligence born of mindlessness, helplessness and moral weakness.

This much at least is occasionally recognized within the new politics of consumption itself. We have already explored the diverse ways in which consumption advocates and activists working in a range of affluent nations negotiate often conflicting visions of consumerism. Activists certainly draw on ideas of greed, socialization, manipulation and emulation in explaining consumer behaviour. But some demonstrate also a productive interpretative hesitancy, not common within the polemical text, that leads to a very firm recognition of the interplay between the psychological and structural forces underlying consumption economies, and of the way that, for many people, consumption gives rise to conflicting values, to intense emotional and moral ambivalence.

This same ambivalence has been generally, though rather fleetingly, recognized by anti-consumerist critics. While some commentators certainly insist that hypermaterialist values have now simply won out and substantially govern the mentality of younger western generations in particular, many other writers recognize a continuing, paradoxical conflict between stated values and actual consumption behaviour across affluent populations. Critics thus draw attention to the fact that people increasingly express postmaterialist sentiments – those that emphasize the importance of health, happiness, social relationships and the environment – while, at the same time, they continue to work and consume in a manner that seemingly valorizes a rank materialism. A recognition of this contradiction between consumption practices and social values has led, as we have seen, to the ready adoption by many critics of a sociologically segmented view of affluent populations in which a numerically growing minority of people – cultural creatives, new humanists, downshifters and so on – are seen to be breaking free of this contradiction and developing a consciousness that challenges a consumerist ethos. Relatedly, though in less 'groupist' terms, western consumers in general are treated as psyches in conflict, the most recent expression of this being Barber's useful notion of divided consciousness.

Both these approaches move towards an understanding of 'liquid modern' consumption as giving rise to personal dilemmas and political contestation. Yet both approaches also lead us back to, rather than beyond, consciousness as an explanatory paradigm. Talk of enlightened minorities importantly recognizes the rise of collectively shared alternative values, but still renders society as peopled by the conscious and the falsely conscious, the moral and the amoral, the self-creating person and the consumer–automaton. Talk of divided consciousness better recognizes that *all* individuals experience forms of emotional and moral conflict in relation to consumption, yet still rests on a vision of the 'wrong consciousness' winning out and of people giving in to a dominant consumerist culture. Strikingly, but unsurprisingly, what these interpretations do not allow for, or even entertain, is the possibility that contemporary western consumerism does not now – and perhaps never did – simply rest on a smooth and successful manipulation of individual and collective consciousness or on the cultural manufacture of subjects – of flesh-and blood people – who simply hold predominantly consumerist values and eagerly live consumer identities.

What is in fact so startling about commodity consumption in the early twenty-first-century West is precisely the generalized evaluative ambivalence surrounding it. We in affluent nations ably demonstrate a seemingly unstoppable propensity to consume but stubbornly withhold a clear belief in or consent for the consumerization of life. We are drawn to commodities and commodified experiences but are repelled by what consumerism and materialism fully unleashed might do to the values and life-ways we hold dear. Undoubtedly, this ambivalence in part reveals our propensity for hypocrisy and self-deception. We speak and do different things, and fool ourselves that we do not. It tells also – to draw on the work of Helga Dittmar – of a process of ideological disguise through which we continue to fundamentally privilege possessions as a source of identity, but distance ourselves from the fact of doing so. This mirrors a duplicitous culture which insists that 'to have is to be', but holds also to a view of individuality as residing in an essential, non-material personhood.[25]

Hypocrisy, self-deception and ideological disguise most probably all underlie the insistence of the average late-modern western citizen that to consume is *not* to accept consumerism. But what remains to be dealt with still is the degree to which this ambivalent evaluation of the pleasures offered up by consumer economies demonstrates not simply excuse-making but also the highly tenuous connection between consciousness and action, values and behaviour, identity and performance. It demonstrates, in other words, that how and what we consume does not necessarily speak for our values, principles and beliefs, or our sense of who we are as a person. Indeed, if we begin, in light of this ambivalence, to seriously rethink a western consumerism and its current manifestations, we are inevitably confronted by the fact that a materialistic psyche, a manipulated consciousness framed by and conditioned into an addictive commodity desire, may figure comparatively little in how contemporary consumerism is maintained. This is not simply populism – or naivety. Hordes of compulsive, emulative and plain greedy consumers are no doubt somewhere out in the shopping landscapes of affluent nations. In wandering the proverbial mega-mall or witnessing a fad for the latest technology, it is, in fact, all too easy for the critical observer to despair at the state of people's minds. But this is thin empiricism and bad theorizing. It fails to grasp that consumerism does not need, nor does it have, unstinting ideological acceptance by individuals to push western societies – through good economic cycles and bad – towards higher and higher levels of consumption over time.

This is, at base, to recognize that commodity consumption in affluent economies – and elsewhere – does not simply work through the production of particular kinds of one-dimensional individuals who value 'stuff' above all else. As the historians John Brewer and Frank Trentmann have recently observed, with great perception, one of the overriding and ever-recurring themes of western commentary has been the assumed bridge between 'the material flow of goods and the identity of consumers'. What needs to be vigorously grasped instead, they rightly insist, is the imperative to 'intellectually decouple the consumer, consumer culture and consumption'. As they succinctly state:

> Instead of a breakthrough of one particular mode of indi-
> vidualistic materialism . . . modernity appears marked by
> gaps and tensions between consumption as practice, the
> identity of the consumer, and social systems and values.[26]

This proposition opens up an extraordinarily rich seam of possible thinking in relation to contemporary consumerism and connects with the recent work of others on the vibrancy of material culture. It is a proposition that implicitly insists that, in seeking to understand what now drives consumerism in affluent nations, we look beyond the prism of socialization, manipulation, emulation and alienation, and grasp instead the possibility that consumption and overconsumption does not take place in auto-response to ideological messages and as a simple product of consumer identity only. On the contrary, contemporary forms of western consumption may be seen as embedded also, at one and the same time, in processes of what might usefully be named *encirclement*, *enablement* and *routinization*. These processes shift our attention from consumer consciousness and consumerist culture to the economic and temporal arrangements, day-to-day material realities and social conventions, that underscore everyday life in the affluent world – and beyond. They seek to grasp consumption as a systemic logic and as human action and interaction, not simply as something driven by a twisted mentality. Moreover, they allow us to examine consumerism, not merely as a framework of mind but also as something that is engaged in – that is *done* – under constraint, with purpose, and in the course of living a contemporary modernity. Let me, then, expand further on these suggestions.

The strength of contemporary anti-consumerist polemic certainly does not lie in its grasp of overconsumption as a product of a systemic, economic logic that shapes social space, everyday time and social conduct in powerful ways. While critics readily invoke images of an economy that rests on overwork and overspending, and of governments that chase after this state of affairs, any deeper analysis of consumption as in some sense systemically *enforced* is more often than not eclipsed within much contemporary commentary by an overriding tendency to individuate responsibility. Overconsumption as driven not by compulsive, emulative or therapeutic individual choices but by the systemic power of global commodity capitalism to organize our lives and shape the places where we work and reside is thus acknowledged but not accentuated. To do so would be to undermine a focus on consumerism as an attitude, and to somehow excuse individuals from the requirement of personally taking hold of their consumption in the interests of their own wellbeing and that of a social morality. The narrowness of this analysis has already been challenged throughout this book; a challenge reiterated by a number of those interviewed who sought to reinstate a sense of the structural, economic imperatives driving contemporary forms of consumption in the affluent world and leaving individuals with little option but to participate in given economic frameworks.

This is a key point to grasp, and to grasp more fully. There is a dire need to re-emphasize within current debates the degree to which, as consumers and workers living in capitalist economies, we are systemically impelled to live, earn, spend and overspend in certain ways. In terms of economic and social action, our options as subjects of capitalism are limited – and these options differ significantly across the categories of class, gender, race, age, sexuality and physical and mental ability. We are to varying degrees compelled to work at certain jobs and for given hours, to live in certain types of housing and use particular types of transport, to consume or overconsume various kinds of products and services, to shop in various places, and to map out our life-course in structured ways. To opt out of conventional patterns of work, mainstream frameworks of consumption and the entrenched infrastructures of contemporary urban life is, for many people, both logistically difficult and economically risky. This is especially so given the fact that an ability to consume or not consume, as Bauman has convincingly argued, now constitutes the marker of social marginality within contemporary capitalist societies.

To write in the readily accepted terms of enforcement, however, as I have done above, is perhaps not the best means of grasping the structural economic logic driving overconsumption. Notions of enforcement can lead us towards a determinism (this time economic rather than cultural) in which our lives are entirely governed by a capitalist system and in which the status of consumerism as a product of cultural dictates is unhelpfully sidelined altogether.[27] In shifting, then, to a slightly different sense of consumerism as embedded in a systemic economic logic, and of overconsumption as structurally encouraged, what should be accentuated is not that we are, for the most part, forced to work and consume in ways that are functional to commodity capitalism, but that it is made inordinately difficult for us to follow different paths. This is to speak not in terms of enforcement but in terms of *encirclement*: a useful descriptor in two respects. Metaphorically, encirclement conveys the sense in which we in affluent nations live our lives through public, private, institutional and commercial space, and through a temporal arrangement of day-to-day activities, that has arisen in intimate connection with a market capitalism and that places us in a life-world that is utterly geared for consumption. This, as much, is accepted by most theorists as fundamental to any conceptualization of the process of commodification under conditions of late modernity. Politically, however, encirclement is a term that invokes a notion of containment and delimitation rather than determination and dominance. It thus provides for the fact that individuals retain an agency, albeit a compromised one, to move in and out of and to accept, embrace, remould, resent and reject the consumption-geared life-world they inhabit. Moreover, encirclement, as used here, implies a process of shaping but not wholly defining everyday life, of propelling individuals to consume, but not guaranteeing that that is all they will do or all they will value.

Of course, the reality is that most of those who live in affluent nations willingly consume the goods and services on offer at a level either relative to their income or their debt. Western populations may well be encircled by socio-economic structures that partially mandate a treadmill of earning and spending, but most of us do not need much prodding to participate. Here too, however, we must look beyond consciousness for explanation and grapple more adeptly than is evident within recent critique with the way that the things and experiences available for purchase within affluent nations, and globally, demonstrably *enable life*, giving it a practical, communicative and embodied material richness. In this sense, we are neither conditioned nor forced to consume, but do so in human response to the fact that the things and experiences our money can buy allow us to live in, enjoy and shape the world in certain ways.

There is a decided silencing of this proposition in at least some streams of contemporary anti-consumerist thinking. In fact, many critics and activists – particularly those advocating downshifting, simplicity and frugality – are drawn into a somewhat awkward espousal of both materialism and idealism. On the one hand, there is an insistence on recognizing nature as a material environment that is both finite and demanding of care. On the other hand, the material realm of industrially produced commodities is partially rejected through the reassertion of a dualism between people and things. Here, commodities, particularly material objects, are anointed only in so far as they are needed – in terms of being essential for living – or, if wanted, are rationally desired and enjoyed. A life that is 'really real' is seen as residing principally in the world of the intellectual, the emotional and the spiritual. Importantly, alternative influences such as Slow Food and the advocacy of consumer citizenship offer greater openness to the commodity as a source of identity, expression and pleasure. Yet, the overriding theme within much of the new politics of consumption, including Slow Food, is unmistakably the falsity of most commodity satisfaction, particularly the ersatz and temporary fulfilment of mass-produced things and media experiences, and of mainstream commercial space such as the shopping mall.

That western populations need to drastically moderate their consumption, to consume differently and to fundamentally re-envisage the material world is not, at least in this book, in question. But a critique of consumerism cannot interpretively rest on evading or denying the fact of *enablement*; the fact that material and cultural commodities are always deployed by individuals to facilitate living, and that the commodities we acquire and experience, however mass-produced and surrounded they are by marketing hype, do deliver qualities that are of functional, symbolic and embodied importance. This is to see everyday consumption for what, in one inescapable sense, it is: a form of material practice – understood as the ways that we think about, utilize, affect and are affected by our material world. This also is to credit individuals, as indeed they should be credited, with motives for consuming that are born of the dynamics of such practice, not simply the caress of the advertisement or the desire for status. One such dynamic remains the communicative use of commodities; another concerns the very materiality of the world, or the embodied interaction between people and material things.

The first dynamic needs little further explication. As touched on above, consumption must clearly be understood as a means of communicating, of saying something about ourselves and our relationship with others. A contemporary politics of consumption well recognizes this fact, though in a way that tends to mirror the assumed division between conscious consumption and conditioned consumerism. Thus Slow Food recognizes certain forms of consumption as symbolizing enjoyment, conviviality and support for local producers; political consumption recognizes the commodity as a mean of ethical statement; and simple living locates the expression of a particular kind of existential awareness in restrained consumption practices. There is less preparedness, however, to recognize the communicative nature of mainstream consumption. The acquisition of mainstream commodities and the peopling of conventional shopping environments is generally interpreted as able only to speak of the pursuit of social status and social conformity, and of the flattening homogeneity of late modernity. Dominant forms of consumption are thus rendered communicatively stunted; alternative purchasing as communicatively rich.

What this reasoning gives rise to is a too easily assumed equation between types of commodities or consumption spaces and degrees of human expression.[28] Branded commodities and highly commercial environments may well seek to engineer the range of ideas and emotions we can feel and communicate, but there is no evidence to suggest that they are entirely successful in this. The assertion otherwise is often little more than an expression of the class sensibility (or, in Bourdieu's terms, the habitus) of the commentator. In the context of everyday social life, commodities and commercial spaces of all types – from the hamburger to the free-range egg, the shopping mall to the farmers' market – offer communicative possibility (as studies of material culture have ably demonstrated). All such commodities and retail environments are able, at various moments, to provide the ground for expressions of status and conformity, belonging and identity, social relationships and ethical belief. The problem to be confronted is not, then, that certain commodities and commercial spaces entirely dictate and devalue what we are able to communicate through their purchase or use, but that in highly commodified economies market products and commercial environments become too prominent or important as things and places of social and emotional expression.[29] The negative promise here is that more and more human communication takes place through an ever-narrower selection of marketed things and retail space. This indeed is why most affluent world 'consumers' are drawn to consumption as constantly enabling expression, but routinely assert also a belief that there are realms of social and emotional communication that are not, and should not be, purely mediated through the stuff we can buy.

If consumption remains communicatively enabling – in bounded terms – it is even more enabling in relation to our sense of human agency and our embodied experience of the world. In taking the essential materiality of life as a point of analytical departure, we can, as the North American theorist Bill Brown suggests, readily characterize dominant traditions of social critique as based on a paradigm of *looking through* commodities, interrogating them symbolically for what their abundance and acquisition says about the individual and society. It is imperative also, however, to confront the very 'thingness' of material commodities themselves, or *look at them* as material objects with which we live in particular embodied ways.[30] The British sociologist Tim Dant has made a similar point in arguing that consumption has generally come to be understood in social and cultural theory (and, I might add, in social commentary) as always and only illustrative of the social features of buying and selling goods. Yet consumption, at least in relation to material commodities, is also about the physical nitty-gritty of living with objects. The commodity objects we live with are by all means surrounded with cultural and ideological meaning: they communicate certain things. But, more than this, commodities as material objects allow us to experience our bodies and act in the world in particular ways. Thus, commodity objects, through being produced, carry human agency and, through being interacted with, extend this agency by allowing us to perform or conduct our everyday life both in a functional way and with a sense of effectiveness and vibrancy.[31]

Much of our interaction with commodity objects, then, is not simply culturally overlaid; it is connected with the pre-symbolic physical and emotional rewards and frustrations of interacting with things (a point, I suggest, that is hardly news to most so-called 'consumers'). In illustrating this we can use here, as Dant does, the example of an automobile. This is a commodity object that is supremely symbolic of consumerist culture, but is also useful and, through interaction with it, enables our body to sense movement through space and time, and perhaps also to experience speed and other sensations such as coordination. Of course, when our car breaks down or operates out of control, the interaction on offer becomes one of anger and alarm.

A similar reality is evident in relation to notions of consumption as novelty and surprise. As theorists and critics rightly point out, consumerism in the affluent world is ensconced in a celebration of the new: we are pushed to always grab the commodities of the moment and discard those of the moment past. That marketing, emulation and the cultures of consumption play a big role here can hardly be disputed. But what these forces play on rather than simply construct, as the Italian economist Marina Bianchi has noted, is the quite fundamental, though qualified, enjoyment humans experience in encountering newness and change. Bianchi thus writes of the attraction to consumers of 'bounded novelty'. Consumption, in other words, is in part driven by the fact that as human beings we are drawn to experiencing things that are new as long as the experience on offer is not too unfamiliar and thus strange or frightening. For this reason, we readily purchase commodities of known type, but which offer novel, 'improved' functions and possibilities.[32] Thus the market success of an item such as the iPod is not simply connected to the commercial hype promoting it, or the fact that we must have one because everyone else does, but because it offers the distant past and the near future: it is a transistor radio with a whole lot of new and surprising workabilities.

To write in these terms is not to celebrate contemporary western, and indeed global, forms of consumption, least of all the ubiquitous iPod. It is to insist that we understand consumption as a fundamental material and human act. Taken as offering forms of enablement, both in terms of how we bodily live in the world and how we communicate with others, consumption and overconsumption become explainable in terms way beyond affluenza. And, as with the realities of encirclement, this understanding of consumption as enabling is crucial to formulating a more sophisticated critique of consumerism itself.[33]

In broaching the dynamics of both encirclement and enablement I have begun to touch necessarily on a third crucial practice-based aspect of contemporary consumption, especially within the Minority World – that of *routinization*. Overwhelmingly, critics and theorists of consumerism have tended to interpret consumption as a spectacular process: as desiring, shopping for and displaying the glittering prizes of affluence. But the bulk of everyday consumption – for food and household goods, for example – must be characterized as mundane rather than spectacular.[34] A good deal of our consumption also is quite inconspicuous rather than undertaken for display – as in the use of household electricity, gas and so on. What is more, consumption is often consequential rather than purely desired, as in the need to facilitate the effective use of one commodity – a dishwasher for instance – through the purchase of another – dishwashing powder, rinse aid and so on. Equally, certain commodities develop the status of the taken-for-granted: their acquisition has a deep normality to it such that the question becomes not whether to own, for example, a television but which brand and type to have. Here, in all of these instances, consumption – and overconsumption – does not primarily involve an acquisitive consciousness or the dogged pursuit of desired and displayed commodities at all. It is, rather, a product of the day-to-day material aspects of living – and this requires, as the British sociologist Alan Warde has rightly insisted, that we seek to understand consumption as a practice that is collective, rather than individual, and is in part expressive of materially framed routines.[35] These routines are embedded in technologies and the social conventions they give rise to, and in our individual, though socially generalized, habits of relating to the material and technological world.

Consumption and overconsumption, particularly in affluent economies, originates in part, then, through the very technological systems and objects with which individuals must interact. These systems and objects frame everyday practice; in a sense they have an agency or power to direct us to certain forms of consumption which then become simply routine, taken-for-granted aspects of living – and which lead us on to further types and levels of commodity acquisition and use. This is to reveal the flipside of the commodity object as enabling; it can also be channelling, not only in the terms of encirclement outlined above, but also in rendering certain forms of consumption, and the acquisition of particular types of commodities, as *customary*.

The work of Elizabeth Shove and others has illustrated this well. As Shove argues, much of our consumption is bound up with the technologies that surround us. These technologies, encompassing both objects and systems of operation, continually develop and, in the process, reshape across generations expectations about how we are to live a material life. As technologies change, so too do customary notions of such things as cleanliness, comfort and convenience.[36] Viewed in this socio-technological sense the contemporary commodities of the household, the workplace and the public sphere – from heating and air-conditioning to communication and information devices – not only afford much valued services and experiences, but also shape conventions of everyday practice and our understanding of what it is to live normally and reasonably. They give rise, in other words, to the customary, routine actions of commodity acquisition and usage for living day to day.

Crucial to note here is the manner in which these technologically framed routines effectively both maintain consumption and escalate it over time. The technological systems and objects routinely engaged with by affluent populations in particular, and the gradual reframing of social convention through technological change, partially scripts our consumption behaviour. Affluent populations especially are thus continually participants in an unfolding socio-technological narrative of commodity acquisition and use, where one commodity depends on the purchase of another and, through continual innovation, consumption itself becomes a process of upgrading. What is being pursued here, however, is not merely social status in the sense of 'keeping up with the Joneses' but a more general need to keep one's life materially in step with the times.

This sense of consumption as connected with the socio-technological routines of living can be taken in a slightly different direction by recourse to the notion of habit. In her exploratory study of people's relationship with consumer waste, the Australian cultural and environmental theorist Gay Hawkins has given us some clues to this understanding. Consumption and the concomitant production of mountains of refuse by affluent societies, Hawkins notes, is connected with certain habits that are 'embedded in the character of social life'. Habit is understood here not in terms of addiction and dependency, but simply as embodied dispositions towards our material environs that are shared with others and expressed through our repeated and routine performance of certain actions. These habitual actions – often as basic as buying our weekly groceries, then throwing a good deal of them out when they go unused and rot – remind us that all life is based on routine bodily performances and habitual ways of acting that 'bind us to the world at the same time as they blind us to it'. Through habit we are blinded to alternative ways of acting precisely because we are engaging in taken-for-granted routine, but we are also bound to others because our habits often mirror the routines of those around us.[37] Forms of consumption and waste can be seen in this formulation as neither pathological nor inescapable; they are the outcome, in part, of shared – and transformable – routines of acquiring, using, living with, forgetting about and discarding commodities. Consumption and overconsumption thus arise in part from particular forms of conventional action that have become usual to us and that we habitually perform – and which speak merely of this bodily habit rather than of a materialistic, manipulated or immoral personhood.

As with the notions of encirclement and enablement, grappling with consumerism and overconsumption as arising from the everyday routines of social life calls for a modification in how we might formulate an interpretation and politics of contemporary consumption. Notions of routinization invite us, once again, to think beyond the construct of consumer consciousness, and direct our attention to consumption as social and human practice connected with both actions and expectations and the changing individual and social awareness of them. Indeed, invitation is the operative word here. What I have attempted to do in the last few pages is not to simply dismiss the strong – and rhetorically useful – theoretical approach of much contemporary anti-consumerist commentary or to deny that the notions of consumer consciousness and consumerist culture have a place in explaining western overconsumption, but to generate parallel ways of identifying the origins of a consumerist logic that take us beyond ideas of manipulation, socialization, emulation, amorality and anomie. In doing so I have accentuated the gaps and tensions – to return to the words of Brewer and Trentmann – between consumption as consciousness and consumption as action, suggesting that what in part drives western overconsumption is not a majority acceptance of the values and mentality, the ideology, of consumerism, but forces lying outside 'consumerist culture' and connected with consumption as systemic reality, material practice and social convention.

OUTSIDE CONSUMPTION

Consumerism – and the overconsumption of the affluent world – is to be opposed, first and foremost, because of its effects and impacts. In environmental terms, there is no question that world production and consumption has reached levels that tax the Earth way beyond its capacity to provide the resources for and deal with the detritus of present forms of global economic activity. Both Minority and Majority World nations are implicated in this destructive process, and all states and peoples are thus obligated to confront change. But affluent nations remain overwhelmingly – even with the rising economic presence of China and India, and even given First World recessionary times – the champion consumers on a per capita basis. This implicates the West not only in environmental degradation but also in fostering a gross global inequality of life opportunity and access to the material and cultural riches that sustain a decent existence. That First World overconsumption helps maintain and worsen this inequality is also beyond question. But, as I have demonstrated throughout this book, western consumption is understood by its contemporary critics, as it has long been understood by theorists, to have other effects and impacts that negatively rebound on the very fabric of our societies and the tenor of our lives; that pull our communities apart and undermine the quality of our existence.

In bringing this chapter to a close, I briefly revisit this sensibility of consumption as decline and tackle some of the specific claims now made about the impact of overconsumption on wellbeing and society more broadly. It is in relation to these impacts that a contemporary western anti-consumerism is, as we have earlier noted, drawn into a decided interpretative irony. While Minority World overconsumption is readily understood by critics to result in environmental damage and global inequality, much contemporary debate is almost exclusively focused on the impact of consumerism on the western life-world: on the life satisfaction of western citizens and the social health of western nations. This results in the contention that consumption in the affluent world, to return to Comeliau's words, has transformed social relations in their entirety. Indeed, this perspective has been put even more forcefully by the British sociologist Colin Campbell, for whom it is now apposite to talk of a 'consumer civilization' rather than simply a consumer society or culture. Here, consumerism – a phenomenon fundamentally connected with desire rather than reason, and individualism rather than communalism – has become a western metaphysics of being; it is no longer simply about selfishness, acquisitiveness or anomie, but embodies the arch wants-driven and self-oriented philosophy of western life.[38]

Whether couched in these rather grand terms or not, late modern consumerism is, as we have seen, constantly made responsible by contemporary critics for both the loss of certain life qualities and social values and the rise of an increasingly depthless and socially disconnected existence. As I have made plain, there is a deeply ethical analysis at work in these observations, one that not only connects with an albeit patchy body of psychological and sociological evidence, but also which importantly resonates with a widely shared distaste for a world governed by the dollar and what it buys. And yet at work also in this identification of the supposed socio-cultural effects of overconsumption is the same lack of interpretative creativity characteristic of the inflexible propensity to locate the chief cause of consumerism in the realm of disturbed consciousness.

Not the least of difficulties in this respect is the way in which the very focus of the new politics of consumption on the realm of everyday exchange – on shopping and spending – means that the desire to consume and the act of doing so becomes obsessively isolated as the key source of various existential and social problems (and centralized, too, as the avenue of our escape from them). Interpretatively, uncontrolled consumption – considerably more so than the profit-motivated adventurism of commodity producers and finance capital – is routinely identified as the chief origin of environmental and social damage. Ill-being and social decline thus emanates from the consumption practices of individuals. Even economic recession is blamed mostly on the consumer, on our erstwhile addiction to shopping – rather than principally on a feral financial system that has served the world so poorly. In the very effort, then, to afford western citizens a political and moral agency, to rightly insist that they can and should act to change themselves and their societies, much of the new politics of consumption becomes cornered into a 'consumption reductionism' in which people's spending behaviour is made to bear the weight of a society gone wrong. At the same time, anti-consumerist commentary in particular can become a process almost of incantation in which, from one text to another, the assumed effects of consumption are formulaically identified and repetitively asserted. In a good deal of critique also this mode of assertion itself results – as in much social theory – in a negative presumptuousness towards the world: a world in which there is apparently nothing that now lies, that is now thought, felt, done or wished for, outside the empire of consumption.

The pitfalls of repetitive assertion – the tendency of this critical strategy to render commentary analytically static and to provide a politics of consumption with thin empirical foundations – can be seen in relation to the central theme of life-satisfaction and wellbeing. There is almost no critical text on consumerism published over the past decade or more that fails to draw on evidence relating to the psycho-social measurement of happiness. A battery of psychometric tests have, as we noted previously, generally demonstrated the limited connection between increasing affluence and greater life-satisfaction. This clearly is a powerful argument against a consumerist, growth-at-all-costs logic. But it is an argument that is constantly made to overreach itself, drawing critical commentary into a highly tenuous mode of interpretative 'spin' that ignores rather than openly deals with the contradictory nature of this evidence. In a purely empirical sense, the psychometrics of wellbeing does not 'prove' terribly much – and what it does prove provides (unfortunately) only awkward support for a shift to simpler and slower living. Measured levels of subjective wellbeing in western countries do not rise with income, but nor do they significantly fall; they tend to remain fairly constant over time, and this constant is relatively high.[39] Moreover, in international terms, wealthy nations tend consistently to exhibit high national average levels of subjective wellbeing relative to other countries.[40]

Beyond the empirical quibble, however, it is the very turn to psychometrics itself, and to the thorny concept of happiness, that is most problematic in efforts to grasp the individual and social impacts of consumerism. A metrics of happiness, one that somehow miraculously allows wide-ranging comparisons to be made of life-satisfaction over time and between cultures, may inform but cannot add much to a nuanced politics of consumption.[41] As the Australian health sociologist Lenore Manderson has ably pointed out, states such as wellbeing and ill-being, happiness and unhappiness, fulfilment and yearning are not simply to be captured through 'scientific' measurement, they have their own particular valence and may be subjectively felt in concert or in contradiction with each other.[42] The contingent relationship between these subjective states and factors such as income and wealth is even harder to ascertain, while meaningful cross-cultural comparison of wellbeing survey results is plagued with difficulty.[43]

But perhaps the most uncertain move of all in relation to the metrics of wellbeing is the suggestion by contemporary critics that to abandon consumerism is to embrace real happiness or, in the more sophisticated terms of some commentators, to facilitate a true flourishing of one's potential. The latter suggestion in particular – indebted to the work of Sen and Nussbaum – is a substantive one. Yet, in rightly challenging the ideological connection between wealth and wellbeing, contemporary anti-consumerist commentary, on the whole, repetitively invokes a taken-for-granted understanding of existential meaning as a product of the satisfied, fulfilled, choosing and individualized self in touch with an essential authenticity. Irresistibly appealing as this is to a late-modern western sensibility, it draws the new politics of consumption into both portraying consumerism as suppressing the true fulfilment of the self while neglecting to sufficiently deal with the fact that this very notion of personhood as a state to be authentically and fully lived is, ironically, itself the cultural product of capitalist consumer modernity. The chief tenor of much anti-consumerist polemic, then, is that we must leave the false choice and ersatz fulfilment of consumerism behind, but take its very idea of the choosing, self-actualizing individual with us. As a consequence, the very notion of modern personhood that commodity capitalism has been deeply embroiled in constructing is not rejected at all – and the more potentially invigorating effort of envisioning how a very different kind of selfhood might be forged beyond a western individualism is left hanging.

In large part, though, what makes the turn to wellbeing so resonant for the new politics of consumption is the image of an all-encompassing *ill-being*. For so many commentators and critics the consumerism underlying overconsumption is understood – just as it is in the more abstract realm of social theory – as a ubiquitous force encasing the contemporary western life-world in an overpowering process of psychic and social dissolution, and threatening other cultures with the same. Indeed, one cannot come away from a reading of the contemporary critical literature on consumption or a perusal of anti-consumerist websites with anything but a sense of contemporary western life – if not that of the globe – as entirely commodified; and now in deep trouble because of it.

As I have insisted throughout this book, this sense of affluent world consumption as something to be energetically contested marks out an essential and highly productive ground of social analysis and political opposition. There is simply no room for complacency here. Overconsumption is most certainly a symptom of broader global socio-economic imperatives, but this still leaves the everyday practices of consumption in the West as deeply entangled not only with environmental degradation and global inequality, but also with a whole set of disturbing phenomena now seemingly characteristic of affluent societies – from overwork and mismanaged debt to increased levels of stress, depression and social isolation, to civic disengagement and individual self-obsession – and, of late, to increased unemployment, bankruptcy and homelessness. The sociological evidence for a number of these trends is shaky, but they are not fiction, and to do anything other than assume that they are bound up with the historically entrenched gearing of the affluent world to higher and higher levels of consumption, and to increasingly dramatic cycles of boom and bust, would be just plain denial.

In recognizing this, however, we are faced with a pressing interpretative dilemma. Must this recognition of consumerism as social destruction lead to a disenchantment with the world, with the societies in which we live and with our fellow citizens? Must we simply view consumerism as an all-powerful process of psycho-social colonization and enclosure – and, if we do, then how do we explain difference, dissent, opposition and resistance or the simple fact that most people share with the critic and theorist the same fundamental distaste for the society that covets things a little bit too eagerly and shops a little bit too much? It is in dealing with this dilemma that the new politics of consumption – once again, not unlike much of the more avowedly theoretical treatments of consumerism – becomes both contradictory and deeply conflicted. Consumerism has, this politics seems to insist, delivered us a society in ruins; a culture in tatters; a morality shredded; a body, mind and soul besieged and destroyed; and yet all happiness and social cohesion can somehow in some way be voluntaristically regained. Unpalatably underlying this confused and confusing couplet of complete dominance and miraculous escape is the ever-present image of the consuming masses: beings to be despised or pitied who affluenzically want everything consumerism offers but don't really want it all, who lack the moral virtues to change but who deserve to be saved, who have morphed into mindless, acquisitive infants but who can, somehow, through a sheer act of will, choose to think and live differently, and who are now deservedly paying the recessionary cost of their consumer greed but who might learn their lesson and reform their ways.

I am, of course, moving here to caricature and a far too biting critique. Deliberately so. I am well aware that the best of contemporary anti-consumerist thinking is more subtle than this and I have demonstrated very clearly that some advocates, activists and critics talk of a world less totally dominated by the commodity and recognize the continued propensity and desire of people in affluent nations to think and act well. Yet after many years now of intellectually and personally engaging with this politics, I remain struck by how unshiftingly imbued the field of anti-consumerist discourse in the West is with a melancholic negativity towards the social world and those who people it, a negativity relieved only by the attention given to the apparent opposition embodied by 'conscious' minorities. Contemporary critics are resolutely intent on offering, to varying degrees, not only a narrative of destruction, but also what Bennett has referred to as a story of disenchantment. This is the tale of modernity as loss, of existence as alienated and of society as decayed. The strength of a disenchantment story is that it sounds the alarm; its weakness is that it not only draws us into the political con-tradictions noted above, but also robs us of the ability to recognize that there is always much about the world, about the societies in which we live and particularly about the lives and actions of people around us that remains good, hopeful and even enchanting. This calls out for a less melancholic, more generous form of interpretation.[44] In relation to the analysis of overconsumption and consumerism, the import of this insight is palpable: the effects of the commodity world are not ubiquitous. Consumerism is not everywhere and in control. For all of us, our existence tracks forward both inside and outside dominant forms of consumption – and this 'out-side' exists both on the ground and in the mind.

In a grounded sense, those of us who would critique and oppose consumerism must finally let go of the notion that

this term can be used to simply define western economic and
social life, and that the world of rampant consumption must
be spoken of as overpowering and omnipresent in order
for it to be made objectionable. As the economic geographers Katherine Gibson and Julie Graham have argued, it
is crucial to see economic life in the West not simply as a
'singular capitalist system or space' but also as proliferating
with economic forms, with different ways of, and reasons for, undertaking labour and engaging in consumption
beyond the logic of a profit-oriented consumerist ideology.
Gibson and Graham, whom I have drawn on earlier, write
of the 'diverse economy' within affluent nations, pointing
to the prevalence of various localized forms of economic
activity – from undertaking unpaid work to participating in
non-market transactions such as donating, gift-giving and
mutual exchange – that involve people in alternative forms
of economic transaction.[45] These forms of non-commodified
economic life, as Colin C. Williams has argued, are not
simply the province of the alternative few but also are generalized across western populations. Williams has been a
constructive critic of what he calls the 'commodification
thesis' – that metanarrative, deeply ingrained in a theoretical
and polemical literature on consumption, that portrays the
world as undergoing an unstoppable transition to a totalized
consumerism. Like Gibson and Graham, Williams reminds
us, and draws on an exhaustive array of empirical evidence in
doing so, that everyday life within so-called consumer societies continues to involve a great deal of non-monetized and
non-commodified activity and labour.[46] This is no apologia
for western life as it currently is. It is an effort to recognize
the practical everyday limits that people in affluent societies
place on profit as the motivator for undertaking work. It is to
acknowledge our need and continuing propensity to engage
with willingness and effort in activities of subsistence, care

and community involvement that have little if anything to do with making and spending money. This not only challenges a sense of consumerism as ideologically ubiquitous but also suggests that social and economic life in the West exhibits trends and involves people in everyday actions that embody, to use Williams's own phrase, an ethic of 'anticommodification', or an ethos that contradicts the imperative to always and forever be a consumer.[47]

This ethos is present also in the imagination. I began this chapter by drawing on my earlier ethnographic work on the everyday, rather than formal, critique of consumerism, noting the tendency of people to both willing participate in, but express disquiet about, consumer economies. None of my research since has altered my long-held understanding that this expression of ambivalence is not simply denial, self-deception or hypocrisy but tells of the deeply affective way in which, faced with an imperative to become consumers and an economy that continually seeks to commodify all aspects of life, people often 'stand back' from the market that encircles them, feel anger at its encroachments, refuse to participate in it or, at the very least, question its relevance to life. This can be seen as an everyday process of imagining an 'outsidedness' in relation to a perceived consumer culture, of distancing ourselves at the level of thought and feeling, just as we do at the level of non-commodified economic activity, from a world in which everything seems to be for sale.[48] This outsidedness in no way undoes consumerism; it is not usually resistance, opposition or challenge in any politicised sense. Yet, like our everyday participation in non-monetized economic action, it attempts to place limits on how much mental and social space consumerism should be allowed to claim. Here, too, we move towards an ethic of anti-commodification and, in the context of this book, towards the conclusion.

5

CONSUMING DIFFERENTLY

In the western world at least, talk of social, political and economic change has, over the last decade or more, become inseparable from a sense of unfolding environmental crisis. As I sit writing in record-breaking summer heat of over 46 degrees Celsius, a day in which nearly two hundred of my fellow citizens have perished in uncontrollable bushfires of unprecedented intensity, this crisis seems horrifically near. It seems near also for those who connect the dots; linking an increasing savagery of the natural world with the barbarism of a globe hostage to money. Change, though, will clearly not be easy. For many critics of the western present, fundamental transformations in how and what the affluent world produces and consumes and in the nature of our working and everyday life will only come – and much too late – as a reluctant but inevitable reaction to resource depletion and climate change, and the social unrest and hardship arising from them. This sentiment is perhaps also one shared in less politicized terms by a western public for whom the future is increasingly felt as a time of environmental uncertainty and risk. Even western governments now readily justify their pitifully inadequate policy responses to environmental realities as 'measures that must be taken' – while not forgetting, of course, to tirelessly spin the mock bravery of their actions.

This sense of change as an inevitability, brought on by environmental breakdown, was frequently demonstrated during the interviews with political activists and advocates undertaken as part of this study. For many of those we spoke with, a certain pessimism about the driving force and especially the timing of socio-economic change sat alongside a less bleak sense of social transformation as the product of purposeful individual and collective action in the here and now. As the Canadian activist Aiden Enns put it:

> I have good days and bad days, or days of optimism and days of pessimism. Pessimistically, I think we are heading for a collapse of the economy, of the way things are. If you just look at the charts of consumption, we cannot sustain what we are doing . . . We are on a crash course of collision . . . a collapse of our current economic structure . . . On the good days, I trust that people will elect new leaders [and adopt] more sustainable ways of living.

The Australian environmentalist Suzie Brown sounded the same alarm:

> I actually think that environmental problems are going to start driving change more and more quickly. So yes, I think change will happen. Who knows if it will be soon enough. But, actually, if I have any hope for large-scale change, I think that that's how it's going to come about – we're going to be forced to [change]. Whilst I believe in the [necessity of] cultural and grassroots shifts, the quickest change

will come from the structural level and from government policy forcing business, the corporate world, to change at the same time. And I only think that that's going to come about through environmental crisis.

This environmentally focused 'tipping point' perspective on socio-economic change, like much of the contemporary politics of consumption itself, is by no means new – though, unfortunately, it will almost certainly be vindicated. Nevertheless, world events have, for the time being at least, overtaken and twisted this narrative. The world has indeed now foundered on the rock of crisis, affluent countries are experiencing relative hardship, and a global economy is being restructured. But this has been driven by the death of an unfettered neo-liberalism, not of the planet. Moreover, if change is underway it is certainly a contradictory brew; laced with a hopeful revival in the USA, Europe and elsewhere of regulatory interventionism and liberal democratic principles, but equally flavoured with the old market orthodoxies of pursuing growth and increasing consumption. The political lesson of this is clear. No politics of change can rest content on visions of inevitability, and least of all on an assumption that we will get the crises we predict and out of them will come the end of one socio-economic system and the birth of another. Guided by this kind of vision alone, a politics of consumption would be rendered nothing more than a statement of pending doom, informed by a naive belief that as global consumerism inevitably implodes we will be necessarily driven towards a new ecologically oriented rationality and humanist enlightenment. Such an apocalyptic romanticism is undoubtedly one aspect of a contemporary anti-consumerist politics in the West, but it is the more purposeful optimism of which Aiden Enns spoke that mostly animates it; a sense that by acting now – through consumption choices, lifestyle decisions, civic participation and, above all, political involvement – we can foster and guide the changes to come. This is to give emphasis to the already ongoing 'grassroots shift' invoked by Suzie Brown – a grassroots response that is perhaps now, in the post 2008 era, all the more recognizable as a crucial politics of the moment.

It is this very shift, evident both in social commentary and in political practice, that I have traced throughout this book. As signalled in the Introduction, the aim here has been to examine why and how certain forms of consumption, particularly those deeply embedded in the character of western life, are now being more vigorously opposed than ever before. Yet my task has been to *contest* as well as explore a re-enlivened politics of consumption presently evident across the affluent world, not in order to undermine its importance but to further generate ways of understanding western consumerism and the job of transforming it. I have thus extensively challenged the now once again dominant interpretation of consumerism as a product of manipulation, emulation and moral disengagement, and I have sought to reinterpret overconsumption through the prism of social and material arrangements and practices. In offering this more expansive framework of explanation I inevitably began to tackle questions of political approach and strategy, gesturing towards ways in which a contemporary politics of consumption might better ground a call for change in a broader sense of the exigencies and dynamics of western material life and in a willingness to more effectively communicate an oppositional perspective. This was to insist – and this has been an underlying theme of the whole book – that interpretation shapes response. In interpreting and reinterpreting what consumerism is and how it is maintained over time, we in fact make and remake our understanding of the individual and collective action needed to reinvent current forms of economic and social life.

At various points throughout the previous chapters I have

discussed contemporary western anti-consumerism as a field of projected and partially enacted solutions to the problem of overconsumption and the environmental, social and cultural damage with which it is connected. In discussing anti-consumerism as political response and strategy, I have both insisted that it is very much a politics in the making and progressively identified its vagaries and contradictions, as well as its attachments to broader political theories and values. I do not need to laboriously rehearse every element of these arguments here. Instead, in this concluding chapter, I simply begin to sketch, by drawing together a number of themes already touched upon, some potentially productive ways in which the task of contesting western overconsumption might be further communicated and conceptualized at a time of global economic and political realignment.

THE ETHICS OF ADDRESS

The political theorist Hannah Arendt long ago rightly chastised the western social sciences for turning humans into automatons rather than acknowledging them as thinking beings who act. This was a conceptual shift, an analytical strategy, to paraphrase Arendt, that reduced human beings in all their complexity and plurality to the level of a conditioned animal almost without consciousness at all.[1] This book has taken contemporary anti-consumerist polemic to task for often blithely adopting this conditioning thesis. A heavy moral tone unmistakably permeates the new politics of consumption, particularly at the level of public commentary, in which the majority of western individuals are far too often envisaged as having let go of virtue and all intelligence; as being content to wallow in shopping and as now, in changed economic circumstances, having to face up to their addiction. This perspective is informed by an unrelenting obsession with consumer consciousness as utterly dominant, displacing all other human values and sentiments. I have established already the inadequacy of this approach through recourse to discussing processes of encirclement, enablement and routinization, and through insisting that we recognize the intense emotional ambivalence – and sense of outsideness as well as inclusion – with which we all experience contemporary economic life.

But the issue here is not only one of interpretation; it is also one of political ethics. Ethics, as theorists point out, must be understood as naming not simply morals – or certain abstract codes of value and principle – but also the way we act towards ourselves, others and the world. In this sense, to speak of ethics is to invoke a relational concept bound up in human conduct; it is to speak of the concrete expression through what we do and how we do it of particular values. To borrow a line from J. K. Gibson-Graham, 'Ethics involves the embodied practices that bring principles into action'.[2] Such embodied practices include the task of commentating. The way critics, theorists and activists write and speak, the way we conceptualize and convey our message, carries an ethical dimension. The ethics of social commentary is contained not merely in the value positions we, as social observers, put forward, but in the underlying ethos of how, through words, we define and treat others. This, then, is to begin to tackle what I will call the ethics of address. By this, I refer to the disposition and the conduct of a particular political discourse, the manner in which it perceives and addresses others in speech and writing, and the way that this disposition and conduct either constrains or facilitates constructive and respectful forms of communication, engagement and understanding.

One of the major failings of contemporary anti-consumerist politics in the West – a failing that contributes to its marginality and condemns it, when all is said and done, to engaging with a vanguard or, at best, a narrow segment of western populations rich in social and cultural capital – is the non-recognition of this subtle ethical dimension. Anti-consumerist commentators are not alone here, but they do tend to excel, as I have insisted, at an overgeneralized and censorious social diagnostics based on disdain or pity for an imagined imbecile called 'the consumer'. Indeed, with some notable exceptions, there is a breathtaking propensity for contemporary critics of consumerism to routinely address western individuals 'living in the mainstream' as easy targets rather than as intellectual equals – or to move awkwardly, in love/hate mode, between the two. A more generous form of consumption politics is sometimes espoused by activists involved in advocacy and educational activities; not least because, unlike the opinion-rich critic, they are often drawn into a face-to-face relationship with a public that enables them to adopt a more self-reflexive and subtle form of anti-consumerism. But this is not, at least in relation to the dominant face of contemporary anti-consumerism in the West, the general rule. Somehow it has become once again *de rigueur* in the context of anti-consumerist commentary to view the public as a degenerate mass and to tell them they are fools.[3]

In large part, this is borne of a confusion between morals and moralism – or a simple lack of concern for the distinction. Clearly, moral judgement – including judgement of people's behaviour – in relation to consumption can hardly be avoided, nor should it be, given the clear levels of over-consumption characteristic of affluent economies over time. Yet, a slide into moralism is a different matter.[4] As Jane Bennett and her colleague Michael Shapiro have argued, moralism is 'a style of speaking, writing and thinking that is too confident about its judgements and thus too punitive in its orientation to others'. This can lead to a ethos of blame, an individualization of social problems and a strategically ineffective rhetoric that chastises people rather than opens out debate and reflexive thinking in relation to issues of social change.[5]

Importantly, this encapsulates at least something of the ethical poverty of a boots-and-all anti-consumerism that berates the affluenzic and celebrates the downshifter. At its worst, this form of critique has proven communicatively and relationally stunted, content to connect with and afford respect to an enlightened few – or those wavering on the edge of enlightenment – but not to most. More so than this, however, an overgeneralizing and punitive form of anti-consumerism neglects to prefigure the ethical landscape of a new society. This is rather ironic, for, as I have emphasized previously, a contemporary western politics of consumption is marked by a deeply ethical concern for the damaging impacts of western material life. The downfall of anti-consumerism as moralism is not that it dares to invoke moral principles and offer judgements, but that it does so by enveloping a valiant call for a more humane, other-regarding and ecologically grounded society in an attitude of current disrespect (or, at most, patronizing lament) for the contemporary western person as social and economic actor. This is a high-handed disregard that – at times with an almost casual aggression – diminishes the intelligence, rationality and moral sensibility of the consuming individual. What, incidentally, is often diminished here also is the experience of poverty in the midst of affluence. Much anti-consumerist polemic has been so intent on characterizing all of western life as excess that it has neglected to adequately address the constrained consumption experiences and life possibilities of the significant and numerically growing ranks of the western poor.[6] This sleight-of-hand has become a glaring inadequacy in the post-2008 era; where western excess has become disguised, the nature and level of global consumerism has altered, and everyday life in the affluent world has turned precarious for many.

The unhelpfully vanguardist nature of this form of ethically conflicted address is potentially compounded in contemporary discussions of overconsumption, particularly those focused on lifestyle change, by a tendency to deal only in visions of gain. A transition to consuming, working and living differently is so often portrayed in the new politics of consumption as unquestionably positive in terms of increased individual wellbeing, even though practices such as downshifting are acknowledged as involving personal struggle. Any resistance to such lifestyle change on the part of a western public is thus variously interpreted as driven by passivity, ignorance, fear or irrationality.

The importance and integrity of the life-oriented politics embedded in and, in fact, substantially definitive of a contemporary western anti-consumerism has been continually underscored throughout this book. Yet, as we have seen, a life politics often slides into a fetishization of the role of individual will in becoming 'conscious' and in altering one's lifestyle. This, as I have made plain, is a strategy that understates the constraints placed on individual change through processes of encirclement. Conversely, what is overstated here is the possibility and desirability of a permanent condition of individual mindfulness in relation to consumption behaviours; an overstatement that forestalls an exploration, alongside this albeit important individualized model of awareness, of the far greater and more encompassing project of transforming collectively shared conventions, routines and habits in relation to the way material life is lived. But, even more than this, the tendency to convey a politics of consumption through visions of change as gain alone eclipses the need to deal with the realities of sustainable consumption as *loss*.

Consuming differently clearly involves a 'giving up' of many of the things that particular commodities currently enable us to do and to experience. Moreover, what is given up is not always easily substituted for by the non-material pleasures of a slower and simpler life – and contemporary western 'consumers' well know it. They know that the comforts and conveniences currently afforded by the technologies and infrastructures surrounding us – from the mobile phone to the airconditioner – and the pleasures of the commodified things and experiences available to us – from global tourism to home renovation – would be drastically altered under conditions of true sustainability.[7]

A world of simplicity and slowness may well produce different modes of wellbeing and communality, but social and economic transformation never simply complements the needs of the contented self and never simply unfolds as the good life attained. Strategically, as we have seen, there are sound reasons why a politics of consumption might promote a vision of change through appealing to a desire for, and promising the realization of, a less pressured and more emotionally rewarding life – and there is unquestionably a very different type of human joy and flourishing to be had in a state beyond consumerism. But such a politics leaves itself open to deserved rejection if it fails to sufficiently acknowledge the realities of reduced consumption as loss as well as gain, and to engage people as conversants, as partners, in identifying workable rather than romanticized ways of somehow preserving the positive uses, pleasures and satisfactions that many commodities presently offer. Any such rejection of anti-consumerism might well be reflective of people's resistance to or fear of change. It will also, however, be the product of good judgement, of a sense by people that an anti-consumerist politics does not address them, but instead a purist and privileged few, and does not, in proffering promises of slowness, simplicity and localism as human wholeness and nirvana-like satisfaction, tell a story that is open enough with others, and itself, about the benefits and costs of change. This, indeed, is why the experience of deep economic recession is a double-edged sword. It is an experience that has certainly led to individual and collective reflection on the past 'decades of greed' and on 'extreme capitalism', but retrenchment, unemployment, bankruptcy and economic restraint are likely to have people beating a path back towards a known prosperity, not voluntarily travelling even further into a landscape of consuming frugally.

This concern with the sentiment of loss directs us also to questioning any simple rejection of excess. Just as the realities of sustainable consumption as loss are generally ignored in the new politics of consumption, the suggestion that material excess is a necessary element of human culture is almost entirely overlooked. Western anti-consumerism is at base a mixture of rationalism and Puritanism; happiness and social cohesion emanates from consuming sensibly, while emotional and environmental health emanates from consuming frugally. In no uncertain terms, then, this is a politics – with the exception perhaps of Slow Food – that devalues the phenomenological attraction and cultural place of the 'splurge' and the 'carnivalesque', whether this takes place in individualized terms (as the shopping spree or the grand world tour), in localized terms (as the feast, the party, the wedding, or the fair), or in national and global terms (as the cultural, sporting or official event). Excess, in these instances, is often both blatant material waste but also physical, emotional and social gain. Indeed, the 'good' moment of excess and waste is not rational or performed with a nagging moral conscience leading to moderation and balance, it is simply 'too much': it is to fleetingly revel in having *beyond what we need* and, in the process, it is a moment that creates embodied human enjoyment and social bonds. Clearly, no politics of over-consumption, if it is to make sense, can tolerate permanent material profligacy. Yet, nor can it simply dismiss the materially excessive in favour of every act of consumption being rational, mindful, reasonable and, oh so boringly, moderate. Unfortunately, it is here that the very language of the new politics of consumption – with its invocations of 'simplicity', 'frugality', 'slowness' and of shifting 'down' – conveys a message that both attracts and repels. This language carries all the worthy promise of a less pressured life that is so appealing to many western individuals but seems to leave little room for a love of the complex, the fast, the cosmopolitan and expansive way of life that also remains deeply valued as part of what modernity offers.

CONSUMPTION AS JUSTICE

If one of the faultlines of the contemporary anti-consumerist critique and politics explored in this book is its ethically conflicted mode of addressing an imagined western populace (and its related failure to adequately tackle questions of loss and excess), one of its strengths is surely its movement towards a treatment of consumption as a key human behaviour that, in its various forms, enacts or violates justice. This is perhaps the principal conundrum of a new politics of consumption in the West; it so often vents disgust for the materialistic western individual, but it holds in principle, and admirably so, to an ecologically framed humanism that looks to consumption carefully pursued as beneficial for all.

Interpretatively, there is a partial degree of consensus among many western critics and activists about the perceived causes of consumerism and the environmental and social consequences of Minority World overconsumption. When it comes to questions of political strategy, however, there is greater diversity. We can in fact identify an array of oppositional responses to western consumerism involving the advocacy and pursuit of semiotic warfare, ethical consumer choice, lifestyle change, policy intervention, economic restructuring and community renewal.

These strategies of resistance to and escape from conventional frameworks of consumption are by no means mutually exclusive, yet they clearly differ and divide in various ways. At times an anti-consumerist politics, in the guise of ethical consumption and consumer citizenship, for instance, utilizes the market as a realm of oppositional action. Alternatively, what receives emphasis also, in simple living for example, is the richness of a life lived beyond the market and uncluttered with commodity choice. At one moment, an anti-consumerism will accept and celebrate forms of hedonistic consumption as pleasurable and convivial, as in Slow Food, while, for those intent on frugal living, enjoyment and social connection is to be largely sought through the non-material realm. Above all, there is an array of adopted reference points from which a politics of consumption begins – and, at times, largely ends. These reference points predominantly involve the pursuit of individual wellbeing and the consumption-based expression of responsibility towards nature and global equity. But they involve also the preservation of local economies and non-corporate forms of production and trade, the reinvigoration of forms of democratic governance and policy making, and the reconnection of people to place and community.

All this undoubtedly makes for an amorphous field of opposition and eco-social renewal. A contemporary western anti-consumerism can at times appear a grab bag of concerns and intentions offering only a diffuse sense of what lower levels and different forms of consumption aim to achieve beyond personal happiness and the individual performance of particular morals. But this, it is imperative to note, disguises an allegiance to a rich and guiding common principle that, while largely unarticulated, both draws together the various strands of anti-consumerist politics and provides a formal basis for addressing how and why consumption can and should be rethought. Indeed, I want to suggest here that a reinvigorated politics of consumption in the West is productively expressive of, and derives much of its import from, a diversely conceptualized idea of just consumption.

In its fundamental Socratic sense, the idea of justice, as the Finnish political economist Heikki Patomäki has outlined, embodies the notion that 'everyone gets and does what he or she deserves, or what rightfully belongs to him or her'.[8] This universalist conception of justice, still highly apposite to the way justice can be understood now, encompasses both the concept of entitlements (what we deserve) and rights (what belongs to us). But indirectly embedded in this conception of justice is the notion also of proper action, of an imperative to *act well* in order to ensure that both ourselves *and others* are granted entitlements and have rights observed. Justice, then, is fairness thought and fairness done, and this sensibility and the concrete realization of fairness is, to return to Patomäki, 'both a virtue of individuals, and a concept routinely used in social practices, particularly when some of their aspects are discussed or disputed publicly, i.e. politicized'.[9]

This is certainly not the place to enter deeply into the realm of moral philosophy, or to discuss the complex notions of duty, consequence and virtue that underlay various theorizations of how justice is realised.[10] Rather, my purpose here is merely to note that an envisioning of consumption as justice – as fairness – is suggestively offered within a contemporary western politics of consumption, and it is done so along three principle axes: in relation to the self, to the other and to nature.

Notably, many of those who critique a contemporary western consumerism do so on the basis of arguing, with credibility, that on an individual level a life positively dominated by the acquisition of money and commodities damages the self physically and mentally. That is, a highly consumer-ist and money-oriented existence bound up in overwork and overspending fails, following the conventional adage, to do justice to oneself, particularly in terms of delivering a flourish-ing life. Beyond the self, however, critics implicitly work with a notion of just consumption in relation to how we as consum-ers of goods and services act towards other people: familial others, societal others and global others. Here, the pursuit of an intensive work and high-consumption lifestyle is seen to lead to a neglect of obligatory relationships of care, particu-larly towards family and friends, while, on a more collective level, an increasingly intense societal emphasis on commodity choice as a field of individual power and expression under-mines a sense of political citizenship and a recognition also of our obligation to engage, beyond the market, in the com-munities of place and in the social networks of which we are a part. Similarly, on a society-wide and especially on a global level, overconsumption clearly contradicts a commitment to fair and equitable distribution of goods and services and, moreover, ignores the exploitative labour practices of domi-nant systems of commodity production.

In moving from the social to the environmental dimensions of consumption, a contemporary anti-consumerism is equally engaged with the imperative to think and act in just ways. Explicit in much critical commentary on overconsumption is an insistence that we are obliged to attend with solicitude to our local, national and global natural environments – and there is a very firm sense in which this insistence embodies ideas of justice. The often invoked concept of environmen-tal justice, for example, points to the way in which Minority World consumption rampantly overuses natural resources at a hugely disproportionate rate to that in the Majority World. Similarly, the concept of sustainable development articulates the key notion of intergenerational justice: that present generations have an obligation to properly manage the natural environments on which future generations will, like us, depend.[11] These environmentally inflected arguments for a just consumption are powerful ones, but they remain an extension of 'other-directed' concern towards our fellow human beings. To these, then, must be added arguments that go beyond a privileging of human benefit as the rationale for responsible consumption. In this regard, some forms of anti-consumerism clearly embrace a sense of justice towards non-human animals as sentient beings.[12] Above all, a contemporary anti-consumerism, across the board, invokes a commonsense notion that we should act justly towards nature for its own sake, or, in more exact terms, that we should embrace an imperative to care for and respect – to live with – the natural environment out of a sense not simply of our own survival but of humility and awe at being in the world, and as a virtue of being human.[13]

If we begin to view western anti-consumerism in these terms, we begin also to make sense of it as field of cultural opposition and alternative action that aims for far more than reduced levels and different forms of consumption.[14] Contemporary critical treatments of Majority World consumerism are very much statements about an essential and universal principle of fairness, and especially about the politics of its violation or enactment through systems of commodity exchange, through forms of human productive labour, and through modes of distributing and allowing access to goods, services and resources. The significance of this cannot be overstated. We live at a point in time in which questions of social justice both within and beyond national boundaries must be more vigorously engaged with than ever before. This is not least the case because, as Martha Nussbaum has demonstrated, the horizons of why, how and to whom and what we should do justice have expanded and are being reframed in the context of rapid social and environmental change and the latest, and perhaps most extensive, wave of globalization.[15] In this context, the need for alternative visions of the just, and a deep commitment to justice itself, is paramount. And, as I hope I have made abundantly clear throughout this book, a contemporary politics of consumption in the West signals one of the most challenging and hopeful elements of this revisioning.

SELF, OTHER AND THE NEW MATERIALISM

To write of justice and, in the process, to insist that a contemporary western anti-consumerism is intent on the task of rethinking fundamental principles and contesting power is by no means to claim too much. It is, though, to sidestep a concluding assessment of the more immediate political dimensions of the commentary and much of the activist dialogue dealt with in previous chapters. As I have made plain, the new politics of consumption is profoundly shaped by a theory of change as the product of individual virtue, modes of living, types of consciousness and personhood itself. This is merely to acknowledge the theoretical parameters within which a contemporary western anti-consumerism tends to work.

What this focus on the aware, principled and fulfilled self has given rise to is a complex dialogue centred on challenging the mental landscape of consumerism (as in culture jamming), directing consumer behaviour towards environmental and social responsibility (as in ethical and political consumption) and identifying the wellbeing to be derived through individuals working less, consuming less and adopting a different sense of temporality (as in downshifting, simplicity and slow living). If we can politically characterize the new politics of consumption – and such a move is always conditional – it is these three fields of response, particularly the latter two, that give it its energy. It is on these grounds that, strategically and conceptually, many of those in affluent nations who now contest western overconsumption clearly feel most comfortable in advocating change.

Strategically, this is driven by a sense of the importance to western individuals of both economic choice and life satisfaction, and of the way these desires can be used to popularize a politics of consuming and living differently. Thus, while anti-consumerism is fundamentally critical of the commodification of our lives, it nevertheless accepts and promotes consumption as a means of stating alternative personal values beyond those mandated by consumer culture. While embroiled in excess, waste, selfishness and amorality, acts of consumption – exercised as a 'just choice' based on considerations of personal, social, environmental and inter-species impact – can express also a political empowerment and an ethical integrity. Similarly, by focusing on the issue of work–life balance, and the broader desire of western individuals for self-actualization, the new politics of consumption can demonstrate a political moderateness by attending to questions of individual wellbeing rather than directly advocating the holus-bolus dismantling of economic systems and political structures.

Conceptually, however, the constructs and notions of individualism and moral choice, self-fulfilment and happiness, existential authenticity and spiritual balance, and especially eco-social equilibrium, that are constantly articulated by the new politics of consumption are not just strategic tools; they provide the normative framework of contemporary western anti-consumerist critique and activism. These values, as we have seen, sit alongside a privileging also of notions of place and community and of civic participation and global cooperation as integral to adopting new forms of material life. This makes for a theoretically rich but often contradictory politics: a politics about which, to echo the language of an earlier paragraph, we might well feel variously pessimistic and optimistic in terms of its ability to realise an alternative future.

On the downside, a reinvigorated politics of consumption in the West seems to demand too much and challenge too little. It demands, by virtue of its very focus on the commodity and its dogged belief in a culture of consumption and money as determining of social life, that the western individual *as consumer and income earner* bears responsibility for change. It thus in part constitutes an 'expenditure-side politics', implicitly accepting the myth of neoclassical economics that it is the consumer that drives global commodity production. It is, then, the act of buying or not buying, rather than the act of producing, that is usually accentuated in contemporary critique. As a consequence the calculated *overproduction* of certain commodities and commodity types, driven by the profit-motivated logic of global capital itself, remains far less exhaustively targeted by the new politics of consumption than the individual act of spending.[16] Likewise, income-generating work is understood as an individual money-focused activity that is to be mostly contested on the basis of 'time famine' and personal stress rather than directly challenged as part of a broader system of production, capital ownership and labour.

It is a similar story of too much and too little in relation to questions of virtue and lifestyle change. As we have seen, anti-consumerist politics tends to demand, at the very least, that people develop and perform, through a process of constant self-governance, a particular moral sensibility. Even more extensively, the demand is made for people to reinvent their self-identity and to live a different life. To reiterate the obvious objections, this dual focus on moral choice and authentic living both rests on an uncontested liberal individualism and narrowly addresses segments of the western bourgeoisie. But more than this, an emphasis in particular on voluntaristically transforming one's consciousness and life in tune with the simple and the slow, raises the task of participating in social change to a level that is potentially both daunting and uninviting. It too tightly binds the formal development of an 'enlightened' state of mind and mode of living with the very substantial actions needed to challenge rich world overconsumption – such as limiting resource use, minimizing the production of waste and pursuing forms of leisure and enjoyment that are not overly dependent on commodities. Change in relation to what, how much and where we consume is thus too rigidly linked to a shared identity, homogenous community and a set way of acting and thinking rather than being more flexibly envisaged as an outcome of everyday actions and material practices, both individually and collectively performed, that avoid overconsumption but preserve a sense of social life as enlivened by a wide range of sensibilities, desires, values, types of community and ways of living.

Most problematic of all, however, is the tendency of a contemporary western anti-consumerism to dwell on the micropolitics of ethical consumer choice and low-consumption lifestyles and thus leave comparatively unexplored the dimensions of broad, or macropolitical, social change. Much of the new politics of consumption simply collapses the distinction between individual and social transformation and personal and collective action in tackling this problem – and, at the same time, assumes that addressing overconsumption is the key to realising a new society. In the case of ethical or responsible consumption, a performance of politics through the act of purchasing is seen to both constitute collectivity and challenge dominant economic and moral frameworks. In the case of downshifting, simplicity and slow living, an alternative life experience – forged through a process of self-examination and the achievement of wellbeing – gives rise, it is assumed, to a new ecologically framed commonsense that is conducive also of a desire for community, egalitarianism and social and global justice. Maybe so. Yet glaringly absent here is a thorough and frank examination of how a care for the self and a performance of virtuous personhood can actually translate into both a care for others and a remaking of social, cultural and economic life. On this score, a contemporary anti-consumerist politics offers little real insight into how enlivened communities of place, new socio-economic arrangements and equitable global relations are made real through responsible consumption and simple/slow living, nor are we offered much exploration of how the different elements of a just consumption – to self, other and nature – interconnect and possibly contradict. Addressing this later issue of contradiction is crucial, otherwise we are left with the vacuous assertion that environmental sustainability, the welfare of our fellow citizens and the needs of a global humanity will be simply met through our own self-actualization – through the achievement of the authentic, contented and frugal living western self.

But all this, of course, is to potentially silence the very real hope embodied in the new politics of consumption. A fine-grained exploration, a generative analysis, of contemporary anti-consumerist critique and activism in the West cannot possibly end on a note of pessimism. Like all stories of transformation, and all political visions that seek a better world, the anti-consumerism explored throughout this book is a partial and unfolding attempt to formulate alternatives to life as currently lived. This makes for a politics that is increasingly plural – but for one also that offers substantive and encompassing possibilities for change at both a personal and collective level.

As we have seen, a reinvigorated politics of consumption in the West emphasizes the need not only for mindful purchasing and altered lifestyles, but also for extensive policy intervention, taxation reform and financial market regulation in the pursuit of sustainability and global justice – and how timely this call has now become. Equally, there is an insistence by both theorists and activists on identifying, maintaining and further constructing spaces of local economic activity and forms of work that operate outside the logic of capitalism. Integral also to some streams of anti-consumerist politics is a direct engagement with questions of production, particularly in terms of resisting the corporatization of agriculture and the destruction of local food systems. Even those who celebrate lifestyle change do not do so one-dimensionally; advocates for simple living explicitly emphasize that a pursuit of personal wellbeing only takes on broader social meaning and impact in the context of both working for legislative reform and building communities of place and shared experience. Likewise, those who advocate forms of responsible consumption do so with a commitment to ensuring that ethical choice constitutes more than a surface expression of personal politics but is ultimately reflective of a deeper, collectively developed sense of obligation to environmental sustainability and global equity. Perhaps most importantly of all, the very attention given in the new politics of consumption to personal lifestyle and ethical action is not easily dismissed by the simple charge of individualism and tokenism. In imagining politics as a product of personhood, western anti-consumerism not only recognizes the importance of the experiential in contemporary political action but also constructively reinvigorates a sense that individuals have a power to govern their existence. In this, a re-enlivened anti-consumerism in the West ably identifies concrete ways in which people can feel and act out sensibilities and needs that contest and partially escape the economic and social arrangements that encircle them. In a highly practical sense, the new politics of consumption thus works to expand the cultural, economic and social territory that always already exists outside dominant economic and social frameworks: a territory that is in some way peopled by us all through our everyday efforts to think, work, spend and live in ways that are not wholly defined by consumerism and commodification.

It is in this practical way also that, purposefully and suggestively, a western politics of anti-consumerism grasps at a new materialism, at the very ground on which a just consumption might be realized. To speak of a new materialism – a valuing of material objects and forms that does not privilege endless accumulation – is to conjure up a different framework of relationship between ourselves and the physical world. This sense of an alternative materiality is, like the critique of consumer modernity itself, hardly new, but it is an immensely productive way of conceptualizing what consuming differently might entail. In their deservedly influential study of the meaning of domestic things, first published in 1981, Mihaly Csikszentmihalyi and Eugene Rochberg-Halton distinguished between a '*terminal materialism*', whereby the 'habit of consumption can become an end in itself, feeding on its autonomous necessity to possess more things, to control more status, to use more energy', and an '*instrumental materialism*', which involves 'the cultivation of objects as essential *means* for discovering and furthering goals', the primary one of which is 'the fuller unfolding of human life'.[17] This latter form of materialism, the authors insisted, was thus to be conjoined with the need to urgently address issues of environmental and social sustainability, and with the obligation to use things well in the interests of oneself, others and the planet.

More recently, the attempt to fathom and describe what new ways of *thinking about* and *living with* the material world might involve has moved in two overlapping directions – and we have touched on both in previous chapters. One formulation envisages, as we have seen, the production of an attitude of care towards the physical world through the conscious adoption of alternative – particularly simple and slow – forms of living.[18] Another formulation invokes not so much life-style change but the more immediate and specific moments in which individuals become aware of material things as *things* and, in doing so, more fully grasp their presence, value and use.[19] The former approach moves towards a new materialism through a reflective process whereby individuals consciously decide to relate in different ways to their mate-rial context. The latter conceptualization calls forth a new materiality through an embodied phenomenological process whereby the object world, by suddenly making us realise that it is there, literally incites us to recognise the material anew – and to treat it better.

In both instances, however, what is being identified is a sense of material reality that does not have to be simply invented from scratch but is already part of who we are and how we act; and thus has to be *maintained and intensified*. An ethos of care towards the objects, resources and landscapes that facilitate life is not absent in the West; it abounds already in the material practices of past generations (for whom thrift and recycling were strategies well utilized), in our continued need to cherish the objects (often ones of no great monetary value) that are most deeply meaningful and useful to us, and in the fact that the natural world – the sand through our toes – still delights us and receives our regard. The pursuit of a new materialism is the revitalization of this ethos, and not simply of the self. The broader hope – an Aristotelian one – is that care is contagious; that attending to an ethics of the material world encourages an attendance to the ethics of the social at a local and global level. Here, we turn or return to a materialism in the philosophical realm: a sense that social relations arise in connection with the material forms life takes. It is thus through a respectful relationship with the material world that one also touches humanity. It is, then, on this ground, a common ground of being with and consuming things differently, that we may well forge different ways of being with each other.

POSTSCRIPT

AFTER THE BOOM, BEYOND THE

WEST

Western excess, it might be imagined, came to an abrupt end in late 2008. Not since the Great Depression had global share markets plummeted with such ferocity. Levels of western consumption followed suit; the longest shopping spree in US history, commencing in 1991 and characterized by an uninterrupted annual increase in household consumption expenditure, was all over by the onset of 2009. The same story was repeated across the affluent world and the long dormant language of recession and even depression was revived and re-entered the political frame.

Revived also was an emboldened critique of neo-liberalism. By early 2009, western political leaders were sounding a little bit like budding anti-consumerists. In rightly identifying the self-inflicted death of neo-liberal, free market economics – at least as a governing ideology – capitalist corporate excess was at last being named by ruling elites for what it is: a money grab underpinned by greed and amorality. In his inaugural presidential address, Barack Obama spoke of

a 'new era of responsibility' where markets would be subject to a watchful eye and citizenship reborn through a sense
of duty to self, nation and the world and to the principles
of distributive fairness and environmental care. Rhetoric,
yes. But the deeper, worthy promise here was and is one of
state and society renewed. Indeed, in face of an imploding
'extreme capitalism', as the Australian prime minister Kevin
Rudd has dubbed it, the interventionist state and the notion
of the social itself have been resuscitated. Market regulation,
both national and global in scope, is back on the agenda as a
way of rebuilding a mixed economy and forging a new 'social
capitalism' able to facilitate the sound operation of free markets while reigning in their perversities and guaranteeing
that communal, rather than purely economic, goals remain
primary.[1] Even conservatives have abandoned the unfettered
market, with Nicholas Sarkozy and Angela Merkel calling,
by early 2009, for a 'moral' form of capitalism and for vigorous global financial regulation.

Cynicism is easy in the face of such positioning. What is
being outlined here is the rescue and revival of consumer
capitalism and, not for the first time, this task has largely
fallen to social democratic regimes in the USA, Europe
and elsewhere. We are, at least in terms of the commodity,
certainly not undergoing a transition from one epoch to
the next, but have been witnessing the preservation, albeit
tempered by vaguely environmental and socio-ethical
concerns, of global consumption as we know it. Western
governments, social democrats in particular, now deal in an
exquisite contradiction; they must talk of socio-economic
responsibility, balance, moderation, collective interests, but
they must also celebrate market demand, induce individual
desire and reinvigorate overconsumption. How else could
it be if levels of hardship now unimaginable to western
majorities are to be avoided? Contemporary capitalism in

free fall is not the ground on which fundamental change can be actualized by governments of any ilk; the fall must be desperately checked, the status quo cautiously modified. And as the globe emerges from crisis perhaps there will, for this very reason, be an effective return to a re-jigged 'business as usual' or even, in the medium term, to a default, insular and dangerous western conservatism as affluent states compete for economic survival, react to the domestic turmoil of recession and respond to population demands for renewed prosperity. There is a possibility also, however, of a more positive, if incremental, shift taking root. Western material excess is not, of course, at an end but it has now been made utterly visible as a damaging force while the realty of limits – economic, social, moral, environmental – has reasserted itself. The re-emergence of the interventionist state and of a mainstream language of balance and responsibility is surely hopeful, especially if it serves to legitimate broader civic action and calls for change both in the West and beyond. One transformation, at least, is palpable. In quite practical terms, any form of rich-world hyper-consumerism driven by easy credit and an ethos of acquisition at all costs, has been rendered less viable both ideologically and structurally.

Yet, as I have argued throughout this book, much anti-consumerist polemic has suffered a similar fate of viability and any simple celebration of market collapse – of the 'shopocalypse' – nudges at the politically negligent. The new politics of consumption continues, in the post-2008 era, to provide a crucial political and moral vision of sustainable and humane forms of commodity use. But global recession does not simply confirm anti-consumerist critique, nor unproblematically move us towards anti-consumerist goals. The global economic downturn in fact highlights the partial failure of a contemporary radical politics of consumption to write of, and to seek to understand, western material life beyond the easy naming and the immediate moment of a 'luxury fever', an 'affluenza' that has now suddenly morphed into something quite different. Global recession highlights also the unpredictable relationship between crisis and change. Aggregate levels of global consumption have fallen for a time and collective reflection on the moment of excess is now the overdue order of the day. But tough economic times are not the ally of experimentation with new forms of economic life, of a shift towards sustainable frameworks of production and exchange, or of the material and psychic frameworks of security and safety that underscore a preparedness to opt for alternatives. These changes, it seems, may have become more distant; postponed until better times. In light of these realities, the impetus of this book has been to suggest that a western politics of consumption, an analysis and critique of affluent world consumerism, must become less beholden to momentary polemic based on dubious analytical orthodoxies about the dominance of consumer culture and the helplessness of those who people it, and build a response on firmer foundations – the bedrock of which must be a questioning of analytical assumptions and a reflexive exploration of political positions, modes of communication and imagined futures.

A further impetus of this book has been to write of the West, and the West only. This has been a very deliberate strategy and I have been keenly aware that it is not one that will please all. The particular forms of commodity consumption discussed throughout the previous chapters are by no means uniquely western, either historically or in a contemporary sense. What is more, a politics of consumption centred on an opposition to the socio-cultural, spiritual and environmental consequences of materialism and commodification is not simply a Minority World phenomenon. If anything, critics and activists in the global South have been even more vocal in identifying the ramifications on their societies, cultures and polities of an encroaching consumerism – and we might note here the advocacy of the Third World Network and of radical consumer groups such as the Consumers' Association of Penang as well as the work of Third World critics such Martin Khor or Vadana Shiva. Khor, for instance, has long critiqued levels of western consumption, and the impact of commodity culture on the integrity and vibrancy of Majority World societies. In this, he joins in a much broader opposition to the global inequality, environmental degradation and suppression of 'the local' that underpins a world production and consumption system. Most recently, Khor has reminded us that a global economic crisis – one manufactured in the corporate headquarters and consumer marketplaces of the West – may well have wreaked havoc in the First World but has been even more devastating for the communities and workers of the Third.[2]

The last thing I have wanted to do in this book is to silence such voices; and my own work has now moved, as always intended, to a fuller subsequent engagement with consumption and anti-consumerism beyond affluent nations. In this monograph, however, it has been crucially important to take the West as a point of departure and to fully analyse a western anti-consumerism in its particularity.

There have been two reasons for this. First, I have wanted to resist the tendency to portray anti-consumerism across the globe as more interpretatively and politically unified than it actually is. Third World critics of a global consumerism most certainly share some of the concerns of western commentators and political activists – and there has long been a vigorous dialogue going on between 'anti-consumerists' across international borders. But Majority World critics offer also some very different perspectives on consumer culture, on notions of self and society, and on the subject of change. In differing from the West, a politics of consumption in a Majority

World context has usually involved not the advocacy of cultural transformation or even lifestyle change, but the defence of what is positive about the local and the traditional, the preservation of cultural difference and of national economic autonomy, and, perhaps most of all, an opposition to imperialism and colonialism in all its modern and postmodern manifestations. Moreover, where an anti-consumerism in the West is broadly aligned with a left-liberal politics, Third World critics are, in many respects, less politically unified. In grappling with this complexity, a very different book would need to have been written.

A second key reason for focusing on the particularity of a contemporary western anti-consumerism is precisely the historical uniqueness of its annunciation, notwithstanding the need to recognize the myriad connections it maintains with a western tradition of opposition and critique. As a 'westerner', I have been simply fascinated and politically invigorated by a set of arguments, practices and dreams that have arisen in an economic and cultural context so malignantly designed to suppress them. As a consequence, I have wanted both to interrogate and wholeheartedly join with this critical and imaginative force; to participate with others in questioning and developing it, and most of all, in lending it vigour.

NOTES

Introduction: Trouble in Consumer Paradise

1 www.buynothingday.co.uk, accessed 13 November 2006.
2 Juliet Schor, 'The new politics of consumption', in Joshua Cohen and Joel Rogers (eds) *Do Americans Shop too Much?*, Beacon Press, Boston, 2000, pp. 3–33.
3 See Liz Minchin, 'All power to you', *The Age*, Melbourne, 7 December 2006, p. 20. A similar ethos is evident in the 'Earth Hour' campaign, launched in 2007 (see www.earthhour.org).
4 Overconsumption has been variously conceptualized but refers essentially to a tendency to consume goods and services at a level over and above that which is necessary to maintain a reasonable standard of living and at a rate that is greater than can be environmentally sustained in terms of resource provision and the handling of waste. In ch. 1 we examine this term much more closely.
5 Most of these books have been published since the late

1990s. I will discuss and reference them fully in the chapter following.

6 Naomi Klein, *No Logo*, Flamingo, London, 2000.

7 For a recent snapshot of such statistics see the *New Internationalist*, November 2006, p. 18.

8 For an accessible discussion of this see Norman Myers and Jennifer Kent, *The New Consumers: The Influence of Affluence on the Environment*, Island Press, Washington, 2004.

9 For a useful survey of the literature on states of wellbeing in the West see Richard Eckersley, *Well & Good: How We Feel & Why it Matters*, Text, Melbourne, 2004.

10 Elizabeth Shove, *Cleanliness, Comfort and Convenience: The Social Organisation of Normality*, Berg, Oxford, 2003, pp. 3–7.

11 See Linda Tuhiwai Smith, *Decolonizing Methodologies: Research and Indigenous Peoples*, Zed Books/University of Otago Press, London and Dunedin, 1999. See also, in this context, Kim Humphery, 'Dirty questions: indigenous health and "western research"', *Australian and New Zealand Journal of Public Health*, vol. 25, no. 3, June 2001, pp. 197–202.

12 Terry Eagleton, *After Theory*, Allen Lane, London 2003.

13 Bruno Latour, 'Why has critique run out of steam? From matters of fact to matters of concern', in Bill Brown (ed.), *Things*, University of Chicago Press, Chicago, 2004, pp. 151–73.

14 Ibid., p. 171.

Chapter 1 The New Politics of Consumption

1 Daniel Miller, *The Comfort of Things*, Polity, Cambridge, 2008.

2 See Juliet B. Schor, *The Overspent American: Why We Want What We Don't Need*, Harper Perennial, New York,

1999 and Juliet B. Schor, *The Overworked American: The Unexpected Decline of Leisure*, Basic Books, New York, 1992. See also, Bill McKibben, 'Introduction', in Juliet B. Schor and Betsy Taylor, *Sustainable Planet: Solutions for the Twenty-First Century*, Beacon Press, Boston, 2002, p. 10.

3 See Klein, *No Logo*, p. xix; and David Boyle, *Authenticity: Brands, Fakes, Spin and the Lust for Real Life*, Harper Perennial, London, 2003, pp. 291–6.

4 See, respectively, John Ralston Saul, *The Unconscious Civilization*, Penguin, Melbourne, 1997; Martha Nussbaum, *Frontiers of Justice: Disability, Nationality, Species Membership*, Harvard University Press, Cambridge, MA, 2006; Richard Sennett, *The Culture of New Capitalism*, Yale University Press, New Heaven, 2006; Klein, *No Logo*; George Monbiot, *Manifesto for a New World Order*, New Press, London, 2006 and his *Heat: How to Stop the Planet from Burning*, Allen Lane, London, 2006; Joel Bakan, *The Corporation: The Pathological Pursuit of Profit and Power*, Constable, London, 2004; Boyle, *Authenticity*; Thomas Frank, *One Market Under God: Extreme Capitalism, Market Populism and the End of Economic Democracy*, Vintage, London, 2002; Carl Honoré, *In Praise of Slow: How a World Movement is Challenging the Cult of Speed*, Orion, London, 2004; and Eric Schlosser, *Fast Food Nation: The Dark Side of the All-American Meal*, Harper Perennial, New York, 2005.

5 A more detailed list of publications, focusing only on the last decade, would have to include John de Graaf, David Wann and Thomas H. Naylor, *Affluenza: The All-Consuming Epidemic*, Berrett-Koehler, San Francisco, 2001; Paul R. Ehrlich and Anne H. Ehrlich, *One With Nineveh: Politics, Consumption, and the Human Future*, Island Press/Shearwater Books, Washington,

2004; James, J. Farrell, *One Nation Under Goods: Malls and the Seductions of American Shopping*, Smithsonian Books, Washington, 2003; Robert H. Frank, *Luxury Fever: Why Money Fails to Satisfy in an Era of Excess*, Free Press, New York, 1999; Jane Hammerslough, *Dematerializing: Taming the Power of Possessions*, Perseus, Cambridge MA, 2001; Daniel Harris, *Cute, Quaint, Hungry and Romantic: The Aesthetics of Consumerism*, Da Capo Press, New York, 2001; Tim Kasser, *The High Price of Materialism*, MIT Press, Cambridge MA, 2002; Kalle Lasn, *Culture Jam*, Eagle Books, New York, 1999: Robert D. Manning, *Credit Card Nation: The Consequences of America's Addiction to Credit*, Basic Books, New York, 2000; Schor, *The Overspent American*; Barry Schwartz, *The Paradox of Choice: Why More is Less*, HarperCollins, New York, 2005. To this list we could add a range of 'solution-oriented' critiques such as Cecile Andrews, *The Circle of Simplicity: Return to the Good Life*, HarperPerennial, New York, 1998; John Drake, *Downshifting: How to Work Less and Enjoy Life More*, Berrett-Koehler, San Francisco, 2000; John de Graaf (ed.), *Take Back Your Time: Fighting Overwork and Time Poverty in America*, Berrett-Koehler, San Francisco, 2003. Many other significant texts that pre-date the last decade will be cited later.

6 In many respects a contemporary anti-consumerist commentary – though not an activism – is a veritable North American publishing phenomenon. Elsewhere, the field of anti-consumerist commentary is more dispersed (while a number of authors take a heavy lead from North American texts). For a very brief list see from France, Christian Comeliau, *The Impasse of Modernity*, Zed Books, London, 2002; from Australia, Clive Hamilton and Richard Denniss, *Affluenza: When Too Much is Never*

Enough, Allen & Unwin, Sydney, 2005; from Britain, Oliver James, *Affluenza: How to be Successful and Stay Sane*, Vermilion, London, 2007.

7 Here, we can selectively cite a range of more specialized texts such as Thomas Princen, Michael Maniates and Ken Conca (eds), *Confronting Consumption*, MIT Press, Cambridge, MA, 2002; Michele Micheletti, *Political Virtue and Shopping: Individuals, Consumerism and Collective Action*, Palgrave Macmillan, New York, 2003; Marius de Geus, *The End of Over-consumption: Towards a Lifestyle of Moderation and Self-Restraint*, International Books, Utrecht, 2003; Rob Harrison, Terry Newholm and Deidre Shaw (eds), *The Ethical Consumer*, Sage, London, 2005; Myers and Kent, *The New Consumers*; Thomas Princen, *The Logic of Sufficiency*, MIT Press, Cambridge, MA, 2005; Robert F. Woollard and Aleck S. Ostry (eds), *Fatal Consumption: Rethinking Sustainable Development*, UBC Press, Vancouver, 2000; Maurie J. Cohen and Joseph Murphy (eds), *Exploring Sustainable Consumption: Environmental Policy and the Social Sciences*, Elsevier, Oxford, 2001; Daniel Doherty and Amitai Etzioni (eds), *Voluntary Simplicity: Responding to Consumer Culture*, Rowman & Littlefield, Lanham, 2003; Schor and Taylor (eds), *Sustainable Planet*; Roger Rosenblatt (ed.), *Consuming Desires: Consumption, Culture and the Pursuit of Happiness*, Island Press/Sherwater Books, Washington, 1999; Laura Westra and Patricia H. Werhane (eds), *The Business of Consumption: Environmental Ethics and the Global Economy*, Rowman & Littlefield, Lanham, 1998. Once again, there are many earlier published texts that will eventually be added to this list.

8 See, for example, Zygmunt Bauman, *Liquid Life*, Polity, Cambridge, 2005; George Ritzer, *The Globalization of Nothing*, Pine Forge Press, Thousand Oaks, 2004.

9 The term 'affluenza' has been somewhat playfully defined as 'a painful, contagious, socially transmitted condition of overload, debt, anxiety, and waste resulting from the dogged pursuit of more'; de Graaf, Wann and Naylor, *Affluenza*, p. 2.

10 Ehrlich and Ehrlich, *One with Nineveh*, pp. 113, 213.

11 Thomas Princen, 'Consumption and its externalities: Where economy meets ecology', in Princen et al. (eds), *Confronting Consumption*, pp. 33–4.

12 On this point see the useful essay on consumption and population by Robert Engelman, 'Hope in numbers', in Schor and Taylor (eds), *Sustainable Planet*, pp. 193–208.

13 Ehrlich and Ehrlich, *One with Nineveh*, p. 213.

14 See John de Graaf, 'Preface' and 'Introduction', in de Graaf (ed.), *Take Back Your Time*; Schor, 'The (even more) overworked American', in de Graaf (ed.), *Take Back Your Time*, pp. 6–11; Stephan Rechtschaffen, 'Timeshifting', in Schor and Taylor (eds), *Sustainable Planet*, pp. 175–92. See also Eckersley, *Well & Good*; Honoré, *In Praise of Slow*. For tabular statistics on differential working hours in affluent nations see, *OECD Factbook 2008*, 'Average annual hours worked per year per person in employment', p.153 (accessible at: http://oberon.sourceoecd. org/pdf/factbook2008/30200811e-06-03-02.pdf).

15 See Carlo Petrini, *Slow Food: The Case for Taste*, Columbia University Press, New York, 2001; and Honoré, *In Praise of Slow*. For an excellent discussion of slow living, offering a particular focus on Slow Food, see Wendy Parkins and Geoffrey Craig, *Slow Living*, Berg, Oxford, 2006.

16 Numerous references could be given here, but see, for example, Schor, *The Overspent American*, pp. 20–1; de Graaf et al., *Affluenza*, chs. 8 and 10; William E. Rees,

'Ecological footprints and the pathology of consumption', in Woollard and Ostry (eds), *Fatal Consumption*, pp. 21–51; Michael Carr, 'Social capital, civil society, and social transformation', in Woollard and Ostry (eds), *Fatal Consumption*, pp. 69–98.

17 See, respectively, Schwartz, *The Paradox of Choice*, and his earlier book *The Costs of Living*, Norton, New York, 1994; Jonathan Rowe, 'Wasted work, wasted time', in de Graaf (ed.), *Take Back Your Time*, p. 60; Herman E. Daly, 'Consumption: the economics of value added and the ethics of value distributed', in Laura Westra and Patricia H. Werhane (eds), *The Business of Consumption: Environmental Ethics and the Global Economy*, Rowman & Littlefield, Lanham, 1998, p. 26; and Paul L. Wachtel, 'Overconsumption', in Roger Keil and David Bell (eds), *Political Ecology: Global and Local*, Routledge, London, 1998, p. 267.

18 A very long list is possible here, but see, for example, Vance Packard, *The Hidden Persuaders*, Penguin, London, 1957; J. K. Galbraith, *The Affluent Society*, Houghton Mifflin, Boston, 1958; D. H. Meadows, D. L. Randers, and W. W. Behrens, *The Limits to Growth*, Universe Books, New York, 1972; E. F. Schumacher, *Small is Beautiful: Economics as if People Mattered*, Harper & Row, New York, 1973; Fred Hirsch, *The Social Limits to Growth*, Harvard University Press, Cambridge, MA, 1976; Tibor Scitovsky, *The Joyless Economy*, Oxford University Press, New York, 1976; William Leiss, *The Limits to Satisfaction*, Marion Boyars, London, 1978; André Gorz, *Paths to Paradise: On the Liberation from Work*, Pluto, London, 1985; F. E. Trainer, *Abandon Affluence!*, Zed Books, London, 1989; Joel Jay Kassiola, *The Death of Industrial Civilization: The Limits to Economic Growth and the Repoliticization of Advanced Industrial Society*, State University of New York Press,

Albany, 1990; and Robert Lane, *The Market Experience*, Cambridge University Press, Cambridge, 1991.

19 For book-length studies see, for example, Paul Wachtel, *The Poverty of Affluence: A Psychological Portrait of the American Way of Life*, Free Press, New York, 1983; Herman E. Daly and John Cobb, *For The Common Good: Redirecting the Economy Toward Community, the Environment, and a Sustainable Future*, Beacon Press, Boston, 1989; Schor, *The Overworked American*; Paul Ehrlich and Anne Ehrlich, *The End of Affluence*, Ballantine Books, New York, 1974.

20 See Alan Durning, *How Much is Enough? The Consumer Society and the Future of the Earth*, Norton, New York, 1992 and, for some of his more recent work, John C. Ryan and Alan Thien Durning, *Stuff: The Secret Life of Everyday Things*, Northwest Environment Watch, Seattle, 1997. 'Enoughness' is a term often invoked within the contemporary anti-consumerist literature. It has been defined by Vicki Robin as 'a stance of material sufficiency and spiritual affluence' (Vicki Robin, 'What's money got to do with it?', in Schor and Taylor (eds), *Sustainable Planet*, p. 80).

21 Rees, 'Ecological foot prints', p. 28.

22 Ibid., p. 29.

23 Jason Venetoulis, Dahlia Chazan and Christopher Gaudet, *Ecological Footprint of Nations*, Redefining Progress, Oakland, 2004.

24 Ibid., pp. 8–12. There is little point in providing detailed up-to-date figures in relation to national footprints as these alter rapidly. The point to note here is the existence of vast differentials. Thus in 2000 the USA had a footprint of 9.57 hectares per capita compared with the lowest of 0.50 hectares per capita in Bangladesh. For the most recently available calculations see www.footprintof nations.org.

25 The focus here is not only on resource consumption but also on what environmental researchers call 'waste-sink capacity', or the ability of the earth to absorb the waste produced through dominant production methods and by way of post-consumption rubbish. As Jennifer Clapp has observed, with much of the waste-sink capacity of rich nations used up and the per capita production of garbage steadily increasing, waste is quite literally 'distanced' in terms of being exported from wealthy to developing countries (and, we might add, from rich to poor neighbourhoods within wealthy nations themselves). See, Jennifer Clapp, 'The distancing of waste: overconsumption in a global economy', in Princen et al. (eds), *Confronting Consumption*, p. 158.

26 On this debate see Maurie J. Cohen, 'The emergent environmental policy discourse on sustainable consumption', in Cohen and Murphy (eds), *Exploring Sustainable Consumption*, pp. 21–7; Ken Conca, 'Consumption and environment in a global economy', in Princen et al. (eds), *Confronting Consumption*, pp. 133–53.

27 On this, see Paul Hawken, Amory Lovins and L. Hunter Lovins, *Natural Capitalism: Creating the Next Industrial Revolution*, Little, Brown, Boston, 1999.

28 See Benjamin Barber, *Jihad vs McWorld*, Ballantine Books, New York, 2001; Jeremy Seabrook, *Consuming Cultures: Globalization and Local Lives*, New Internationalist, Oxford, 2004.

29 These figures are cited in, respectively, Farrell, *One Nation Under Goods*, p. xi; de Graaf, Wann and Naylor, *Affluenza*, p. 14.

30 Greg Crister, *Fat Land: How Americans Became the Fattest People in the World*, Houghton Mifflin, New York, 2003. See also Schlosser, *Fast Food Nation*, and for a more recent perspective, Jane Dixon and Dorothy Broom

(eds), *The Seven Deadly Sins of Obesity: How the Modern World is Making us Fat*, University of New South Wales Press, Sydney, 2007.

31 Reported in Marilyn Bordwell, 'Jamming culture: Adbusters' hip media campaign against consumerism', in Princen, et al. (eds), *Confronting Consumption*, pp. 237–53.

32 This can be seen in relation to Australia, for example, where considerable effort has been devoted to documenting a similar set of propensities towards shopping, overeating, larger housing and so on. See Hamilton and Denniss, *Affluenza*, and Eckersley, *Well & Good*.

33 For tabular statistics relating to OECD countries from 1993 to 2006 see *OECD Factbook 2008*, 'Gross national income per capita', p. 37 (accessible at: http://puck.sourceoecd.org/pdf/factbook2008/30200811e-02-01-02.pdf). On income differentials from the mid-1980s to the mid-2000s see *OECD Factbook 2008*, 'Distribution of household disposable income among individuals – measured by gini coefficients', p. 249 (accessible at: http://lysander.sourceoecd.org/pdf/factbook2008/30200811e-11-03-02.pdf).

34 For evidence and discussion of these income, savings, debt and expenditure trends in relation to the largest consumer economy, the USA, see Frank, *Luxury Fever*; Schor, *The Overspent American*; Manning, *Credit Card Nation*; Lizabeth Cohen, *A Consumers' Republic: The Politics of Mass Consumption in Postwar America*, Vintage, New York, 2004. For general tabular statistics on savings rates in OECD countries from 1993 to 2006 see *OECD Factbook 2008*, 'Household net savings rates as a percentage of household disposable income', p. 43 (accessible at: http://lysander.sourceoecd.org/pdf/factbook2008/30200811e-02-02-02.pdf).

35 Yiannis Gabriel and Tim Lang, *The Unmanageable Consumer*, 2nd edn, Sage, London, 2006, pp. 19–20.

Gabriel and Lang note also the recent consumer boom experienced within some transitional economies of Eastern Europe and in the developing economies of China and India. This is in stark contrast to the under-development of South American and African economies. On this, see also Myers and Kent, *The New Consumers*.

36 See, respectively, Hamilton and Denniss, *Affluenza*; James, *Affluenza*; Comeliau, *The Impasse of Modernity*, p. 58; Lasn, *Culture Jam*; Petrini, *Slow Food*, pp. xxiii, 23; and Wachtel, 'Overconsumption', pp. 266–7. This latter text reiterates Wachtel's much more detailed exploration offered in *The Poverty of Affluence*.

37 See Frank, *Luxury Fever*, and also Robert H. Frank, 'Market failures', in Cohen and Rogers (eds), *Do Americans Shop Too Much?*', pp. 37–43.

38 For an encapsulation of her approach see Schor's intro-duction to *The Overspent American*, pp. 3–24. As one of the most thorough of commentators, Schor is very care-ful to acknowledge the roots of her theory in the work of Thorsten Veblen, and the similarity of her thesis to other contemporary critics such as Galbraith, Hirsch, Scitovsky and Amartya Sen. See also, for perhaps the clearest statement of Schor's thesis, Douglas B. Holt, 'An interview with Juliet Schor', *Journal of Consumer Culture*, vol. 5, no. 1, March 2005, pp. 5–21.

39 See, respectively, Rosenblatt, 'Introduction', *Consuming Desires*; Schwartz, *The Paradox of Choice*, and Schwartz, *The Costs of Living*, p. 379.

40 See, respectively, Myers and Kent, *The New Consumers*, pp. 121–5; Bordwell, 'Jamming culture' p. 242; and Michael Maniates, 'In search of consumptive resistance: the voluntary simplicity movement', in Princen et al. (eds), *Confronting Consumption*, p. 204.

41 This rather hopeful line emerged soon after the credit-

crunch of 2008 and was well articulated by the British writer Jeanette Winterson, 'The bank crash is an opportunity to think about the way we live and why', *The Times*, 18/10/08, books section, p. 3

42 Such surveys of public opinion (and often the exact same ones) have been noted, for example, by de Graaf et al., *Affluenza*, p. 3; Douglas B. Holt and Juliet B. Schor, 'Introduction', in Juliet B. Schor and Douglas B. Holt (eds), *The Consumer Society Reader*, New Press, New York, pp. vii–viii; Robert. F. Woollard, 'Introduction', in Woollard and Ostry (eds), *Fatal Consumption*, p. 11; Farrell, *One Nation Under Goods*, p. 269; and, for similar survey evidence relating to Australia, Eckersley, *Well & Good*, pp. 110–17.

43 See www.wvs.isr.umich.edu. As we later explore, this does not simply imply a lowering of levels of individual consumption within post-materialist societies or subcultures.

44 For a careful reading of Inglehart's data that suggests the need for caution in assuming a transition from materialist to post-materialist values see Shinobu Majima and Mike Savage, 'Unpacking Culture Shifts in Post-War Britain: A Critical Encounter with Ronald Inglehart', Working Paper no.17, Centre for Research on Socio-Cultural Change, University of Manchester, 2006.

45 Etzioni, in 'Introduction', Doherty and Etzioni (eds), *Voluntary Simplicity*, p. 17.

46 See, for example, de Graaf et al., *Affluenza*, ch. 13; Hamilton and Denniss, *Affluenza*, p. 15.

47 Comeliau, *The Impasse of Modernity*, pp. 45 and 44 respectively.

48 See Holt, 'An interview with Juliet Schor', pp. 5–8.

49 See Richard Easterlin, 'Does economic growth improve the human lot?' in Paul David and Melvin Reder (eds), *Nations and Households in Economic Growth: Essays in*

Honour of Moses Abramovitz, Academic Press, New York, 1974; Amartya Sen, *Commodities and Capabilities*, Oxford University Press, New Delhi, 1999 (first published 1987).

50 For earlier work see Jeremy Seabrook, *What Went Wrong? Why Hasn't Having More Made People Happier?* Pantheon, New York, 1978; Michael Argyle, *The Psychology of Happiness*, Methuen, New York, 1987; Wachtel, *The Poverty of Affluence*; David G. Myers, *The Pursuit of Happiness: Who is Happy – and Why?*, Washington Square Press, New York, 1992; Stanley Lebergott, *Pursuing Happiness: American Consumers in the Twentieth Century*, Princeton University Press, Princeton, 1993.

51 McKibben, 'Introduction', p. 3.

52 Etzioni, in Doherty and Etzioni (eds), *Voluntary Simplicity*, p. 14.

53 Ehrlich and Ehrlich, *One with Nineveh*, p. 215. See also Eckersley, *Well & Good*, p. 84.

54 Cited in Eckersley, *Well & Good* p. 83. Indeed, a range of commentators contend that life-satisfaction levels, regardless of external circumstances, always reach a constant homeostatic state over time.

55 See David G. Myers, 'Wealth and happiness: a limited relationship', in Doherty and Etzioni (eds), *Voluntary Simplicity*, pp. 44–5. This is a reproduced chapter from Myers's book *The American Paradox: Spiritual Hunger in the Age of Plenty*, Yale University Press, New Haven, 2000. Myers draws directly on Ingelhart's work with the World Values Survey, which has in fact linked the growth of post-materialist values with this phenomenon of diminishing returns.

56 Myers, 'Wealth and happiness', pp. 49–50; Schwartz, *The Paradox of Choice*, ch. 10.

57 See Kasser, *The High Price of Materialism*, ch. 2, for a useful discussion of this work.

58 Ibid., p. 5.
59 Betsy Taylor, 'How do we get from here to there?', in Schor and Taylor (eds), *Sustainable Planet*, p. 237.
60 Holt, 'An interview with Juliet Schor', p. 8.
61 Many commentators note some or all of these impacts of consumerism. See, for example, Schor, *The Overspent American*; Schwartz, *The Paradox of Choice*; de Graaf et al., *Affluenza*, ch. 8.
62 See, for example, de Graaf et al., *Affluenza*, p. 66; Schor, *Overspent American*, p. 2. One such measure, the Genuine Progress Indicator, has been developed by the Redefining Progress group (referred to earlier), while another, the Index of Social Health, has been developed by Marc Maringoff at Fordham University.
63 See, for example, Durning, *How Much is Enough*, p. 34; de Graaf et al., *Affluenza*, p. 57. Perhaps predictably, given the dominance of generational thinking within critiques of consumption, young people are often targeted as the culprits here.
64 Eckersley, *Well & Good*, p. 51.

Chapter 2 Anti-Consumerism in Action

1 See, for example, Schor, *The Overspent American*, ch. 6; de Graaf et al., *Affluenza*, p. 3; Myers and Kent, *The New Consumers*, ch. 9; Farrell, *One Nation Under Goods*, ch. 14; Kasser, *The High Price of Materialism*, ch. 9; Schwartz, *The Paradox of Choice*, ch. 11.
2 Andrew Leyshon and Roger Lee, 'Introduction: alternative economic geographies', in Andrew Leyshon, Roger Lee and Colin C. Williams (eds), *Alternative Economic Spaces*, Sage, London, 2003, p. 6.
3 Tim Jordan, *Activism!: Direct Action, Hacktivism and the Future of Society*, Reaktion Books, London, 2002, p. 102.

4 On culture jamming, consumerism and the role of Adbusters see Bordwell, 'Jamming culture'; Joseph D. Rumbo, 'Consumer resistance in a world of advertising clutter', *Psychology and Marketing*, vol. 19, no. 2, 2002, pp. 127–48; and on culture jamming generally, Klein, *No Logo*, ch. 12. For examples of these 'subvertisements' and 'uncommercials' see the Media Foundation website www.adbusters.org.

5 The reverend has gone into print also. See Bill Talen, *What Should I do if Reverend Billy is in my Store?*, New Press, New York, 2003; and the website www.revbilly. com, for the latest.

6 Jordan, *Activism!*, p. 117. See also Klein, *No Logo*, ch. 12, for a constructive critique of jamming.

7 This argument is at the core of the vociferous polemic against culture jamming by the Canadian academics Joseph Heath and Andrew Potter in *The Rebel Sell: Why the Culture Can't be Jammed*, Capstone, Chichester, 2005.

8 See Alberto Melucci, *The Playing Self: Person and Meaning in a Planetary Society*, Cambridge University Press, Cambridge, 1996.

9 See Schor, *The Overspent American*, pp. 145 and 155–7; de Graaf, Wann and Naylor, *Affluenza*, ch. 25; Farrell, *One Nation Under Goods*, pp. 271–2; Eckersley, *Well & Good*, p. 265; Kasser, *The High Price of Materialism*, pp. 111–12; Myers and Kent, *The New Consumers*, p. 134; and Durning, *How Much is Enough?*, ch. 10.

10 Mary Rayner, Rob Harrison and Sarah Irving, 'Ethical consumerism – democracy through the wallet', *Journal of Research for Consumers*, issue 3, 2002. It shoud be noted at this point that the term 'consumerism' has long been used, particularly in the USA, UK and elsewhere, to name a political movement advocating consumer rights

and interests and pursued through consumer associations. Clearly, this still current, but rather specialized, utilization of the term runs up against the much more usual understanding of consumerism as a form of excess (and, as such, its continued use by consumer advocates and organizations is, I would argue, of dubious value). I have opted throughout this book to utilize the phrase 'ethical consumption' as a way of avoiding this conflation of meaning.

11 Harrison, Newholm and Shaw, 'Introduction', in Harrison, Newholm and Shaw (eds), *The Ethical Consumer*, pp. 1–8.

12 On the growing popularity and market share of organic and local foods in various western economies, and the motivations behind both their increased consumption and the factors precluding this, see, for example, Stewart Lockie, Kristen Lyons, Geoffrey Lawrence and Kerry Mummery, 'Eating "green": motivations behind organic food consumption in Australia', *Sociologia Ruralis*, vol. 42, no. 1, January 2002, pp. 23–39; Charlotte Weatherell, Angela Tregear and Johanne Allinson, 'In search of the concerned consumer: UK public perceptions of food, farming and buying local', *Journal of Rural Studies*, vol. 19, 2003, pp. 233–44; M. G. McEachern and P. McClean, 'Organic purchasing motivations and attitudes; are they ethical?', *International Journal of Consumer Studies*, vol. 26, no. 2, June 2002, pp. 85–92. See also Alan Warde, *Consumption, Food and Taste*, Sage, London, 1997, who has explored the manner in which food purchasing under conditions of late modernity has become partially detached from the determinants of class and income. Food selection on the basis of particular principles and concerns thus becomes expressive of fluidly constituted consumer groupings or 'neo-tribes'.

13 On this point see Lockie et al., *Sociologia Ruralis*, p. 36, and Harrison et al., *The Ethical Consumer*, p. 2.

14 This is to paraphrase Jess Worth, 'Buy now, pay later', *New Internationalist*, November 2006, p. 4.

15 See Josée Johnston, 'Consuming global justice: fair trade shopping and alternative development', in James Goodman (ed.), *Protest and Globalisation*, Pluto Press, Sydney, 2001; Raymond L. Bryant and Michael K. Goodman, 'Consuming narratives: the political ecology of "alternative" consumption', *Transactions of the Institute of British Geographers*, NS 29, 2004, pp. 344–66; David Goodman and Michael Goodman, 'Sustaining foods: organic consumption and the socio-ecological imaginary', in Cohen and Murphy (eds), *Exploring Sustainable Consumption*, pp. 97–119; Julie Guthman, 'The "organic commodity" and other anomalies in the politics of consumption', in Alex Hughes and Suzanne Reimer (eds.) *Geography of Commodity Chains*, Routledge, London, pp. 233–49; Julie Guthman, 'Fast food/organic food: reflexive tastes and the making of "yuppie chow"', *Social & Cultural Geography*, vol. 4, no. 1, 2003, pp. 45–58.

16 On this point see Clive Barnett, Paul Cloke, Nick Clarke and Alice Malpass, 'Consuming ethics: articulating the subjects and spaces of ethical consumption', *Antipode*, vol. 37, no. 1, 2005, pp. 23–45. On the moral nature of consumption, particularly 'provisioning', see also Daniel Miller, *A Theory of Shopping*, Cornell University Press, New York, 1998.

17 On the points made in this paragraph, and for quotations, see Michele Micheletti, *Political Virtue and Shopping: Individuals, Consumerism and Collective Action*, Palgrave Macmillan, New York, 2003, preface, ch. 2 and, on phronesis, p. 150. Once again, the use of the term 'consumerism' here, while it draws on a long political

tradition, leads I think to an unhelpful conflation of meaning.

18 Roberta Sassatelli, 'Virtue, responsibility and consumer choice: framing critical consumerism', in John Brewer and Frank Trentman (eds), *Consuming Cultures, Global Perspectives: Historical Trajectories, Transnational Exchanges*, Berg, Oxford, 2006, pp. 219–50.

19 On the points made in this paragraph, and for quotations, see Kate Soper, 'Rethinking the "good life": The consumer as citizen', *Capitalism, Nature, Socialism*, vol. 15, no. 3, 2004, pp. 111–17.

20 Sassatelli, 'Virtue, responsibility and consumer choice', p. 225. On a broader note, an excellent historical investigation of the rise of the consumer as citizen is provided in Frank Trentmann, 'The modern genealogy of the consumer: meanings, identities and political synapses', in Brewer and Trentmann (eds), *Consumer Cultures*. pp. 19-69.

21 See Andy Scerri, 'Not just the warm, fuzzy feeling you get from buying free-range eggs: paradoxes of increased individuation and public awareness of environmental issues in the contemporary West', *Environmental Politics*, (forthcoming, 2009).

22 For this criticism, see Worth, 'Buy now, pay later'; Johnston, 'Consuming global justice'.

23 See Harrison et al., *The Ethical Consumer*, p. 3; Deirdre Shaw and Terry Newholm, 'Voluntary simplicity and the ethics of consumption', *Psychology & Marketing*, vol. 19, no. 2, February 2002, pp. 167–85.

24 Soper, 'Rethinking the "good life"', p. 116.

25 See Anthony Giddens, *Modernity and Self-Identity: Self and Society in the Late Modern Age*, Polity, Cambridge, 1991.

26 For one of the classic statements on the personal as

political see Sheila Rowbotham, Lynne Segal and Hilary Wainwright, *Beyond the Fragments: Feminism and the Making of Socialism*, Merlin, London, 1979. See also Melucci, cited in Parkins and Craig, *Slow Living*, p. 5.

27 See, for example, Hammerslough, *Dematerializing*, ch. 11; and John D. Drake, *Downshifting*.

28 Etzioni, in Doherty and Etzioni, *Voluntary Simplicity*, pp. 8–12.

29 On the points made in this paragraph, and for quotations, see Schor, *The Overspent American*, pp. 22–4 and pp. 146–63. For a similar 'steps-towards-change' approach see Kasser, *The High Price of Materialism*, ch. 9.

30 Schor, *The Overspent American*, pp. 138–9.

31 For the definitive history of the simplicity movement in the USA, see David Shi, *The Simple Life: Plain Living and High Thinking in American Culture*, Oxford University Press, New York, 1985.

32 For an early and influential example of this see Richard Gregg, *The Value of Voluntary Simplicity*, first published in 1936, part of which is reproduced in Doherty and Etzioni, *Voluntary Simplicity*, pp. 131–44.

33 On these points, and for quotations, see Duane Elgin, *Voluntary Simplicity: Towards a Way of Life that is Outwardly Simple, Inwardly Rich*, revised edn, Harper, New York, 1993, p. 28 and pp. 41–2.

34 Joe Dominguez and Vicki Robin, *Your Money or Your Life: Transforming Your Relationship with Money and Achieving Financial Independence*, Penguin, New York, 1999 (first published 1992). Sales of the book finance the Seattle-based New Road Map Foundation that further promotes a frugal lifestyle.

35 See Andrews, *The Circle of Simplicity*, and her, 'The simple solution', in de Graaf (ed.), *Take Back Your Time*, pp. 139–44.

36 Etzioni 'Introduction', in Doherty and Etzioni, *Voluntary Simplicity*, pp. 3–9.
37 Schor, *The Overspent American*, p. 113.
38 See Clive Hamilton, *Downshifting in Britain: A Sea-Change in the Pursuit of Happiness*, Australia Institute, Discussion paper no. 58, 2003; and Hamilton and Denniss, *Affluenza*, p. 154.
39 Schor, *The Overspent American*, p. 115.
40 In the late 1970s Duane Elgin and his colleague Arnold Mitchell undertook a survey of types of voluntary simplicity but this yielded qualitative rather than quantitative information, and estimates of the extent and possible growth of voluntary simplicity in the USA were speculative. See Elgin, *Voluntary Simplicity*, ch. 2; and also Duane Elgin and Arnold Mitchell, 'Voluntary simplicity: a movement emerges', in Doherty and Etzioni, *Voluntary Simplicity*, pp. 145–71.
41 'pop soc' = popular sociology.
42 See Paul H. Ray and Sherry Ruth Anderson, *The Cultural Creatives: How 50 Million People are Changing the World*, Three Rivers Press, New York, 2001 (first published 2000); Richard Florida, *The Rise of the Creative Class . . . and how it's Transforming Work, Leisure, Community and Everyday Life*, Basic Books, New York, 2004 (first published 2002).
43 Boyle, *Authenticity*, p. 40. See also the sociological best-seller of the 1950s, David Riesman's, *The Lonely Crowd: A Study of the Changing American Character*, Yale University Press, New Haven, 1969 (first published 1950).
44 Boyle, *Authenticity*, pp. 40–2. A less complimentary term coined to describe these social groupings is 'bobos' (bourgeois bohemians), now associated with the work of the American critic David Brooks. His witty polemic does not reject the cultural values of this supposed 'new elite' but,

through a form of what Brooks calls 'comic sociology', it examines the way in which an educated, liberal upper-middle class in the USA lives an ideology that combines a wealthy high-consumption lifestyle with an accompanying allegiance to post-materialist values. See David Brooks, *Bobos in Paradise: The New Upper Class and How They Got There*, Simon & Schuster, New York, 2000, Introduction.

45 Boyle, *Authenticity*, pp. 286–96. See also Farrell, *One Nation Under Goods*, pp. 274–6, who writes of the need to promote post-materialist values with a focus on 'whole-systems thinking', 'groundedness' and a 'new materialism'. The last concept revives ideas of thrift, frugality and sufficiency, and gives life to a 'a new kind of worldliness' involving a global care and concern.

46 On these points, and for quotations, see Maniates, in Princen et al. (eds), *Confronting Consumption*, pp. 202 and 233; see also Maniates, 'Individualization: plant a tree, buy a bike, save the world?', in ibid., *Confronting Consumption*, pp. 43–66.

47 See the Slow Food manifesto reproduced in Petrini, *Slow Food*, pp. xxiii–xxiv. See also the Slow Food website at www.slowfood.com.

48 Petrini, *Slow Food*, p. xxi.

49 For a discussion of this difference see Parkins and Craig, *Slow Living*, pp. 2–3.

50 Wendy Parkins, 'Out of time: fast subjects and slow living', *Time & Society*, vol. 13, no. 2/3, 2004, p. 371.

51 See the Society for the Deceleration of Time website at www.zeitverein.com, and the Take-Back-Your-Time website at www.takebackyourtime.org. See also de Graaf, 'Take back your time day', in de Graaf (ed.), *Take Back Your Time*, pp. viii–xii. Other 'slow' groups or networks include the Sloth Club, based in Japan (www.sloth.gr.jp) and the Long Now Foundation (www.longnow.org).

52 On these points, and for quotations, see Honoré, *In Praise of Slow*, pp. 4–5 and pp. 273–82.

53 Parkins and Craig, *Slow Living*, p. ix; their emphasis.

54 Ibid., p. 4.

55 See Julie Labelle, 'A recipe for connectedness: bridging production and consumption with slow food', *Food, Culture & Society*, vol. 7, no. 2, 2004, pp. 81–96.

56 Kelly Donati, 'The pleasure of diversity in slow food's ethics of taste', *Food, Culture & Society*, vol. 8, no. 2, 2005, p. 237.

57 This is pursued through events such as the Terra Madre: World Meeting of Food Communities. The first of these was held in 2004 in Turin, and brought together over 5,000 food producers from 131 countries. On this, see Donati, 'The pleasure of diversity', pp. 237–9; and, on the link between production and consumption, see Labelle, 'A recipe for connectedness'.

58 Parkins and Craig, *Slow Living*, p. 133. This difference is also clearly connected to the deep suspicion of collectivism and to the religiosity characteristic of the North American liberal democratic tradition in contrast to the socialist ethos of European radical political thought and action.

59 Schor, *The Overspent American*, pp. 163–5. See also, Holt, 'How consumers consume', p. 9. Schor insists on the crucial linkage between production and consumption and acknowledges that many critiques of consumerism fail to deal with the former. Interestingly, however, Schor tends to conflate production and work, such that she deals with the issue of working hours and productivity, but does not broach questions concerning the ownership and organization of the means of production.

60 For an example of this attention to community renewal and changes in production and work practices that comes close to a reformist, even democratic socialist,

anti-consumerist manifesto, see the various essays in Schor and Taylor, *Sustainable Planet*.

61 Schwartz, *The Paradox of Choice*, p. 217.

62 The best exception to this rule is the sophisticated analysis of overconsumption offered by de Geus, *The End of Over-Consumption*. De Geus strongly advocates for simple living, but does so in the context of outlining in detail the accompanying need for and potential shape of government regulation and intervention in support of individual moderation and sustainability.

63 Schwartz, *The Paradox of Choice*, pp. 222–35.

64 Hamilton and Denniss, *Affluenza*, p. 190. This undermines what is, in many respects, a well argued case for political change.

65 Maniates, 'Individualization: plant a tree, buy a bike, save the world?', pp. 45–7. Maniates in no uncertain terms rejects what he calls the 'consumption-as-social-action' thesis as dangerously diverting attention from the need for collective political effort to effect social change.

66 On these points, and for quotations, see Etzioni, in Doherty and Etzioni, *Voluntary Simplicity*, pp. 23–4. On communitarianism, which emphasizes a balance between personal autonomy and social responsibility, between individualism and communalism, see the website of the Institute for Communitarian Policy Studies at www.gwu.edu/~icps.

67 See Frank, *Luxury Fever*, and also Robert H. Frank, 'Achieving collective wellbeing through greater simplicity: a simple proposal', in Doherty and Etzioni (eds), *Voluntary Simplicity*, pp. 83–98.

68 Ehrlich and Ehrlich, *One with Nineveh*, pp. 229–34.

69 See for example Jeffrey Hollender, 'Changing the nature of commerce', in Schor and Taylor, *Sustainable Planet*, pp. 61–77; Paul Hawken, Amory Lovins and Hunter L.

Lovins, *Natural Capitalism: Creating the Next Industrial Revolution*, Little, Brown, Boston, 1999.

70 On these points see Herman E. Daly, 'Five policy recommendations for a sustainable economy', in Schor and Taylor (eds.), *Sustainable Planet*, pp. 209–21.

71 See Comeliau, *The Impasse of Modernity*, particularly ch. 13.

72 See Sarah Anderson and John Cavanagh, 'Another world is possible: new rules for the global economy', in Schor and Taylor (eds), *Sustainable Planet*, pp. 155–73.

73 Bakan, *The Corporation*, pp. 149–53.

74 See the ATTAC 'platform' at www.attac.org (accessed 22 August 2006). A Tobin tax is a currency transaction tax, named after the American economist and Nobel Laureate James Tobin. As the ATTAC website points out, even a levy of 0.1% on speculative currency market transactions, implemented by the governments of industrialized countries, would raise tens of billions of dollars annually that, the ATTAC platform suggests, could be used to support the sustainable development of poor countries and to discourage speculation.

75 On these points, and for the above quotations, see Leyshon and Lee, 'Introduction: alternative economic geographies', pp. 4 and 13.

76 See J. K. Gibson-Graham, *The End of Capitalism (As We Knew It): A Feminist Critique of Political Economy*, Blackwell, Oxford, 1996. Gibson and Graham write under the one authorial name.

77 On these points, and for quotations, see Princen, *The Logic of Sufficiency*, pp. vii–viii.

78 Ted Trainer, 'The global ecovillage movement: the simpler way for a sustainable society', *Social Alternatives*, vol. 19, no. 3, July 2000, pp. 19–24. See also Trainer, *Abandon Affluence!*

79 See also Elgin, *Voluntary Simplicity*, pp. 198–201, who outlines the kinds of alternative economic practices characteristic of ecovillages or what he calls 'microcommunities'.

80 See Helena Norberg-Hodge, 'Shifting direction: from global dependence to local interdependence', in Jerry Mander and Edward Goldsmith (eds), *The Case Against the Global Economy: And for a Return to the Local*, Sierra Club, San Francisco, 1996, pp. 393–406. See also her *Ancient Futures: Learning From Ladakh*, Rider, London, 2000 (first published 1992) and, for some of the main localization movement websites aimed at promoting community responses to climate change www.transitiontowns.org (in the UK) and www.communitysolution.org (in the USA).

Chapter 3 Encountering Anti-Consumerism

1 See 'The subversive strikes back', The *Guardian* (London), 16 September 2004, p. 16. In a somewhat different context, the film *Czech Dream*, directed by Vít Klusák and Filip Remunda and released in 2004, offers a biting critique of an emerging consumerism in a 'transitional economy' (see the film website at www.czech-dream.com). See also the Swedish anti-consumerist film *Surplus*, directed by Erik Gadini and released in 2003.

2 Kevin McDonald, *Global Movements, Action and Culture*, Blackwell, Oxford, 2006.

3 This is not to suggest that the activist and the commentator or critic are always different. On the contrary, a number of people interviewed for this study were authors of some of the texts previously discussed.

4 On Slow Food (www.slowfood.com), Adbusters (www.adbusters.org) and ATTAC (www.attac.org), see ch. 3. Greenpeace (www.greenpeace.org), founded in Canada in 1971, now has a presence in over forty countries

and campaigns, using non-violent direct action, to 'ensure a just, peaceful, sustainable environment for future generations'. Friends of the Earth (www.foe.org) is a 'social and environmental justice organization' founded in the USA in 1969 and has a presence in over seventy-two countries. Consumers International (www.consumersinternational.org), founded in the early 1960s, is the international umbrella body for over 250 consumer unions and organizations worldwide. It 'strives to promote a fairer society through defending the rights of all consumers' and has a strong Third World representation and focus on poverty, marginalization and disadvantage. The Fair Trade Federation (www.fairtradefederation.org) is an association of fair trade wholesalers, retailers and producers 'committed to providing fair wages and good employment opportunities to economically disadvantaged artisans and farmers worldwide'. All of these organizations are involved in campaigns for sustainable and responsible consumption.

5 See the essays in Martha McCaughey and Michael D. Ayers (eds), *Cyberactivism: Online Activism in Theory and Practice*, Routledge, New York, 2003; and in Wim van de Donk, Brian D. Loader, Paul G. Nixon and Dieter Rucht (eds), *Cyberprotest: New Media, Citizens and Social Movements*, Routledge, London, 2004. For the now classic statement of the rise of the electronically mediated network as embodying contemporary social relations in the West and globally, see Manuel Castells, *The Rise of Network Society*, 3 vols., vol. I: *(The Information Age: Economy, Society and Culture)*, Blackwell, Oxford, 1996.

6 See www.nologo.org and www.thecorporation.tv.

7 Redefining Progress (www.redefiningprogress.org) was discussed in ch. 1, and the Ethical Consumer Research Association (www.ethicalconsumer.org) and International

Society for Ecology and Culture (www.isec.org.uk) in ch. 2. The London-based New Economics Foundation (www.neweconomics.org), founded in 1986, is an independent think tank that promotes 'innovative solutions that challenge mainstream thinking on economic, environmental and social issues'. It engages in research, campaigning, policy discussion and local projects promoting alternative economic practices. The Center for the New American Dream (www.newdream.org) is an advocacy organization that 'helps Americans consume responsibly to protect the environment, enhance quality of life, and promote social justice'. The organization works with individuals, institutions, communities and business on campaigns that further these aims, and auspices a 'conscious consumer' webpage (www.newdream.org/consumer/). The US-based Worldwatch Institute (www.worldwatch.org), founded in 1974, distributes interdisciplinary information on environmental, social and economic trends. Its work focuses on 'the transition to an environmentally sustainable and socially just society'. The Consumer Citizenship Network (www.hihm.no/concit/), centred in Norway, is an interdisciplinary network of educators from over 120 institutions in 37 countries focused on the need for 'constructive action by individuals in order to achieve sustainable consumption and global solidarity'. It coordinates research about, and develops good teaching practice for, 'consumer citizenship'. Finally, the Association of Conscious Consumers (www.tve.hu), based in Hungary and established in 2000, is one of the major Eastern European organizations focused on advocacy and education relating to sustainable consumption.

8 Delocator (www.delocator.net) originated in the USA in 2005 but now has sister sites in Canada and the United Kingdom. The site targets Starbucks but also other

coffee chains by providing an alternative 'store locator' that, with constant input from site users, identifies and operates as an advocate for local and independently owned cafes. This action is conceptualized not only as a defence of small businesses but as a cultural politics aimed at resisting standardization. Sprawl-Busters (www. sprawl-busters.com) is a US-based 'consultancy' group that assists 'local community coalitions on-site to design and implement successful campaigns against megastores'. Whirl-Mart Ritual Resistance (www.breathingplanet.net/ whirl/), conceived in the USA in 2001, is described as a 'participatory art and action experiment'. The ritual involves groups gathering in superstores and silently pushing empty shopping carts around the aisles. This action 'utilizes tactics of occupation and reclamation of private consumer-dominated space for the purposes of creating a symbolic spectacle'.

9 Reverend Billy and the Church of Stop Shopping (www.revbilly.com) was discussed in ch. 2. Résistance à l'Agression Publicitaire (www.antipub.org) is a leading French anti-consumerism group that undertakes activities similar to Adbusters, with the principal object of resisting 'the negative effects, direct and indirect, of advertising on the environment and citizens'. Action Consommation (www.actionconsommation.org) is a French group formed in 2001 in order to promote responsible forms of consumption. It focuses on raising awareness of the power and responsibility of consumers to address environmental and social issues through their purchasing behaviour, but also promotes broader action to bring about economic, institutional and ideological change. Food Not Bombs (www.foodnotbombs.net) originated in the USA in the 1990s but is now an international network of hundreds of 'autonomous

chapters' working to 'end hunger' and to 'support actions
to stop globalization of the economy, restrictions to the
movement of people, and the exploitation and destruction
of the earth'. Food Not Bombs groups recover waste
food (from dumpsters and other locations) and serve free
vegetarian meals to the public and at protests and events.
ConsumeHastaMorir (www.consumehastamorir.com) is
a Spanish group similar, once again, to Adbusters, while
the Associazione per i Consumi Etici ed Alternativi
(www.consumietici.it/acea.) is a Milan-based consumer
organization that makes available information on ethical
and ecological consumption and promotes social action
to further these practices.

10 Freegan.info (www.freegan.info) is the major world site
promoting a freegan lifestyle and politics focused on
'revealing human overconsumption and waste'. Freeganism
(a combination of 'free' and 'vegan') employs 'alternative
strategies for living based on limited participation in
the conventional economy and minimal consumption
of resources'. As with Food Not Bombs, a key freegan
strategy is 'urban foraging' or 'dumpster diving' whereby
waste food is reclaimed. The Simple Living Network
(www.simpleliving.net) was founded in 1985 and has
since become a major clearinghouse for information and
resources relating to simple living practices and events. The
Compact (http://sfcompact.blogspot.com) originated in
San Francisco in 2004 as a group of individuals who vowed
to forgo the consumption of new goods and to simplify
their lives (through borrowing, bartering and buying
second-hand) for six months in order to 'counteract the
negative global environmental and socioeconomic impacts
of US consumption'. Similar local groups, committed to
escaping 'the consumer grid' for a twelve-month period,
now exist across the USA and in other western countries.

Mutual support is provided by groups meeting monthly. Bilanci di Giustizia (www.bilancidigiustizia.it) is an Italian-wide collective of over 500 families/households that have come together in a 'joint action' to reduce consumption and consume carefully in the interests of personal health, the environment and global justice. Even more so than the Compact, emphasis is placed here on simplification as a collective enterprise.

11 A number of recent studies, some already cited, have utilized interviews in order to explore a politics of consumption. However, researchers have tended to focus on one national context and/or on specific movements – especially culture jamming or simple living. A particularly celebratory approach is offered in commentary that utilizes interviews in order to advocate for model practices such as downshifting. See, for example, Schor, *The Overspent American* and Hamilton and Denniss, *Affluenza*. In contrast, an often politically confused empiricism is evident within marketing scholarship centred on the qualitative exploration of what the American marketing psychologist Stephen Zavestoski has called 'anti-consumption attitudes'. While yielding useful insights, much of this work is wedged between a 'radical' intent focused on supporting responsible consumption and a dubious need to identify 'anti-consumption' as a niche, an understanding of which will assist marketers to sell to these new non-consumers. On this score see Stephen Zavestoski, 'The social–psychological bases of anticonsumption attitudes', *Psychology & Marketing*, vol. 19, no. 2, February 2002, pp. 149–65; and, in the same edition, Margaret Craig-Lees and Constance Hill, 'Understanding voluntary simplifiers', pp. 187–210. See also Robert V. Kozinets and Jay M. Handelman, 'Adversaries of consumption: consumer movements,

activism, and ideology', *Journal of Consumer Research*, vol. 31, December 2004, pp. 691–704; and, for one of the best of such essays, Hélène Cherrier, 'Using existential–phenomenological interviewing to explore meanings of consumption' in Harrison et al. (eds.), *The Ethical Consumer*, pp. 125–35. Finally, beyond both popular advocacy and marketing research, a more theoretically oriented literature has drawn on interviews and immersed observation in order to sympathetically interrogate various anti-consumerist actions as political strategy. See, for example, Maniates, 'In search of consumptive resistance'; Sassatelli, 'Virtue, responsibility and consumer choice', pp. 219–50; Parkins and Craig, *Slow Living*; Gabriel and Lang, *The Unmanageable Consumer*.

12 There is little need here to go into great methodological detail. Interviews were conducted by a research team comprising myself, Ferne Edwards and Kelly Donati, using an interview schedule but with considerable flexibility in how this was followed. These conversations were digitally recorded and fully transcribed, with transcripts returned to interviewees for amendment, approval or withdrawal. Conduct of the research was overseen by a university research ethics committee and almost all those interviewed requested that their real names be used rather than a pseudonym. The age of participants ranged from 29 to 65, with most aged in their 30s and 40s.

13 Interview with Kalle Lasn, The Media Foundation, Vancouver, 6 April 2006.

14 Interview with Joel Bakan, author of *The Corporation*, Canada, 6 October 2006. All further quotations of Joel are from this interview.

15 Interview with Rob Harrison, Ethical Consumer Research Association, Manchester, UK, 20 July 2007.

16 Interview with Helena Norberg-Hodge, International Society for Ecology and Culture, London, 30 March 2007. All further quotations of Helena are from this interview. It should be noted that, unlike most of those interviewed, much of her activism is Third-World based. However, I draw here on her comments targeted at the dynamics of western consumerism.

17 Interview with Suzie Brown, Australian Conservation Foundation, Sydney, 20 February 2006. All further quotations of Suzie are from this interview. The Australian Conservation Foundation (www.acfonline. org.au) was formed in 1966 and focuses on research and advocacy. It is the leading not-for-profit environmental organization in Australia.

18 Interview with Danni Zuvela, Food Not Bombs, Australia, 6 March 2006. All further quotations of Danni are from this interview. For a detailed discussion of Food Not Bombs in Australia and other 'dumpster diving' groups see Ferne Edwards and David Mercer, 'Gleaning from Gluttony: An Australian Youth Subculture confronts the Ethic of Waste', *Australian Geographer*, vol. 38, no. 3, 2006, pp. 279-96.

19 Interview with Lewis Akenji, Association of Conscious Consumers, Budapest, 1 May 2007. All further quotations of Lewis are from this interview. Although strictly speaking a 'transitional' rather than wealthy western economy, Hungary is undergoing rapid economic change and is among the most consumer-oriented of contemporary Eastern European nations.

20 I have commented in more detail on this elsewhere. See Kim Humphery, 'After affluenza', *Arena Magazine*, no. 75, February–March 2005, pp. 11–12.

21 Interview with Erika Lesser, Slow Food (USA), 6 December 2006.

22 Importantly, this turn to community for Helena Norberg-Hodge entailed also a reconnection with nature.

23 Interview with Véronique Gallais, Action Consommation, 31 October 2007. All further quotations of Véronique are from this interview.

24 For a useful overview of French consumption politics see Samy Sanches, 'Sustainable consumption à la Française? Conventional, innovative, and alternative approaches to sustainability and consumption in France', *Sustainability: Science, Practice, & Policy*, vol. 1, no. 1, 2005, pp. 43–57.

25 Interview with Victoria Thoresen, Consumer Citizenship Network, Norway, 4 May 2007.

26 Interview with Aiden Enns, *Geez* magazine, Vancouver, 22 September 2006. *Geez* magazine (www.geezmagazine. org), launched in December 2005, has a radical agenda to question consumer capitalism, but does so from a spiritual perspective.

27 Interview with Xtine Hanson, Delocator, San Francisco, 2 October 2006.

28 For some of the classics within this tradition see Sydney Tarrow, *Power in Movement: Social Movements, Collective Action and Politics*, Cambridge University Press, Cambridge, 1994; and Douglas McAdam, Sydney Tarrow and Charles Tilly, *Dynamics of Contention*, Cambridge University Press, New York, 2001.

29 See, for example, Melucci, *The Playing Self*; and his *Nomads of the Present: Social Movements and Individual Needs in Contemporary Society*, edited by John Keane and Paul Mier, Hutchinson Radius, London, 1989. On Touraine, see McDonald, *Global Movements*, pp. 24–6.

30 See Francesca Polletta, *Freedom is an Endless Meeting: Democracy in American Social Movements*, University of Chicago Press, Chicago and London, 2004. Importantly also, Polletta demonstrated that this has not been at the

cost of strategic effectiveness: that highly personalized, participatory forms of political action have successfully developed innovative strategies for bringing about institutional and policy reforms.

31 See McDonald, *Global Movements*, ch. 10, in particular.

Chapter 4 Interpreting Material Life

1 See Humphery, *Shelf Life: Supermarkets and the Changing Cultures of Consumption*, Cambridge University Press, Melbourne, 1998, p. 197.

2 See Conca, 'Consumption and environment in a global economy'; Cohen, 'The emergent environmental policy discourse on sustainable consumption'; Meadows et al., *The Limits to Growth*.

3 See Conca, 'Consumption and environment in a global economy', p. 134; World Commission on Environment and Development, *Our Common Future*.

4 Mary Douglas and Baron Isherwood, *The World of Goods: Towards an Anthropology of Consumption*, Allen Lane, London, 1979 (first published 1978). All quotations are from the Preface, pp. 3–12.

5 Pierre Bourdieu, *Distinction: A Social Critique of the Judgement of Taste* (trans. Richard Nice), Routledge, London, 1986 (first published 1979).

6 Michel de Certeau, *The Practice of Everyday Life* (trans. Steven Rendall), University of California Press, Berkeley, 1988 (first published in translation 1984). All quotations are from pp. xii–xiii.

7 See, for example, Jean Baudrillard, *Simulations* (trans. Paul Foss, Paul Patton and Philip Beitchman), Semiotext, New York, 1983.

8 There is little point in providing an exhaustive list of references here. For some of the classic cultural studies texts in this genre, see Dick Hebdige, *Subculture: The Meaning*

of Style, Methuen, London, 1979; Angela McRobbie and
Mica Nava (eds), *Gender and Generation*, Macmillan,
London, 1984; and, for the most eager adoption of
the 'resistant consumer' thesis, John Fiske, *Reading the
Popular*, Unwin Hyman, Boston, 1989. For one of the
better early critiques of this approach see Jim McGuigan,
Cultural Populism, Routledge, London, 1992. See also
Celia Lury, *Consumer Culture*, Polity, Cambridge, 1996,
who provides an excellent survey of consumption theory
from the 1970s to the mid-1990s.

9   See the essays in Arjun Apadurai, *The Social Life of Things:
Commodities in Cultural Perspective*, Cambridge University
Press, New York, 1986. This theme was to be taken up
also in cultural studies: see Dick Hebdige, *Hiding in the
Light: On Images and Things*, Routledge, London, 1988.
See also the important work of Mihaly Csikszentmihalyi
and Eugene Rochberg-Halton, *The Meaning of Things:
Domestic Symbols and the Self*, Cambridge University
Press, Cambridge, 1981.

10 See Daniel Miller, 'Why some things matter', in Daniel
Miller (ed.), *Material Cultures: Why Some Things Matter*,
UCL Press, London, 1998, pp. 3–21; and Miller, *A
Theory of Shopping*. See also James Carrier, *Gifts and
Commodities: Exchange and Western Capitalism since 1700*,
Routledge, London, 1995.

11 See Chandra Mukerji, *From Graven Images: Patterns
of Modern Materialism*, Columbia University Press,
New York, 1983. Other works of note here include
Neil McKendrick, John Brewer and J. H. Plumb (eds),
*The Birth of Consumer Society: The Commercialisation of
Eighteenth-Century England*, Indiana University Press,
Bloomington, 1982; Rosalind Williams, *Dream Worlds:
Mass Consumption in Late Nineteenth-Century France*,
University of California Press, Berkeley, 1982; John

Brewer and Roy Porter, *Consumption and the World of Goods*, Routledge, London, 1993.

12 On these geographical approaches, see Louise Crewe, 'Geographies of retailing and consumption', *Progress in Human Geography*, vol. 24, no. 2, 2000, pp. 275–90; Juliana Mansvelt, *Geographies of Consumption*, Sage, London, 2006; and Alex Hughes and Suzanne Reimer (eds), *Geographies of Commodity Chains*, Routledge, London, 2004. See also Ben Fine and Ellen Leopold, *The World of Consumption*, Routledge, London, 1993; Daniel Miller, Peter Jackson, Nigel Thrift, Beverley Holbrook and Michael Rowlands, *Shopping, Place and Identity*, Routledge, London, 1998.

13 For some notable efforts to cross the divide, particularly between environmentalist scholarship and social theory, see Luke Martell, *Ecology and Society: An Introduction*, Polity, Cambridge, 1994; Michael Redclift and Ted Benton (eds) *Social Theory and the Global Environment*, Routledge, London, 1994.

14 See Don Slater, 'Cultures of consumption', in Kay Anderson, Mona Domosh, Steve Pile and Nigel Thrift (eds), *Handbook of Cultural Geography*, Sage, London, 2003, p. 147.

15 This is to quote, respectively, Don Slater, 'Consumer culture and the politics of need', in Mica Nava, Andrew Blake, Iain MacRury and Barry Richards (eds), *Buy This Book: Studies in Advertising and Consumption*, Routledge, London, 1997, p. 51; Peter Jackson, 'Commodity cultures: the traffic in things', *Transactions of the Institute of British Geography*, vol. 24, 1999, p. 97; Jackson Lears, 'Reconsidering abundance: a plea for ambiguity', in Susan Strasser, Charles McGovern and Matthias Judt (eds), *Getting and Spending: European and American Consumer Societies in the Twentieth Century*, Cambridge University Press, New York, 1998, p. 466.

16 See, for example, Andrew Ross, *No Sweat: Fashion, Free Trade and the Rights of Garment Workers*, Verso, London, 1997; Angela McRobbie, *In the Culture Society: Art, Fashion and Popular Music*, Routledge, London, 1999. See also, Paul du Gay (ed.), *Production of Culture, Cultures of Production*, Sage, London, 1997; and, for a more recent statement of the so-called 'cultural economy' approach, Paul du Gay and Michael Pryke (eds), *Cultural Economy: Cultural Analysis and Commercial Life*, Sage, London, 2002. On efforts to re-centre questions of social inequality see Tim Edwards, *Contradictions of Consumption: Concepts, Practices and Politics in Consumer Society*, Open University Press, Buckingham, 2000.

17 For the literature on consumer citizenship and alternative economic spaces, see ch. 2. On consumption and morality, see Daniel Miller, 'The poverty of morality', *Journal of Consumer Culture*, vol. 1, no. 2, 2001, pp. 225–43; and in the same edition, the reply by Richard Wilk, 'Consuming morality', pp. 245–60. See also Andrew Sayer, '(De)commodification, consumer culture, and moral economy', in *Environment and Planning D: Society and Space*, vol. 21, 2003, pp. 341–57. See below for literature on the contemporary study of material practices and person–object relations.

18 Jane Bennett, *The Enchantment of Modern Life: Attachments, Crossing and Ethics*, Princeton University Press, Princeton, 2001, pp. 160–6. Bennett's articulation of this sensibility follows, but builds on, the work of Hayden White. Others have drawn alternatively on the work of Eve Sedgwick in exploring the possibilities of weak theory. See, for example, the excellent discussion of the concept provided in J. K. Gibson-Graham, *A Postcapitalist Politics*, University of Minnesota Press, Minneapolis, 2006, pp. 3–9.

19 Louise Crewe, 'Geographies of retailing and consumption: markets in meltdown', in *Progress in Human Geography*, vol. 27, no. 3, 2003, p. 354.

20 On Ritzer, see George Ritzer, *The McDonaldization of Society: An Investigation into the Character of Contemporary Social Life*, Pine Forge Press, Thousand Oaks, 1993; and *The Globalization of Nothing*. See also the essays in Barry Smart (ed.), *Resisting McDonaldization: Theory, Process and Critique*, Sage, London, 1999.

21 See Zygmunt Bauman, *Work, Consumerism and the New Poor*; Open University Press, Buckingham, 2001; and *Liquid Life*.

22 Zygmunt Bauman, *Consuming Life*, Polity, Cambridge, 2007; Benjamin R. Barber, *Consumed: How Markets Corrupt Children, Infantilize Adults, and Swallow Citizens Whole*, Norton, New York, 2007.

23 Susan Sontag, *Illness as Metaphor*, Vintage, New York, 1979.

24 Susan Sontag, *Aids and its Metaphors*, Allen Lane, London, 1989, p. 8.

25 Helga Dittmar, *The Social Psychology of Material Possessions: To Have is to Be*, Harvester Wheatsheaf, Hemel Hempstead, 1992, ch. 8.

26 All the above quotes are from John Brewer and Frank Trentmann, 'Introduction: space, time and value in consuming cultures', in Brewer and Trentmann (eds), *Consuming Cultures*. p. 6.

27 This is demonstrated in the recent work of Conrad Lodziak, who insists that, for the western majority, consumption has nothing to do with identity, desire, status or meaning at all, but is an obligatory response to contemporary living conditions governed by the planned obsolescence of products, the growth of smaller households, rising working hours and so on. There is

some truth in this contention, but the force of it is lost by the unsupportable dismissal of consumption as cultural and by the portrayal of western populations as unwilling consumers, when quite the opposite is the case. See Conrad Lodziak, 'On explaining consumption', *Capital & Class*, no. 72, Autumn 2000, pp. 111–33.

28 This is a view common to a broader stream of scholarship on consumption, place and space. See, for example, Robert Sack, *Place, Modernity and the Consumer's World: A Relational Framework for Geographical Analysis*, John Hopkins University Press, Baltimore, 1992; Marc Augé, *Non-Places: An Introduction to an Anthropology of Supermodernity*, Verso, London, 1995; and, more recently, Ritzer, *The Globalization of Nothing*. For a contrary treatment of commercial space as communicatively rich, see Miller et al., *Shopping, Place and Identity*.

29 I have discussed these themes more fully in 'Beyond borders: the politics and place of the global shop', in Daniel Thomas Cook (ed.), *Live Experiences of Public Consumption: Encounters with Value in Marketplaces on Five Continents*, Palgrave Macmillan, Basingstoke, 2008, pp. 161–78.

30 Bill Brown, 'Thing theory', in Bill Brown (ed.), *Things*, University of Chicago Press, Chicago, 2004, p. 4.

31 See Tim Dant, 'Consumption caught in the cash nexus', *Sociology*, vol. 34, no. 4, 2000, pp. 655–70; and his more recent *Materiality and Society*, Open University Press, Buckingham, 2005, ch. 1.

32 In this, Bianchi follows the work of Tibor Scitovsky and of D. E. Berlyne – who emphasized the human tendency to be drawn to the novel rather than the constantly known, while being also perturbed by the utterly unfamiliar. For more on this, see Marina Bianchi, 'Taste for novelty and novel tastes: the role of human agency in consumption', in Marina Bianchi (ed.), *The Active Consumer: Novelty and*

Surprise in Consumer Choice, Routledge, London, 1998, pp. 64–86.

33 Particularly, as I will come later to discuss, in dealing with alternative consumption practices as involving felt elements of loss as well as emotional, social and environmental gain.

34 See Humphery, *Shelf Life*.

35 See Alan Warde, 'Consumption and theories of practice', *Journal of Consumer Culture*, vol. 5, no. 2, July 2005, pp. 131–153.

36 Shove, *Cleanliness, Comfort and Convenience*.

37 The quotations above are from Gay Hawkins, *The Ethics of Waste: How We Relate to Rubbish*, University of New South Wales Press, Sydney, 2006, p. viii and p. 14 respectively.

38 See Colin Campbell, 'I shop therefore I know that I am: the metaphysical basis of modern consumerism', in Karin M. Ekström and Helene Brembeck (eds), *Elusive Consumption*, Berg, Oxford, 2004, pp. 27–44.

39 At the level of subjective wellbeing, wealth in the form of capital (such as savings, investments and home ownership), rather than simply income, is also important with some researchers, suggesting that if both are measured together a greater correlation between affluence and happiness is evident. See Bruce Heady and Mark Wooden, 'Economic wellbeing and subjective wellbeing: the effects of income and wealth', in Lenore Manderson (ed.), *Rethinking Wellbeing*, API Network, Perth, pp. 91–108.

40 For a critical treatment of this point, see Aaron C. Ahuvia, 'Individualism/collectivism and cultures of happiness: a theoretical conjecture on the relationship between consumption, culture and subjective well-being at the national level', *Journal of Happiness Studies*, vol. 3, 2002, pp. 23–36.

41 Nor can the turn to the social–psychological invention and study of the person with a 'materialistic values orientation' (MVO). Once again there is certainly psychometric evidence to suggest that an extremely materialistic approach to life results in an unhappy and unlovable person, but there is very little evidence presented to suggest that we are all turning into such monsters. Nevertheless, the latter is often implied. In his *High Price of Materialism*, Kasser, for example, usefully reports on a range of studies of materialism and wellbeing, but neglects to identify what proportion of western populations squarely fall into the MVO category (and to what extent and in what context), nor does he question if such a speculative identification of an apparently pathological personality type is all that useful in actually understanding the dynamics of overconsumption.

42 See Lenore Manderson, 'Introduction: the social context of wellbeing', in Manderson, *Rethinking Wellbeing*, pp. 1–25.

43 My colleagues and I at the Globalism Research Centre in Melbourne have explored these and other aspects of current approaches to wellbeing in Martin Mulligan, Kim Humphery, Paul James, Christopher Scanlon, Pia Smith and Nicky Welch, *Creating Community: Celebrations, Arts and Wellbeing Within and Across Local Communities*, Globalism Institute, Melbourne, 2006.

44 For more on these ideas see Bennett, *The Enchantment of Modern Life*, pp. 3–16. I am taking liberties with Bennett's work here, condensing her sophisticated theorizations in order to utilize them in relation to overconsumption. I am drawing here also on the similarly invigorating discussion of the need to pursue different forms of social interpretation provided in Gibson-Graham, *A Postcapitalist Politics*, pp. 3–9.

45 Gibson-Graham, *A Postcapitalist Politics*. (Katherine Graham and Julie Gibson write as one author.)

46 Colin C. Williams, *A Commodified World?: Mapping the Limits of Capitalism*, Zed Books, London, 2005. Williams specifically identifies the realms of subsistence activities (or domestic work), of unpaid community and voluntary work, and of the activities of the not-for-profit sector as comprising the sphere of non-commodified economic practices – and as constituting a major, indeed expanding, sphere of economic life. For a somewhat less encompassing challenge to the commodification thesis, see Paul Ransome, *Work, Consumption and Culture: Affluence and Social Change in the Twenty-First Century*, Sage, London, 2005, which provides ample evidence to suggest that work (both paid and unpaid) remains both an important source of identity and, above all, a central everyday activity for affluent populations, thus undercutting the validity of labelling western nations 'consumer societies'.

47 This term is borrowed from Williams, *A Commodified World?*, p. 272.

48 Humphery, *Shelf Life*, pp. 11–12.

Chapter 5 Consuming Differently

1 Hannah Arendt, *The Human Condition*, University of Chicago Press, Chicago, 1998, p. 45.

2 Gibson-Graham, *A Postcapitalist Politics*, p. xxviii.

3 It might be noted here that, conveyed as humour, the portrayal of people as duped consumers works as useful communication. The Reverend Billy and the Church of Stop Shopping is effective and fun precisely because it is an open type of observation. It does not parade as expertise. It allows people to laugh at themselves and the world, as well as to interact with and challenge the critic.

The formal discourse of anti-consumerism is not this; it trades on the authority of the text and the assuredness of the social observer to offer a distanced judgement. When it condemns the mindlessness of others, it does so without good humour.

4 The moralizing nature of the new politics of consumption has been the subject of earlier debate. See Miller in *Journal of Consumer Culture*, pp. 225–43; and in the same volume, the reply to Miller by Richard Wilk, 'Consuming morality', pp. 245–60. On the complex moral status of consumption, see Sayer, '(De)commodification', pp. 341–57.

5 See Jane Bennett and Michael J. Shapiro, 'Introduction', in Jane Bennett and Michael J. Shapiro (eds), *The Politics of Moralizing*, Routledge, New York, 2002, pp. 4, 8.

6 That a confrontation with questions of class is not the strong suit of the new politics of consumption is evident, for example, in relation to the issue of obesity. Commentators tirelessly invoke the high incidence of obesity in western nations as metaphoric of the degeneracy of consumerism. Obesity is certainly in part connected to the affordability and consequent overconsumption of foods high in sugars and fats (particularly processed foodstuffs). But the subtleties of the statistics are often ignored by critics. In western nations obesity tends to be more correlated with low rather than high socio-economic status, while the western wealthy tend to have better health and health care than the less economically well off. Obesity in the West is thus not a simple issue of affluence; it is one of social stratification. For a useful discussion of the politics of food in the USA in particular, see Marion Nestle, *Food Politics: How the Food Industry Influences Nutrition and Health*, University of California Press, Berkeley, 2002.

7 This is to recognize that altering consumption may well
   be experienced as diminishing rather than facilitating
   wellbeing. This point is discussed in Clive Barnett,
   Philip Cafaro and Terry Newholm, 'Philosophy and
   ethical consumption', in Harrison et al. (eds), *The
   Ethical Consumer*, p. 14. See also Kersty Hobson,
   'Sustainable lifestyles: rethinking barriers and behaviour
   change', in Cohen and Murphy (eds), *Exploring
   Sustainable Consumption*, pp. 191–209, who ably
   demonstrates how sustainable consumption messages
   are continually contested by a public, not through
   simple resistance to change, but because messages are
   questioned in the context of everyday existence while
   any restylization of life is often perceived as restrictive
   and disadvantageous.
8 Heikki Patomäki, 'Global justice: a democratic perspective', *Globalizations*, vol. 3, no. 2, 2006, p. 101.
9 Ibid., pp. 99–100.
10 See Barnett et al., 'Philosophy and ethical consumption',
   for a useful discussion of some of the moral philosophical
   approaches informing this intent.
11 For the classic statement of this see World Commission
   on Environment and Development, *Our Common Future*.
12 Some of the clearest recent statements of this principle
   in relation to consumption have been provided by
   moral philosophers, albeit from different philosophical
   viewpoints. See Peter Singer, *How Are We To Live?:
   Ethics in the Age of Self-Interest*, Oxford University Press,
   Oxford, 1997; and Nussbaum, *Frontiers of Justice*.
13 This mirrors, as Nussbaum points out, an essentially
   Aristotelian position of wonder and awe towards the
   world. But as Nussbaum goes on to argue, a respect for
   nature is an ethic rather than a point of justice (the latter
   being affordable strictly only to sentient beings rather

than the inanimate world) and does not necessarily imply that we are obliged to leave nature as it is. See Nussbaum, *Frontiers of Justice*, pp. 94, 357–8.

14 In a similar vein, the overlapping politics of sustainability embodies the same scope. Some have written of the concept of 'just sustainability' in an attempt to grasp a more encompassing sense of what the dual goals of environmental sustainability and social sustainability entails. See Julian Ageyman and Bob Evans, '"Just sustainability": the emerging discourse of environmental justice in Britain?', *The Geographical Journal*, vol. 170, no. 2, June 2004, pp. 155–64. Expressed, here, is a concern to address sustainability issues as encompassing 'the need to ensure a better quality of life for all, now and into the future, in a just and equitable manner, whilst living within the limits of supporting ecosystems'.

15 See Nussbaum, *Frontiers of Justice*.

16 To make a basic point, this logic operates in part autonomously of direct consumer demand; a fact demonstrated through the process of the production system deliberately rendering certain technological goods obsolete or in the enormous number of products produced in the hope of finding a market, but which never do so.

17 Csikszentmihalyi and Rochberg-Halton, *The Meaning of Things*, pp. 230–1.

18 One can see this line of argument, for example, in Etzioni, 'Introduction', in Doherty and Etzioni, *Voluntary Simplicity*, and in the whole tradition of simplicity on which he draws, particularly Gregg, *The Value of Voluntary Simplicity*, and Elgin, *Voluntary Simplicity*.

19 Bill Brown, in his 'thing theory', suggests that at moments when things themselves force us to recognize their physicality – when they stop functioning, for

example – we recognize also the possibility of differently experiencing materiality. It is, however, Gay Hawkins, in her *Ethics of Waste*, who has provided one of the best recent explications of this process, connecting it to notions of a new materialism. For Hawkins, waste represents a key cultural moment in the cycle of consumption in which accumulation turns to loss or rejection. Refuse, however, has an irritating habit of making itself noticeable, and when it does, it forces us to recognize its material nature. This recognition can lead to changed dispositions and sensibilities concerning what constitutes rubbish and how to handle it. What gives rise to this, Hawkins suggests, is not simply a morality of recycling, but the embodied enjoyment of enacting routines that challenge a consumerist disregard for waste and that are born of recognizing that we can connect with the material world in different and enlivening ways.

Postscript: After the Boom, Beyond the West

1 See Kevin Rudd, 'The global financial crisis', *The Monthly*, February 2009, pp. 20–9.
2 See Martin Khor, 'Effects of the global economic crisis on developing countries', Informal Note 42, Global Governance for Development Programme, South Centre, 13 March 2009 (www.southcentre.org).

BIBLIOGRAPHY

Agyeman, Julian and Evans, Bob, '"Just sustainability": the emerging discourse of environmental justice in Britain?', *The Geographical Journal*, vol. 170, no. 2, June 2004, pp.155–64.

Ahuvia, Aaron C., 'Individualism/collectivism and cultures of happiness: a theoretical conjecture on the relationship between consumption, culture and subjective well-being at the national level', *Journal of Happiness Studies*, vol. 3, 2002, pp. 23–36.

Albert, Michael, *Parecon: Life After Capitalism*, London and New York: Verso, 2003.

Anderson, Sarah and Cavanagh, John, 'Another world is possible: new rules for the global economy', in Juliet B. Schor and Betsy Taylor (eds.), *Sustainable Planet: Solutions for the Twenty-First Century*, Boston: Beacon Press, 2002, pp. 155–73.

Andrews, Cecile, *The Circle of Simplicity: Return to the Good Life*, New York: HarperPerennial, 1998.

——, 'The simple solution', in John de Graaf (ed.), *Take Back Your Time: Fighting Overwork and Time Poverty in America*, San Francisco: Berrett-Koehler, 2003, pp. 139–44.

Apadurai, Arjun, *The Social Life of Things: Commodities in Cultural Perspective*, New York: Cambridge University Press, 1986.

Arendt, Hannah, *The Human Condition*, Chicago: University of Chicago Press, 1998.

Argyle, Michael, *The Psychology of Happiness*, New York: Methuen, 1987.

Augé, Marc, *Non-Places: An Introduction to an Anthropology of Supermodernity*, London: Verso, 1995.

Bakan, Joel, *The Corporation: The Pathological Pursuit of Profit and Power*, London: Constable, 2004.

Barber, Benjamin R., *Jihad vs. McWorld*, New York: Ballantine Books, 2001.

——, *Consumed: How Markets Corrupt Children, Infantilize Adults, and Swallow Citizens Whole*, New York: Norton, 2007.

Barnett, Clive, Cafaro, Philip and Newholm, Terry, 'Philosophy and ethical consumption', in Rob Harrison, Terry Newholm and Deirdre Shaw (eds), *The Ethical Consumer*, London: Sage, 2005, pp.11–24.

Barnett, Clive, Cloke, Paul, Clarke, Nick and Malpass, Alice, 'Consuming ethics: articulating the subjects and spaces of ethical consumption', *Antipode*, vol. 37, no. 1, 2005, pp. 23–45.

Baudrillard, Jean, *Simulations* (trans. Paul Foss, Paul Patton and Philip Beitchman), New York: Semiotext, 1983.

Bauman, Zygmunt, *Work, Consumerism and the New Poor*, Buckingham: Open University Press, 2001.

——, *Liquid Life*, Cambridge: Polity, 2005.

——, *Consuming Life*, Cambridge: Polity, 2007.

Bennett, Jane, *The Enchantment of Modern Life: Attachments,*

Crossing and Ethics, Princeton: Princeton University Press, 2001.

Bennett, Jane and Shapiro, Michael J., 'Introduction', in Jane Bennett and Michael J. Shapiro (eds), *The Politics of Moralizing*, Routledge, New York, 2002, pp. 1–9.

Bianchi, Marina, 'Taste for novelty and novel tastes: the role of human agency in consumption', in Marina Bianchi (ed.), *The Active Consumer: Novelty and Surprise in Consumer Choice*, London: Routledge, 1998, pp. 64–86.

Bordwell, Marilyn, 'Jamming culture: Adbusters hip media campaign against consumerism', in Thomas Princen, Michael Maniates and Ken Conca (eds), *Confronting Consumption*, Cambridge, MA: MIT Press, 2002, pp. 237–53.

Bourdieu, Pierre, *Distinction: A Social Critique of the Judgement of Taste* (trans. Richard Nice), London: Routledge, 1986.

Boyle, David, *Authenticity: Brands, Fakes, Spin and the Lust for Real Life*, London: Harper Perennial, 2003.

Brewer, John and Trentmann, Frank, 'Introduction: space, time and value in consuming cultures', in John Brewer and Frank Trentmann (eds), *Consuming Cultures, Global Perspectives: Historical Trajectories, Transnational Exchanges*, Oxford: Berg, 2006, pp. 1–17.

Brewer, John and Porter, Roy, *Consumption and the World of Goods*, London: Routledge, 1993.

Brooks, David, *Bobos in Paradise: The New Upper Class and How They Got There*, New York: Simon & Schuster, 2000.

Brown, Bill, 'Thing theory', in Bill Brown (ed.), *Things*, Chicago: University of Chicago Press, 2004, pp. 1–21.

Bryant, Raymond L. and Goodman, Michael K., 'Consuming narratives: the political ecology of "alternative" consumption', *Transactions of the Institute of British Geographers*, NS 29, 2004, pp. 344–66;

Campbell, Colin, 'I shop therefore I know that I am: the

metaphysical basis of modern consumerism', in Karin M. Ekström and Helene Brembeck (eds), *Elusive Consumption*, Oxford: Berg, 2004, pp. 27–44.

Carr, Michael, 'Social capital, civil society, and social transformation', in Robert F. Woollard, and Aleck S. Ostry (eds), *Fatal Consumption: Rethinking Sustainable Development*, Vancouver: UBC Press, 2000, pp. 69–98.

Carrier, James, *Gifts and Commodities: Exchange and Western Capitalism since 1700*, London: Routledge, 1995.

Castells, Manuel, *The Rise of Network Society*, 3 vols, vol. I: *The Information Age: Economy, Society and Culture*, Oxford: Blackwell, 1996.

Cherrier, Hélène, 'Using existential–phenomenological interviewing to explore meanings of consumption', in Rob Harrison, Terry Newholm and Deirdre Shaw (eds), *The Ethical Consumer*, London: Sage, 2005, pp. 125–35.

Clapp, Jennifer, 'The distancing of waste: overconsumption in a global economy', in Thomas Princen, Michael Maniates and Ken Conca, (eds), *Confronting Consumption*, Cambridge, MA: MIT Press, 2002, pp. 155–76.

Cohen, Joshua and Rogers, Joel (eds), *Do Americans Shop too Much?*, Boston: Beacon Press, 2000.

Cohen, Lizabeth, *A Consumers' Republic: The Politics of Mass Consumption in Postwar America*, New York: Vintage, 2004.

Cohen, Maurie, 'The emergent environmental policy discourse on sustainable consumption', in Maurie Cohen and Joseph Murphy, (eds), *Exploring Sustainable Consumption: Environmental Policy and the Social Sciences*, Oxford: Elsevier, 2001, pp. 21–37.

Cohen, Maurie J. and Murphy, Joseph (eds), *Exploring Sustainable Consumption: Environmental Policy and the Social Sciences*, Oxford: Elsevier, 2001.

Comeliau, Christian, *The Impasse of Modernity*, London: Zed Books, 2002.

Conca, Ken, 'Consumption and environment in a global economy', in Thomas Princen, Michael Maniates and Ken Conca, (eds), *Confronting Consumption*, Cambridge, MA: MIT Press, 2002, pp. 133–53.

Craig-Lees, Margaret and Hill, Constance, 'Understanding voluntary simplifiers', *Psychology & Marketing*, vol. 19, no. 2, February 2002, pp. 187–210.

Crewe, Louise, 'Geographies of retailing and consumption', *Progress in Human Geography*, vol. 24, no. 2, 2000, pp. 275–90;

——, 'Geographies of retailing and consumption: markets in meltdown', *Progress in Human Geography*, vol. 27, no. 3, 2003, pp. 352–62.

Crister, Greg, *Fat Land: How Americans Became the Fattest People in the World*, New York: Houghton Mifflin, 2003.

Csikszentmihalyi, Mihaly and Rochberg-Halton, Eugene, *The Meaning of Things: Domestic Symbols and the Self*, Cambridge: Cambridge University Press, 1981.

Daly, Herman, E. 'Consumption: the economics of value added and the ethics of value distributed', in Laura Westra and Patricia H. Werhane (eds), *The Business of Consumption: Environmental Ethics and the Global Economy*, Lanham: Rowman & Littlefield, 1998, pp. 17–29.

——, 'Five policy recommendations for a sustainable economy', in Juliet B. Schor and Betsy Taylor (eds), *Sustainable Planet: Solutions for the Twenty-First Century*, Boston: Beacon Press, 2002, pp. 209–21.

Daly, Herman E. and Cobb, John, *For the Common Good: Redirecting the Economy Toward Community, the Environment, and a Sustainable Future*, Boston: Beacon Press, 1989.

Dant, Tim, 'Consumption caught in the cash nexus', *Sociology*, vol. 34, no. 4, 2000, pp. 655–70.

——, *Materiality and Society*, Buckingham: Open University Press, 2005.

de Certeau, Michel, *The Practice of Everyday Life* (trans. Steven Rendall), Berkeley: University of California Press, 1988.

de Geus, Marius, *The End of Over-Consumption: Towards a Lifestyle of Moderation and Self-Restraint*, Utrecht: International Books, 2003.

de Graaf, John (ed.), *Take Back Your Time: Fighting Overwork and Time Poverty in America*, San Francisco: Berrett-Koehler, 2003.

de Graaf, John, 'Take back your time day', in John de Graaf (ed.), *Take Back Your Time: Fighting Overwork and Time Poverty in America*, San Francisco: Berrett-Koehler 2003. pp. viii–xii.

de Graaf, John, Wann, David and Naylor, Thomas H., *Affluenza: The All-Consuming Epidemic*, San Francisco: Berrett-Koehler, 2001.

Dittmar, Helga, *The Social Psychology of Material Possessions: To Have is to Be*, Hemel Hempstead: Harvester Wheatsheaf, 1992.

Dixon, Jane and Broom, Dorothy (eds), *The Seven Deadly Sins of Obesity: How the Modern World is Making us Fat*, Sydney: University of New South Wales Press, 2007.

Doherty, Daniel and Etzioni, Amitai (eds), *Voluntary Simplicity: Responding to Consumer Culture*, Lanham: Rowman & Littlefield, 2003.

Dominguez, Joe and Robin, Vicki, *Your Money or Your Life: Transforming Your Relationship with Money and Achieving Financial Independence*, New York: Penguin, 1999.

Donati, Kelly, 'The pleasure of diversity in slow food's ethics of taste', *Food, Culture & Society*, vol. 8, no. 2, 2005, pp. 227–42.

Douglas, Mary and Isherwood, Baron, *The World of Goods: Towards an Anthropology of Consumption*, London: Allen Lane, 1979.

Drake, John, *Downshifting: How to Work Less and Enjoy Life More*, San Francisco: Berrett-Koehler, 2000.

du Gay, Paul (ed.), *Production of Culture, Cultures of Production*, London: Sage, 1997.

du Gay, Paul and Pryke, Michael (eds), *Cultural Economy: Cultural Analysis and Commercial Life*, London: Sage, 2002.

Durning, Alan, *How Much is Enough? The Consumer Society and the Future of the Earth*, New York: Norton, 1992.

Eagleton, Terry, *After Theory*, London: Allen Lane, 2003.

Easterlin, Richard, 'Does economic growth improve the human lot?', in Paul David and Melvin Reder (eds), *Nations and Households in Economic Growth: Essays in Honour of Moses Abramovitz*, New York: Academic Press, 1974.

Eckersley, Richard, *Well & Good: How We Feel & Why it Matters*, Melbourne: Text, 2004.

Edwards, Ferne and Mercer, David, 'Gleaning from Glutony: An Australian Youth Subculture confronts the Ethic of Waste', *Australian Geographer*, vol. 38, no. 3, 2006, pp. 279–96.

Edwards, Tim, *Contradictions of Consumption: Concepts, Practices and Politics in Consumer Society*, Buckingham: Open University Press, 2000.

Ehrlich, Paul R. and Ehrlich, Anne H., *The End of Affluence*, New York: Ballantine Books, 1974.

——, *One With Nineveh: Politics, Consumption, and the Human Future*, Washington: Island Press/Shearwater Books, 2004.

Elgin, Duane, *Voluntary Simplicity: Towards a Way of Life that is Outwardly Simple, Inwardly Rich*, revised edn, New York: Harper, 1993.

Elgin, Duane and Mitchell, Arnold, 'Voluntary simplicity: a movement emerges', in Daniel Doherty and Amitai Etzioni, *Voluntary Simplicity: Responding to Consumer Culture*, Lanham: Rowman & Littlefield, 2003, pp. 145–71.

Engelman, Robert, 'Hope in numbers', in Juliet B. Schor and Betsy Taylor (eds), *Sustainable Planet: Solutions for the Twenty-First Century*, Boston: Beacon Press, 2002, pp. 193–208.

Farrell, James J., *One Nation Under Goods: Malls and the Seductions of American Shopping*, Washington: Smithsonian Books, 2003.

Fine, Ben and Leopold, Ellen, *The World of Consumption*, London: Routledge, 1993.

Fiske, John, *Reading the Popular*, Boston: Unwin Hyman, 1989.

Florida, Richard, *The Rise of the Creative Class . . . and how it's Transforming Work, Leisure, Community and Everyday Life*, New York: Basic Books, 2004.

Frank, Robert H., *Luxury Fever: Why Money Fails to Satisfy in an Era of Excess*, New York: Free Press, 1999.

——, 'Market failures', in Joshua Cohen and Joel Rogers (eds), *Do Americans Shop too Much?*, Boston: Beacon Press, 2000, pp. 37–43.

Frank, Thomas, *One Market Under God: Extreme Capitalism, Market Populism and the End of Economic Democracy*, London: Vintage, 2002.

Gabriel, Yiannis and Lang, Tim, *The Unmanageable Consumer*, 2nd edn, London: Sage, 2006.

Galbraith, John Kenneth, *The Affluent Society*, Boston: Houghton Mifflin, 1958.

Gibson-Graham, J. K., *The End of Capitalism (As We Knew It): A Feminist Critique of Political Economy*, Oxford: Blackwell, 1996.

Gibson-Graham, J. K., *A Postcapitalist Politics*, Minneapolis: University of Minnesota Press, 2006.

Giddens, Anthony, *Modernity and Self-Identity: Self and Society in the Late Modern Age*, Cambridge: Polity, 1991.

Goodman, David and Goodman, Michael, 'Sustaining foods:

organic consumption and the socio-ecological imaginary', in Maurie Cohen, and Joseph Murphy (eds), *Exploring Sustainable Consumption: Environmental Policy and the Social Sciences*, Oxford: Elsevier, 2001, pp. 97–119;

Gorz, André, *Paths to Paradise: On the Liberation from Work*, London: Pluto, 1985.

Gregg, Richard B., *The Value of Voluntary Simplicity*, in Daniel Doherty and Amitai Etzioni (eds), *Voluntary Simplicity: Responding to Consumer Culture*, Lanham: Rowman & Littlefield, 2003, pp. 131–44.

Guthman, Julie, 'Fast food/organic food: reflexive tastes and the making of "yuppie chow"', *Social & Cultural Geography*, vol. 4, no. 1, 2003, pp. 45–58.

Guthman, Julie, 'The "organic commodity" and other anomalies in the politics of consumption', in Alex Hughes and Suzanne Reimer (eds), *Geography of Commodity Chains*, London: Routledge, 2004, pp. 233–49.

Hamilton, Clive, *Downshifting in Britain: A Sea-Change in the Pursuit of Happiness*' Canberra, Australia Institute, Discussion paper no. 58, 2003.

Hamilton, Clive and Denniss, Richard, *Affluenza: When Too Much is Never Enough*, Sydney: Allen & Unwin, 2005.

Hammerslough, Jane, *Dematerializing: Taming the Power of Possessions*, Cambridge, MA: Perseus, 2001.

Harris, Daniel, *Cute, Quaint, Hungry and Romantic: The Aesthetics of Consumerism*, New York: Da Capo Press, 2001.

Harrison, Rob, Newholm, Terry and Shaw, Deirdre (eds), *The Ethical Consumer*, London: Sage, 2005.

——, 'Introduction', in Rob Harrison, Terry Newholm and Deirdre Shaw (eds), *The Ethical Consumer*, London: Sage, 2005, pp. 1–8.

Hawken, Paul, Lovins, Amory, and Lovins, L. Hunter, *Natural Capitalism: Creating the Next Industrial Revolution*, Boston: Little, Brown, 1999.

Hawkins, Gay, *The Ethics of Waste: How We Relate to Rubbish*, Sydney: University of New South Wales Press, 2006,

Heady, Bruce and Wooden, Mark, 'Economic wellbeing and subjective wellbeing: the effects of income and wealth', in Lenore Manderson (ed.), *Rethinking Wellbeing*, Perth: API Network, 2005, pp. 91–108.

Heath, Joseph and Potter, Andrew, *The Rebel Sell: Why the Culture Can't be Jammed*, Chichester: Capstone, 2005.

Hebdige, Dick, *Subculture: The Meaning of Style*, London: Methuen, 1979.

——, *Hiding in the Light: On Images and Things*, London: Routledge, 1988.

Hirsch, Fred, *The Social Limits to Growth*, Cambridge, MA: Harvard University Press, 1976.

Hobson, Kersty, 'Sustainable lifestyles: rethinking barriers and behaviour change', in Maurie Cohen and Joseph Murphy (eds), *Exploring Sustainable Consumption: Environmental Policy and the Social Sciences*, vol. 1, Elsevier, 2001, pp.191–209.

Hollender, Jeffrey, 'Changing the nature of commerce', in Juliet B. Schor and Betsy Taylor (eds), *Sustainable Planet: Solutions for the Twenty-First Century*, Boston: Beacon Press, 2002, pp. 61–77.

Holt, Douglas B., 'How consumers consume: a typology of consumption practices', *Journal of Consumer Research*, vol. 22, June 1995, pp. 1–16.

——, 'An interview with Juliet Schor', *Journal of Consumer Culture*, vol. 5, no. 1, March 2005, pp. 5–21.

Holt, Douglas B. and Schor, Juliet B., 'Introduction', in Juliet B. Schor and Douglas B. Holt (eds), *The Consumer Society Reader*, New York: New Press, 2000, pp. vii–viii.

Honoré, Carl, *In Praise of Slow: How a World Movement is Challenging the Cult of Speed*, London: Orion, 2004.

Hughes, Alex and Reimer, Suzanne (eds), *Geographies of Commodity Chains*, London: Routledge, 2004.

Humphery, Kim, *Shelf Life: Supermarkets and the Changing Cultures of Consumption*, Melbourne: Cambridge University Press, 1998.

——, 'Dirty questions: indigenous health and "western research"', *Australian and New Zealand Journal of Public Health*, vol. 25, no. 3, June 2001, pp. 197–202.

——, 'After affluenza', *Arena Magazine*, no. 75, February–March 2005, pp. 11–12.

——, 'Beyond borders: the politics and place of the global shop', in Daniel Thomas Cook (ed.), *Live Experiences of Public Consumption: Encounters with Value in Marketplaces on Five Continents*, Basingstoke: Palgrave Macmillan, 2008, pp. 161–78.

Jackson, Peter, 'Commodity cultures: the traffic in things', *Transactions of the Institute of British Geography*, vol. 24, 1999, pp. 95–108.

James, Oliver, *Affluenza: How to be Successful and Stay Sane*, London: Vermilion, 2007.

Johnston, Josée, 'Consuming global justice: fair trade shopping and alternative development', in James Goodman (ed.), *Protest and Globalisation*, Sydney: Pluto Press, 2001.

Jordan, Tim, *Activism!: Direct Action, Hacktivism and the Future of Society*, London: Reaktion Books, 2002.

Kasser, Tim, *The High Price of Materialism*, Cambridge, MA: MIT Press, 2002.

Kassiola, Joel Jay, *The Death of Industrial Civilization: The Limits to Economic Growth and the Repoliticization of Advanced Industrial Society*, Albany: State University of New York Press, 1990.

Khor, Martin, 'Effects of the global economic crisis on developing countries', Informal Note 42, Global Governance for Development Programme, South Centre, 13 March 2009.

Klein, Naomi, *No Logo*, London: Flamingo, 2000.

Kozinets Robert V. and Handelman, Jay M., 'Adversaries of consumption: consumer movements, activism, and ideology', *Journal of Consumer Research*, vol. 31, December 2004, pp. 691–704;

Labelle, Julie, 'A recipe for connectedness: bridging production and consumption with slow food', *Food, Culture & Society*, vol. 7, no. 2, 2004, pp. 81–96.

Lane, Robert, *The Market Experience*, Cambridge: Cambridge University Press, 1991.

Lasn, Kalle, *Culture Jam*, New York: Eagle Books, 1999.

Latour, Bruno 'Why has critique run out of steam? From matters of fact to matters of concern', in Bill Brown (ed.), *Things*, Chicago: University of Chicago Press, 2004, pp. 151–73.

Lears, Jackson, 'Reconsidering abundance: a plea for ambiguity', in Susan Strasser, Charles McGovern and Matthias Judt (eds), *Getting and Spending: European and American Consumer Societies in the Twentieth Century*, New York: Cambridge University Press, 1998, pp. 449–66.

Lebergott, Stanley, *Pursuing Happiness: American Consumers in the Twentieth Century*, Princeton: Princeton University Press, 1993.

Leiss, William, *The Limits to Satisfaction*, London: Marion Boyars, 1978.

Leyshon, Andrew and Lee, Roger, 'Introduction: alternative economic geographies', in Andrew Leyshon, Roger Lee and Colin C. Williams (eds), *Alternative Economic Spaces*, London: Sage, 2003, pp. 1–26.

Lockie, Stewart, Lyons, Kristen, Lawrence, Geoffrey and Mummery, Kerry, 'Eating "green": motivations behind organic food consumption in Australia', *Sociologia Ruralis*, vol. 42, no. 1, January 2002, pp. 23–39;

Lodziak, Conrad, 'On explaining consumption', *Capital & Class*, no. 72, Autumn 2000, pp. 111–33.

Lury, Celia, *Consumer Culture*, Cambridge: Polity, 1996.

Majima, Shinobu and Savage, Mike, 'Unpacking culture shifts in post-war Britain: a critical encounter with Ronald Inglehart', Working Paper no. 17, Centre for Research on Socio-Cultural Change, University of Manchester, Manchester, 2006.

Manderson, Lenore, 'Introduction: the social context of well-being', in Lenore Manderson (ed.), *Rethinking Wellbeing*, Perth: API Network, 2005, pp. 1–25.

Maniates, Michael, 'In search of consumptive resistance: the voluntary simplicity movement', in Thomas Princen, Michael Maniates, and Ken Conca, (eds), *Confronting Consumption*, Cambridge, MA: MIT Press, 2002, pp. 199–235.

——, 'Individualization: plant a tree, buy a bike, save the world?', in Thomas Princen, Michael Maniates and Ken Conca, (eds), *Confronting Consumption*, Cambridge, MA: MIT Press, 2002, pp. 43–66.

Manning, Robert D., *Credit Card Nation: The Consequences of America's Addiction to Credit*, New York: Basic Books, 2000.

Mansvelt, Juliana, *Geographies of Consumption*, London: Sage, 2006.

Martell, Luke, *Ecology and Society: An Introduction*, Cambridge: Polity, 1994.

McAdam, Douglas, Tarrow, Sydney and Tilly, Charles, *Dynamics of Contention*, New York: Cambridge University Press, 2001.

McCaughey, Martha and Ayers, Michael D. (eds), *Cyberactivism: Online Activism in Theory and Practice*, New York: Routledge, 2003.

McDonald, Kevin, *Global Movements, Action and Culture*, Oxford: Blackwell, 2006.

McEachern, M. G and McClean, P., 'Organic purchasing motivations and attitudes: are they ethical?, *International*

Journal of Consumer Studies, vol. 26, no. 2, June 2002, pp. 85–92.

McGuigan, Jim, *Cultural Populism*, London: Routledge, 1992.

McKendrick, Neil, Brewer, John and Plumb, J. H. (eds), *The Birth of Consumer Society: The Commercialisation of Eighteenth-Century England*, Bloomington: Indiana University Press, 1982.

McKibben, Bill, 'Introduction', in Juliet B. Schor and Betsy Taylor (eds), *Sustainable Planet: Solutions for the Twenty-First Century*, Boston: Beacon Press, 2002, pp. 1–11.

McRobbie, Angela, *In the Culture Society: Art, Fashion and Popular Music*, London: Routledge, 1999.

McRobbie, Angela and Nava, Mica (eds), *Gender and Generation*, London: Macmillan, 1984.

Meadows, D. H., Meadows, D. L., Randers, J. and Behrens, W. W., *The Limits to Growth*, New York: Universe Books, 1972.

Melucci, Alberto, *Nomads of the Present: Social Movements and Individual Needs in Contemporary Society*, edited by John Keane and Paul Mier, London: Hutchinson Radius, 1989.

——, *The Playing Self: Person and Meaning in a Planetary Society*, Cambridge: Cambridge University Press, 1996.

Micheletti, Michele, *Political Virtue and Shopping: Individuals, Consumerism and Collective Action*, New York: Palgrave Macmillan, 2003.

Miller, Daniel, *A Theory of Shopping*, New York: Cornell University Press, 1998.

——, 'Why some things matter', in Daniel Miller (ed.), *Material Cultures: Why Some Things Matter*, London: UCL Press, 1998, pp. 3–21.

——, 'The poverty of morality', *Journal of Consumer Culture*, vol. 1, no. 2, 2001, pp. 225–43.

——, *The Comfort of Things*, Cambridge: Polity, 2008.

Miller, Daniel, Jackson, Peter, Thrift, Nigel, Holbrook, Beverley and Rowlands, Michael, *Shopping, Place and Identity*, London: Routledge, 1998.

Monbiot, George, *Heat: How to Stop the Planet from Burning*, London: Allen Lane, 2006.

——, *Manifesto for a New World Order*, London: New Press, 2006.

Mukerji, Chandra, *From Graven Images: Patterns of Modern Materialism*, New York: Columbia University Press, 1983.

Mulligan, Martin, Humphery, Kim, James, Paul, Scanlon, Christopher, Smith, Pia and Welch, Nicky, *Creating Community: Celebrations, Arts and Wellbeing Within and Across Local Communities*, Melbourne: Globalism Institute, 2006.

Myers, David, *The American Paradox: Spiritual Hunger in the Age of Plenty*, New Haven: Yale University Press, 2000.

Myers, David, G., *The Pursuit of Happiness: Who is Happy – and Why?*, New York: Washington Square Press, 1992.

——, 'Wealth and happiness: a limited relationship', in Daniel Doherty and Amitai Etzioni (eds), *Voluntary Simplicity: Responding to Consumer Culture*, Lanham: Rowman & Littlefield, 2003, pp. 44–5.

Myers, Norman and Kent, Jennifer, *The New Consumers: The Influence of Affluence on the Environment*, Washington: Island Press, 2004.

Nestle, Marion, *Food Politics: How the Food Industry Influences Nutrition and Health*, Berkeley: University of California Press, 2002.

Norberg-Hodge, Helena, 'Shifting direction: from global dependence to local interdependence', in Jerry Mander and Edward Goldsmith (eds), *The Case Against the Global Economy: And for a Return to the Local*, San Francisco: Sierra Club, 1996, pp. 393–406.

——, *Ancient Futures: Learning for Ladakh*, London: Rider, 2000.

Nussbaum, Martha, *Frontiers of Justice: Disability, Nationality, Species Membership*, Cambridge, MA: Harvard University Press, 2006.

Packard, Vance, *The Hidden Persuaders*, London: Penguin, 1957.

Parkins, Wendy, 'Out of time: fast subjects and slow living', *Time & Society*, vol. 13, no. 2/3, 2004, pp. 363–82.

Parkins, Wendy and Craig, Geoffrey, *Slow Living*, Oxford: Berg, 2006.

Patomäki, Heikki, 'Global justice: a democratic perspective', *Globalizations*, vol. 3, no. 2, 2006, pp. 99–120.

Petrini, Carlo, *Slow Food: The Case for Taste* (trans. William McCuaig), New York: Columbia University Press, 2001.

Polanyi, Karl, *The Great Transformation: The Political and Economic Origins of our Time*, Boston: Beacon Press, 2001.

Polletta, Francesca, *Freedom is an Endless Meeting: Democracy in American Social Movements*, Chicago and London: University of Chicago Press, 2004.

Princen, Thomas, 'Consumption and its externalities: Where economy meets ecology', in Thomas Princen, Michael Maniates and Ken Conca, (eds), *Confronting Consumption*, Cambridge, MA: MIT Press, 2002, pp. 23–42.

——, *The Logic of Sufficiency*, Cambridge, MA: MIT Press, 2005.

Princen, Thomas, Maniates, Michael and Conca, Ken (eds), *Confronting Consumption*: Cambridge, MA: MIT Press, 2002.

Ralston Saul, John, *The Unconscious Civilization*, Melbourne: Penguin, 1997.

Ransome, Paul, *Work, Consumption and Culture: Affluence and Social Change in the Twenty-First Century*, London: Sage, 2005.

Ray, Paul H. and Anderson, Sherry Ruth, *The Cultural*

Creatives: How 50 Million People are Changing the World,
New York: Three Rivers Press, 2001.

Rayner, Mary, Harrison, Rob and Irving, Sarah, 'Ethical
consumerism – democracy through the wallet', *Journal of
Research for Consumers*, Issue 3, 2002.

Rechtschaffen, Stephan, 'Timeshifting', in Juliet B. Schor
and Betsy Taylor (eds), *Sustainable Planet: Solutions for
the Twenty-First Century*, Boston: Beacon Press, 2002, pp.
175–92.

Redclift, Michael and Ted Benton (eds) *Social Theory and the
Global Environment*, London: Routledge, 1994.

Rees, William E., 'Ecological footprints and the patho-
logy of consumption', in Robert F. Woollard and Aleck
S. Ostry (eds), *Fatal Consumption: Rethinking Sustainable
Development*, Vancouver: UBC Press, 2000, pp. 21–51.

Riesman, David, *The Lonely Crowd: A Study of the Changing
American Character*, New Haven: Yale University Press,
1969.

Ritzer, George, *The McDonaldization of Society: An Investigation
into the Character of Contemporary Social Life*, Thousand
Oaks: Pine Forge Press, 1993.

——, *The Globalization of Nothing*, Thousand Oaks: Pine
Forge Press, 2004.

Robin, Vicki, 'What's money got to do with it?', in Juliet B.
Schor and Betsy Taylor (eds), *Sustainable Planet: Solutions
for the Twenty-First Century*, Boston: Beacon Press, 2002,
pp. 79–91.

Robinson, Joe, *Work to Live: the Guide to Getting a Life*, New
York: Perigree, 2003.

Rosenblatt, Roger, 'Introduction', in Roger Rosenblatt (ed.),
*Consuming Desires: Consumption, Culture and the Pursuit
of Happiness*, Washington: Island Press/Sherwater Books,
1999.

——, *The Comfort of Things*, Cambridge: Polity, 2008.

(ed.), *Consuming Desires: Consumption, Culture and the Pursuit of Happiness*, Washington: Island Press/Sherwater Books, 1999.

Ross, Andrew, *No Sweat: Fashion, Free Trade and the Rights of Garment Workers*, London: Verso, 1997.

Rowbotham, Sheila, Segal, Lynne and Wainwright, Hilary *Beyond the Fragments: Feminism and the Making of Socialism*, London: Merlin, 1979.

Rowe, Jonathan, 'Wasted work, wasted time', in John de Graaf (ed.), *Take Back Your Time: Fighting Overwork and Time Poverty in America*, San Francisco: Berrett-Koehler, 2003, pp. 58–65.

Rudd, Kevin, 'The global financial crisis', *The Monthly*, February 2009, pp. 20–9.

Rumbo, Joseph, D., 'Consumer resistance in a world of advertising clutter', *Psychology and Marketing*, vol. 19, no. 2, 2002, pp. 127–48.

Ryan, John C. and Durning, Alan Thien, *Stuff: The Secret Life of Everyday Things*, Seattle: Northwest Environment Watch, 1997.

Sack, Robert, *Place, Modernity and the Consumer's World: A Relational Framework for Geographical Analysis*, Baltimore: John Hopkins University Press, 1992.

Sanches, Samy, 'Sustainable consumption à la Française? Conventional, innovative, and alternative approaches to sustainability and consumption in France', *Sustainability: Science, Practice, & Policy*, vol. 1, no. 1, 2005, pp. 43–57.

Sassatelli, Roberta, 'Virtue, responsibility and consumer choice: framing critical consumerism', in Brewer and Trentmann, *Consuming Cultures*, pp. 219–50.

Sayer, Andrew, '(De)commodification, consumer culture, and moral economy', in *Environment and Planning D: Society and Space*, vol. 21, 2003, pp. 341–57.

Scerri, Andy, 'Not just the warm, fuzzy feeling you get from buying free-range eggs: paradoxes of increased individuation and public awareness of environmental issues in the contemporary West', *Environmental Politics*, (forthcoming, 2009).

Schlosser, Eric, *Fast Food Nation: The Dark Side of the All-American Meal*, New York: Harper Perennial, 2005.

Schor, Juliet B., *The Overworked American: The Unexpected Decline of Leisure*, New York: Basic Books, 1992.

——, *The Overspent American: Why We Want What We Don't Need*, New York: Harper Perennial, 1999.

——, 'The new politics of consumption', in Joshua Cohen and Joel Rogers (eds), *Do Americans Shop too Much?*, Boston: Beacon Press, 2000, pp. 3–33.

——, 'The (even more) overworked American', in John de Graaf (ed.), *Take Back Your Time: Fighting Overwork and Time Poverty in America*, San Francisco: Berrett-Koehler, 2003, pp. 6–11.

—— and Taylor, Betsy (eds), *Sustainable Planet: Solutions for the Twenty-First Century*, Boston: Beacon Press, 2002.

Schumacher, E. F., *Small is Beautiful: Economics as if People Mattered*, New York: Harper & Row, 1973.

Schwartz, Barry, *The Costs of Living*, New York: Norton, 1994.

——, *The Paradox of Choice: Why More is Less*, New York: HarperCollins, 2005.

Scitovsky, Tibor, *The Joyless Economy*, New York: Oxford University Press, 1976.

Seabrook, Jeremy, *What Went Wrong? Why Hasn't Having More Made People Happier?*, New York: Pantheon, 1978.

——, *Consuming Cultures: Globalization and Local Lives*, Oxford: New Internationalist, 2004.

Sen, Amartya, *Commodities and Capabilities*, New Delhi: Oxford University Press, 1999.

Sennett, Richard, *The Culture of New Capitalism*, New Haven: Yale University Press, 2006.

Shaw, Deirdre and Newholm, Terry, 'Voluntary simplicity and the ethics of consumption', *Psychology & Marketing*, vol. 19, no. 2, February 2002, pp. 167–85.

Shi, David, *The Simple Life: Plain Living and High Thinking in American Culture*, New York: Oxford University Press, 1985.

Shove, Elizabeth, *Cleanliness, Comfort and Convenience: The Social Organisation of Normality*, Oxford: Berg, 2003.

Singer, Peter, *How Are We to Live?: Ethics in the Age of Self-Interest*, Oxford: Oxford University Press, 1997.

Slater, Don, 'Consumer culture and the politics of need', in Mica Nava, Andrew Blake, Iain MacRury and Barry Richards (eds), *Buy This Book: Studies in Advertising and Consumption*, London: Routledge, 1997, pp. 51–63.

——, 'Cultures of consumption', in Kay Anderson, Mona Domosh, Steve Pile and Nigel Thrift (eds), *Handbook of Cultural Geography*, London: Sage, 2003, pp. 147–63.

Smart, Barry (ed.), *Resisting McDonaldization: Theory, Process and Critique*, London: Sage, 1999.

Sontag, Susan, *Illness as Metaphor*, New York: Vintage, 1979.

——, *Aids and its Metaphors*, London: Allen Lane, 1989.

Soper, Kate, 'Rethinking the "good life": The consumer as citizen', *Capitalism, Nature, Socialism*, vol. 15, no. 3, 2004, pp. 111–17.

Talen, Bill, *What Should I do if Reverend Billy is in my Store?*, New York: New Press, 2003.

Tarrow, Sydney, *Power in Movement: Social Movements, Collective Action and Politics*, Cambridge: Cambridge University Press, 1994.

Taylor, Betsy, 'How do we get from here to there?', in Juliet B. Schor and Betsy Taylor (eds), *Sustainable Planet:*

Solutions for the Twenty-First Century, Boston: Beacon Press, 2002, pp. 233–51.

Trainer, F. E. *Abandon Affluence!*, London: Zed Books, 1989.

Trainer, Ted, 'The global ecovillage movement: the simpler way for a sustainable society', *Social Alternatives*, vol. 19, no. 3, July 2000, pp. 19–24.

Trentmann, Frank, 'The modern genealogy of the consumer: meanings, identities and political synapses', in John Brewer and Frank Trentmann (eds), *Consuming Cultures, Global Perspectives: Historical Trajectories, Transnational Exchanges*, Oxford: Berg, 2006, pp. 19–69.

Tuhiwai Smith, Linda, *Decolonizing Methodologies: Research and Indigenous Peoples*, London and Dunedin: Zed Books/ University of Otago Press, 1999.

van de Donk, Wim, Loader, Brian D., Nixon, Paul G. and Rucht, Dieter (eds), *Cyberprotest: New Media, Citizens and Social Movements*, London: Routledge, 2004.

Venetoulis, Jason, Chazan, Dahlia and Gaudet, Christopher, *Ecological Footprint of Nations*, Oakland: Redefining Progress, 2004.

Wachtel, Paul, L.,'Overconsumption', in Roger Keil, David Bell (eds), *Political Ecology: Global and Local*, London: Routledge, 1998.

Wachtel, Paul, *The Poverty of Affluence: A Psychological Portrait of the American Way of Life*, New York: Free Press, 1983.

Warde, Alan, *Consumption, Food and Taste*, London: Sage, 1997.

——, 'Consumption and theories of practice', *Journal of Consumer Culture*, vol. 5, no. 2, July 2005, pp.131–53.

Weatherell, Charlotte, Tregear, Angela and Allinson, Johanne, 'In search of the concerned consumer: UK public perceptions of food, farming and buying local', *Journal of Rural Studies*, vol. 19, 2003, pp. 233–44.

Westra, Laura and Werhane, Patricia H. (eds), *The Business of Consumption: Environmental Ethics and the Global Economy*, Lanham: Rowman & Littlefield, 1998.

Wilk, Richard, 'Consuming morality', *Journal of Consumer Culture*, vol. 1, no. 2, 2001, pp. 245–260.

Williams, Colin, C., *A Commodified World?: Mapping the Limits of Capitalism*, London: Zed Books, 2005.

Williams, Rosalind, *Dream Worlds: Mass Consumption in Late Nineteenth-Century France*, Berkeley: University of California Press, 1982.

Winterson, Jeanette, 'The bank crash is an opportunity to think about the way we live and why', *The Times*, 18/10/08, books section, p. 3.

Woollard, Robert, 'Introduction', in Robert F. Woollard and Aleck S. Ostry (eds), *Fatal Consumption: Rethinking Sustainable Development*, Vancouver: UBC Press, 2000.

Woollard, Robert F. and Ostry, Aleck S. (eds), *Fatal Consumption: Rethinking Sustainable Development*, Vancouver: UBC Press, 2000.

World Commission on Environment and Development, *Our Common Future*, New York: Oxford University Press, 1987.

Worth, Jess, 'Buy now, pay later', *New Internationalist*, November 2006, pp. 2–5.

Zavestoski, Stephen, 'The social–psychological bases of anti-consumption attitudes', *Psychology & Marketing*, vol. 19, no. 2, February 2002, pp. 149–65.

Websites

Action Consommation: www.actionconsommation.org

Association for a Tobin Tax for the Aid of Citizens: www.attac.org

Association of Conscious Consumers: www.tve.hu

Associazione per i Consumi Etici ed Alternativi:

www.consumietici.it/acea

Australian Conservation Foundation: www.acfonline.org.au

Bilanci di Giustizia: www.bilancidigiustizia.it

Buy Nothing Day: www.buynothingday.co.uk

Centre for the New American Dream: www.newdream.org

Community Solutions: www.communitysolution.org

ConsumeHastaMorir: www.consumehastamorir.com

Consumer Citizenship Network: www.hihm.no/concit/

Delocator: www.delocator.net

Ethical Consumer Research Association:
    www.ethicalconsumer.org

Fair Trade Federation: www.fairtradefederation.org

Food Not Bombs: www.foodnotbombs.net

Freegan Info: www.freegan.info

Friends of the Earth: www.foe.org

Geez magazine: www.geezmagazine.org

Greenpeace: www.greenpeace.org

Institute for Communitarian Policy Studies:
    www.gwu.edu/~icps

International Society for Ecology and Culture:
    www.isec.org.uk

Long Now Foundation: www.longnow.org

Media Foundation: www.adbusters.org

New Economics Foundation: www.neweconomics.org

No Logo: www.nologo.org

Redefining Progress: www.redefiningprogress.org

Résistance à l'Agression Publicitaire: www.antipub.org

Reverend Billy and the Church of Stop Shopping:
    www.revbilly.com

Simple Living Network: www.simpleliving.net

Sloth Club: www.sloth.gr.jp

Slow Food: www.slowfood.com

Society for the Deceleration of Time: www.zeitverein.com

Sprawl-Busters: www.sprawl-busters.com

Take-Back-Your-Time: www.takebackyourtime.org.

The Compact: http://sfcompact.blogspot.com

The Corporation: www.thecorporation.tv.

Transition Towns: www.transitionstowns.org

Whirl-Mart Ritual Resistance: www.breathingplanet.net/whirl/

World Values Survey: www.wvs.isr.umich.edu.

Worldwatch Institute: www.worldwatch.org

INDEX